池本幹雄

Regarding the line "my dad's and my story" in the prologue of chapter one, that story, as many of you probably already knew, followed the plot of *Boruto: Naruto the Movie*. It wraps up in this volume with a slightly different ending than the film version, and leads to Boruto's "my story."

From here on out is unknown territory that no one has ever seen. Of course, I'm not going to spoil it here.

Other than to say that it'll be super cool.

–Mikio Ikemoto, 2017

小太刀右京

My father is a kind of superhuman whose report cards were all A's. He's a university professor, and there is nothing that he does not know.

While it's something I am proud of now, it was tiresome when, as a child, I would only hear, "Well, aren't you your father's son," no matter how hard I worked.

However, once I became an adult and surpassed the age he had been back then, I came to realize, "Ah, my old man had experienced lots of hardship." That it's not a cakewalk at all. Such feelings have been heavily piled on Boruto. I feel like I'm some weird relative who gives unwelcome advice. (*laughs*)

–Ukyo Kodachi, 2017

BORUTO
=NARUTO NEXT GENERATIONS=

VOLUME 3

SHONEN JUMP MANGA EDITION

Creator/Supervisor MASASHI KISHIMOTO
Art by MIKIO IKEMOTO
Script by UKYO KODACHI

Translation: Mari Morimoto
Touch-up Art & Lettering: Snir Aharon
Design: Alice Lewis
Editor: Alexis Kirsch

Printed in the U.S.A.

Published by VIZ Media, LLC
P.O. Box 77010
San Francisco, CA 94107

10 9 8 7 6 5 4 3 2 1
First printing, March 2018

viz.com

shonenjump.com

PARENTAL ADVISORY
BORUTO is rated T for Teen and is recommended
for ages 13 and up. This volume contains fantasy
violence.
ratings.viz.com

BORN FROM DESPAIR

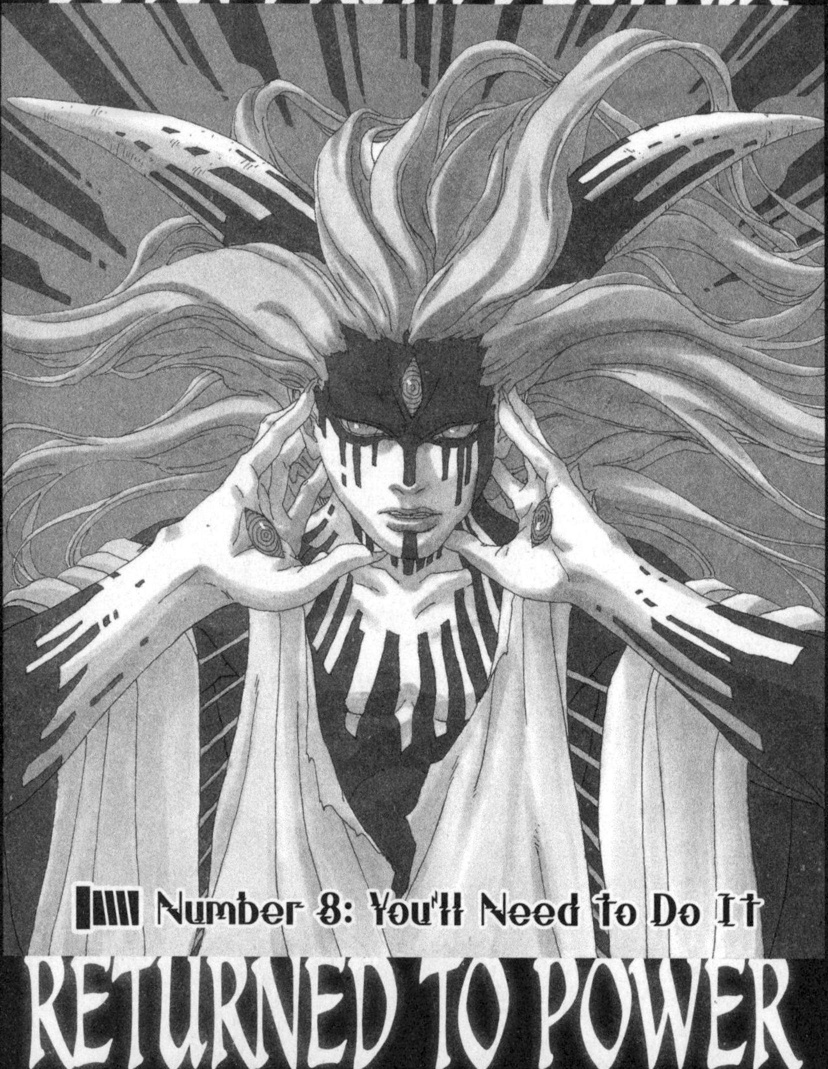

Number 8: You'll Need to Do It

RETURNED TO POWER

BORUTO
-NARUTO NEXT GENERATIONS-

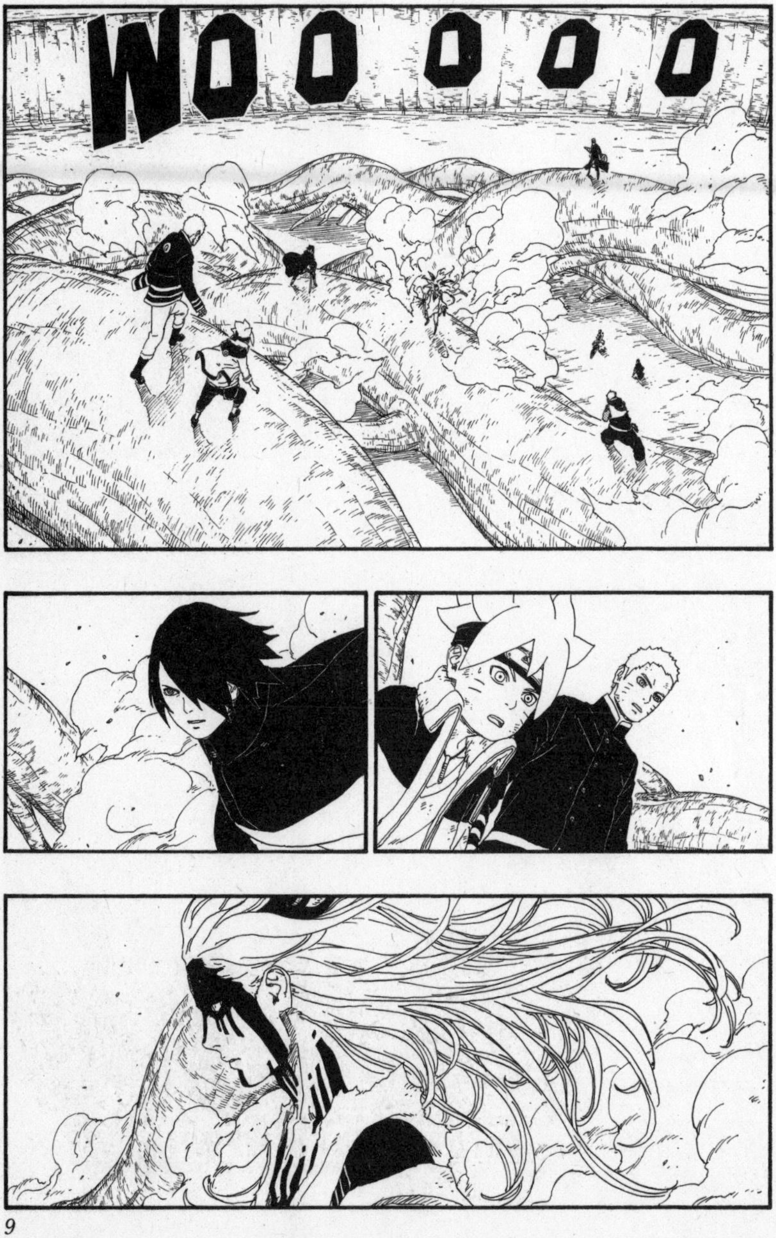
WOOOOO

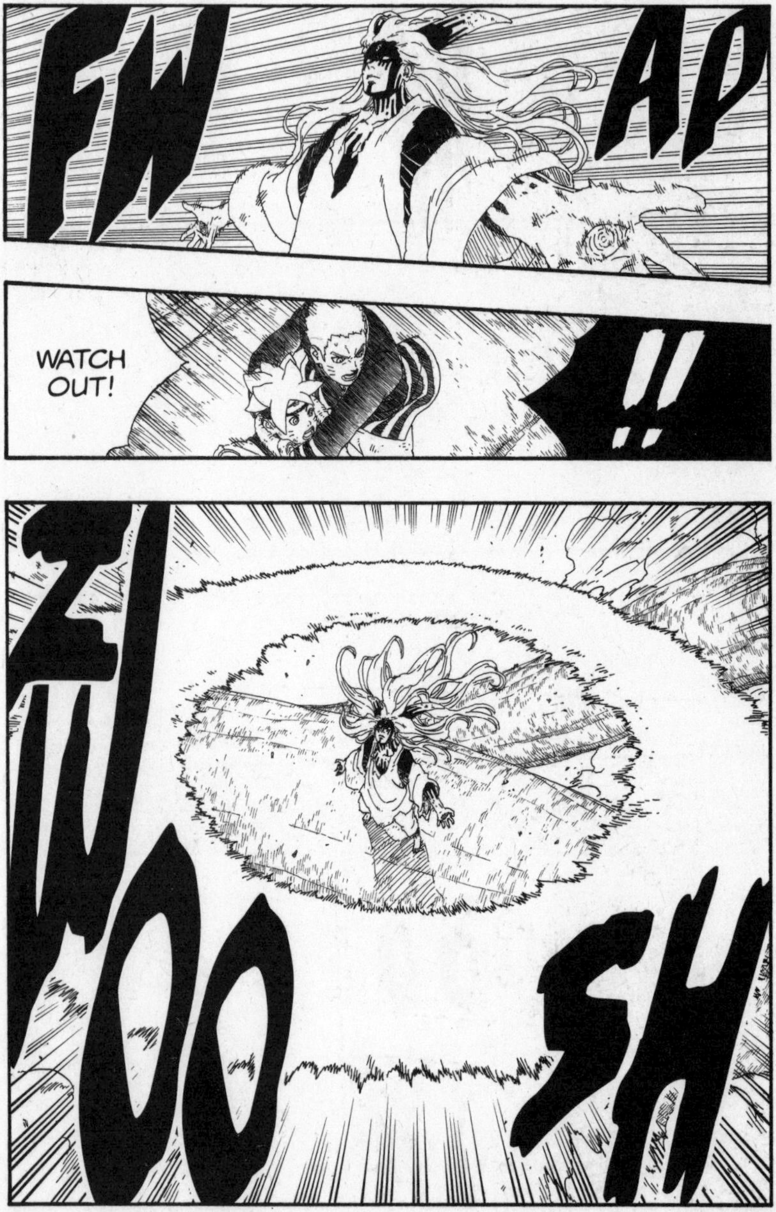
FWAP
!!
WATCH OUT!
ZWOOSH

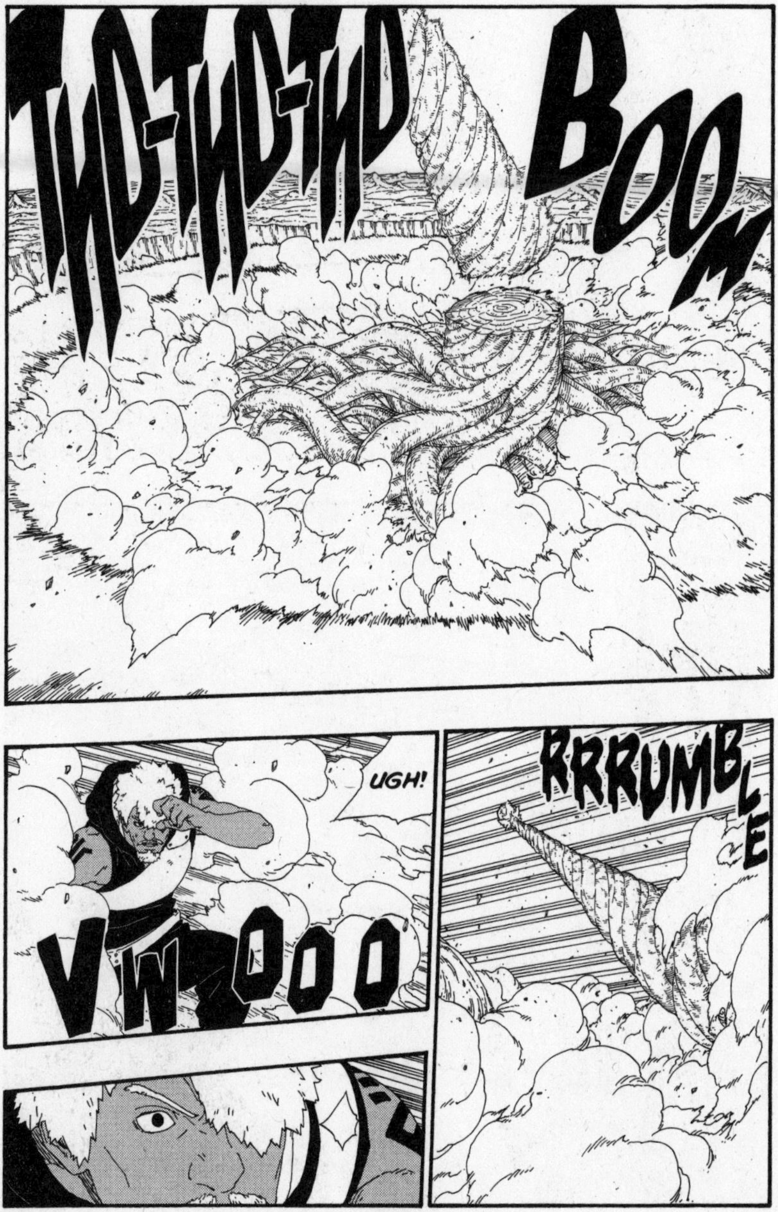
BOOM
THD-THD-THD
RRRUMBLE
UGH!
VWOOO

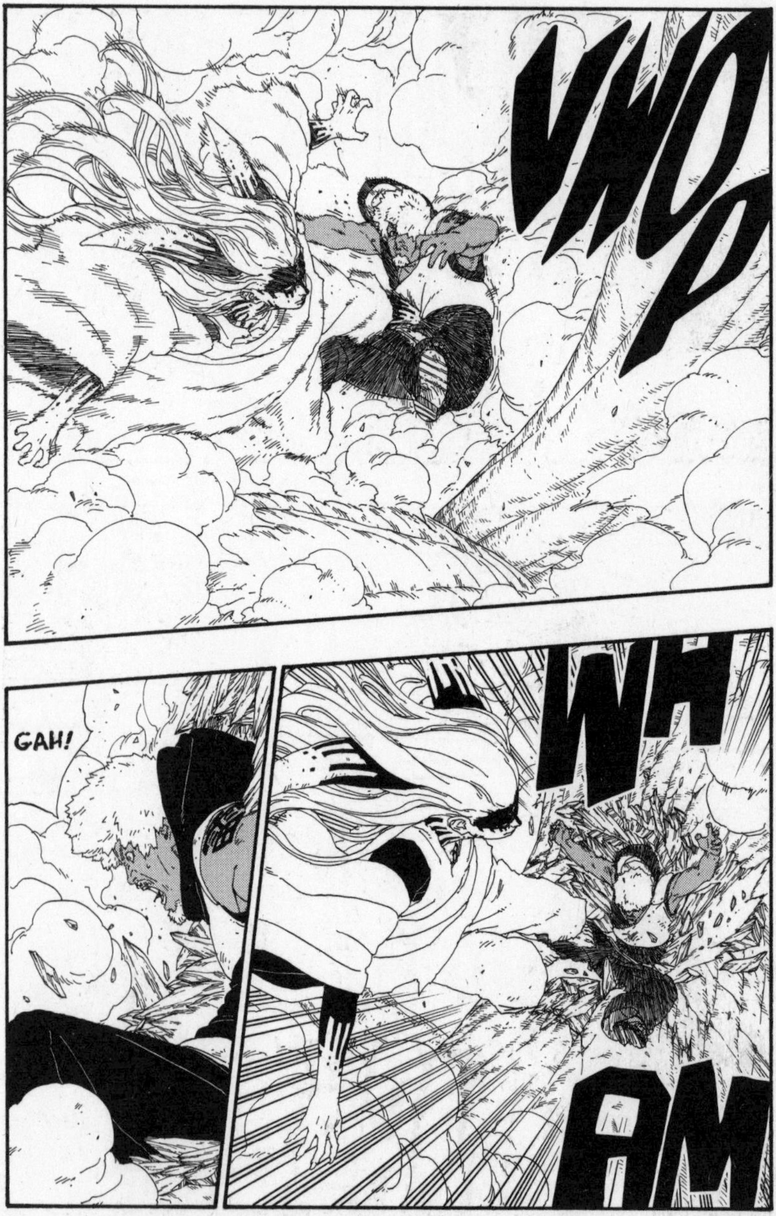
WHAM
GAH!

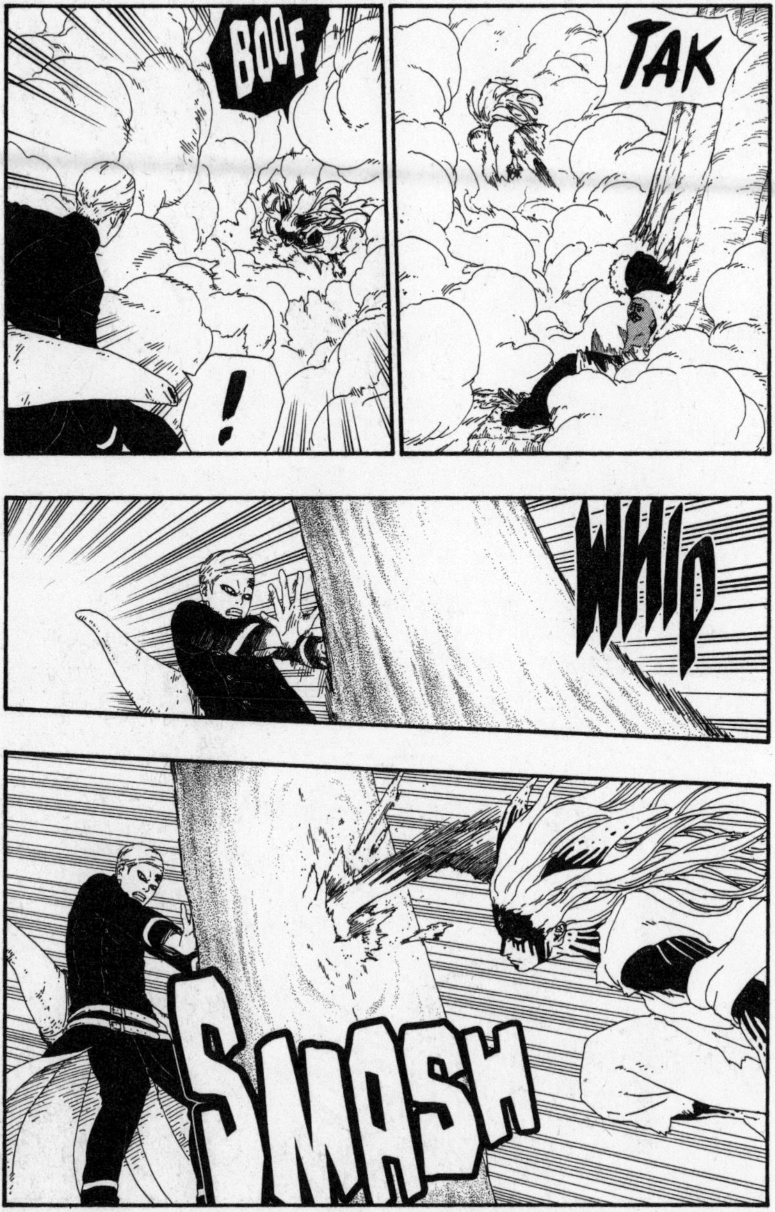
TAK
BOOF
!
WHIP
SMASH

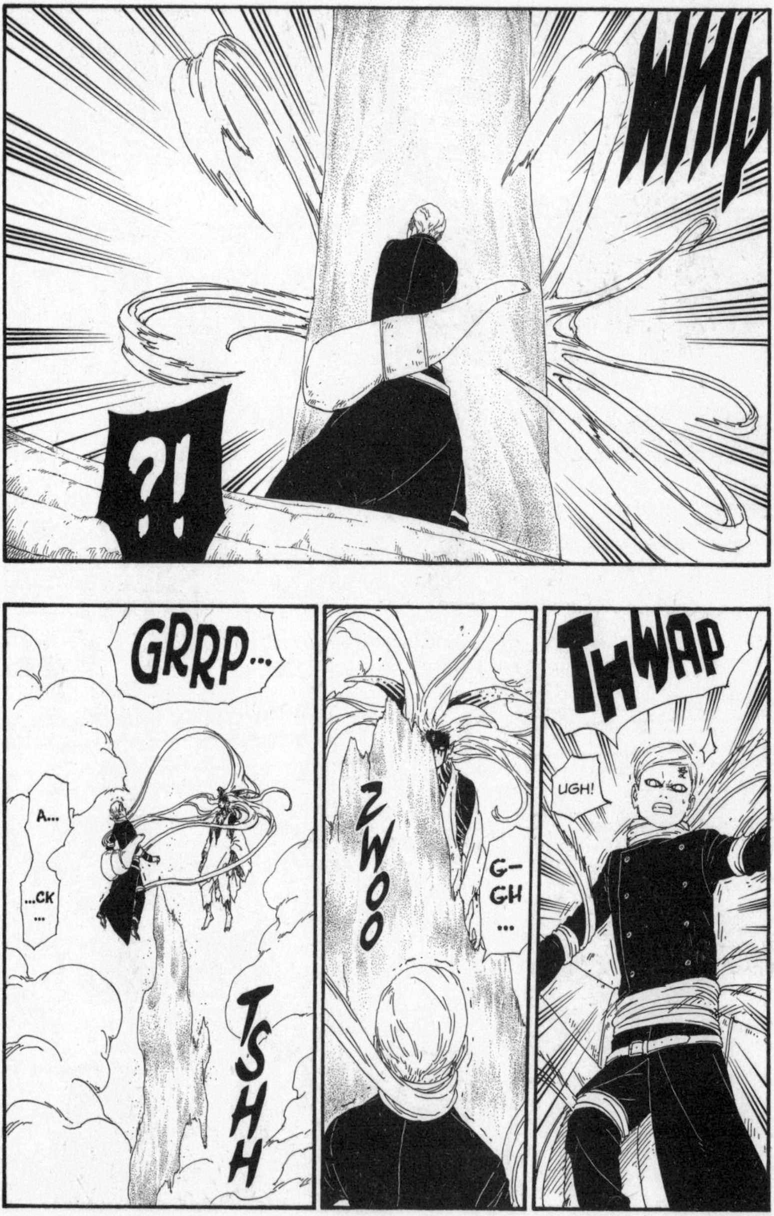
WHIP
?!
THWAP
UGH!
ZWOO
G-GH...
GRRP...
A...
...CK...
TSHH

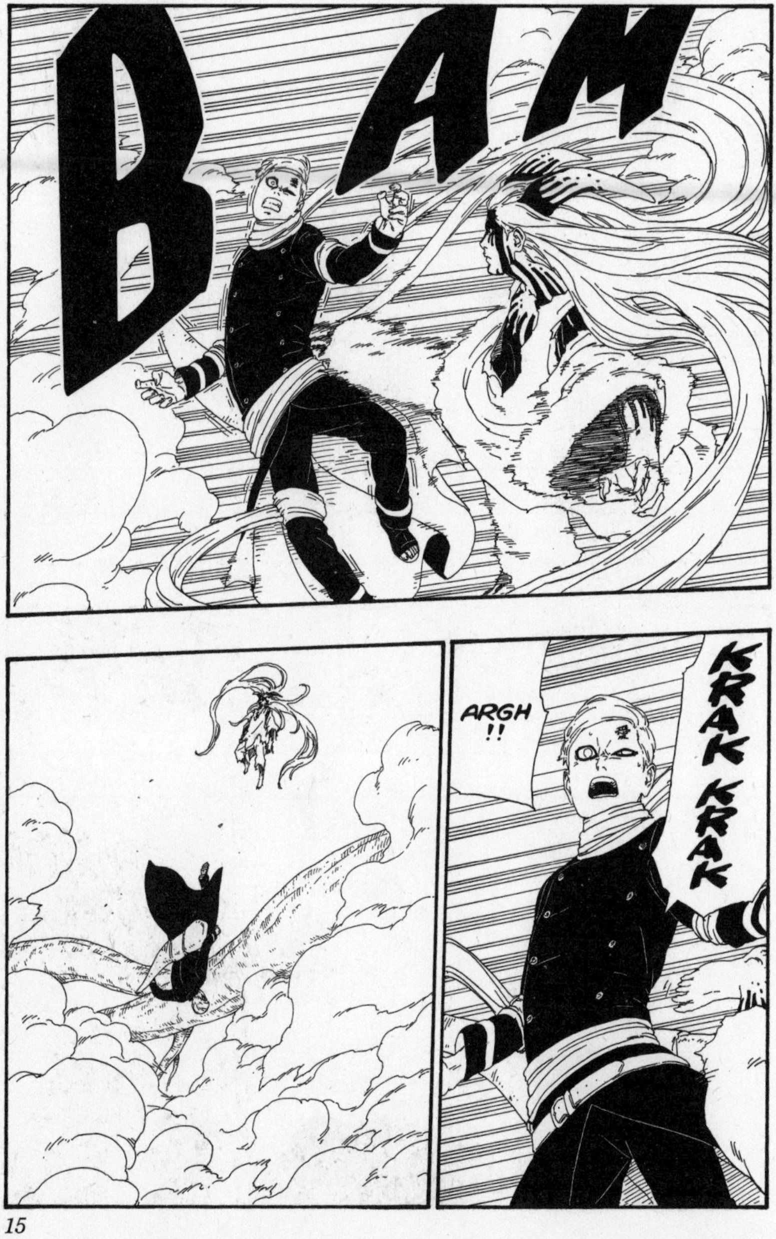
BAM
KRAK KRAK
ARGH!!

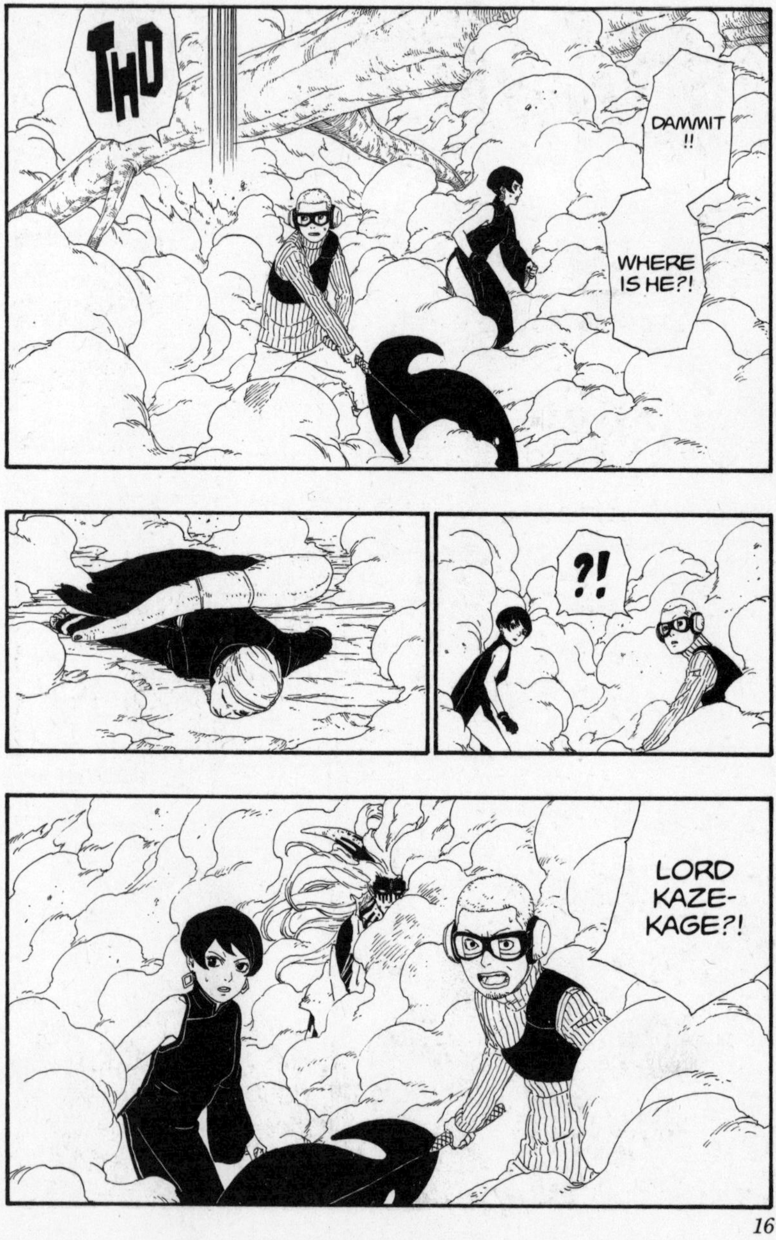
THD
DAMMIT !!
WHERE IS HE?!
?!
LORD KAZE-KAGE?!

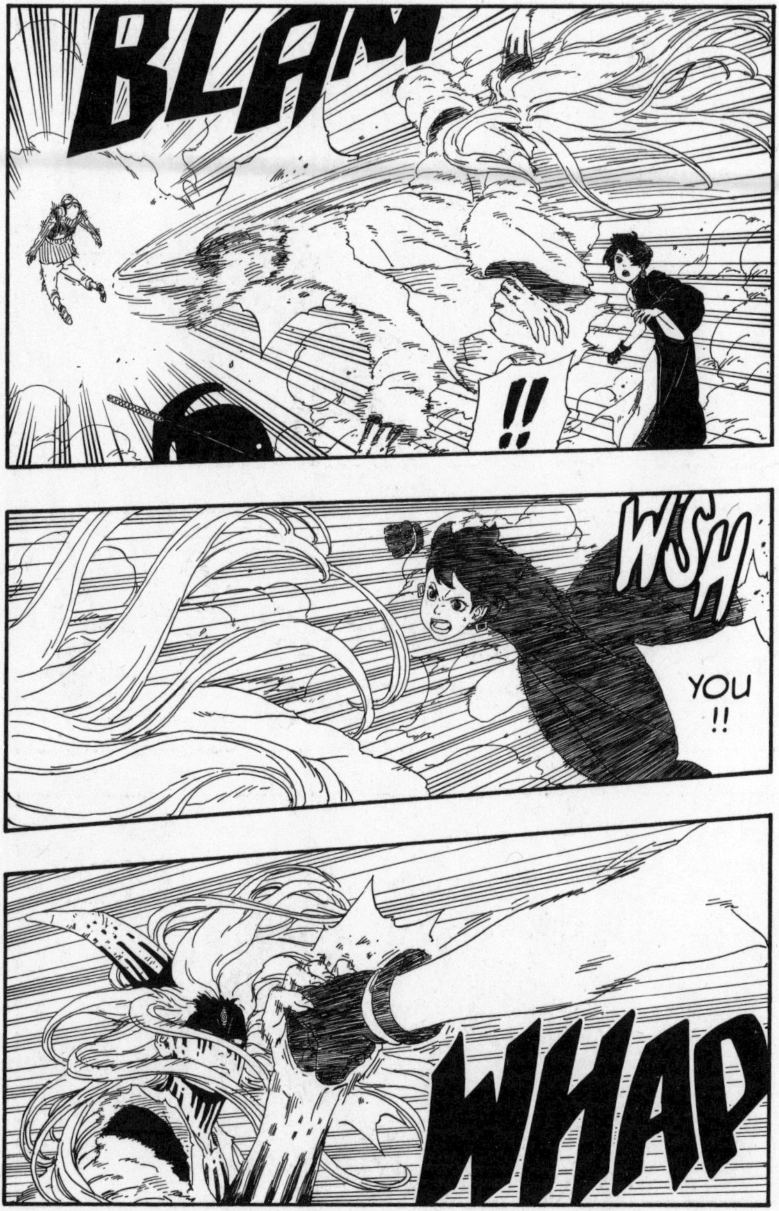
BLAM
!!
WSH
YOU !!
WHAP

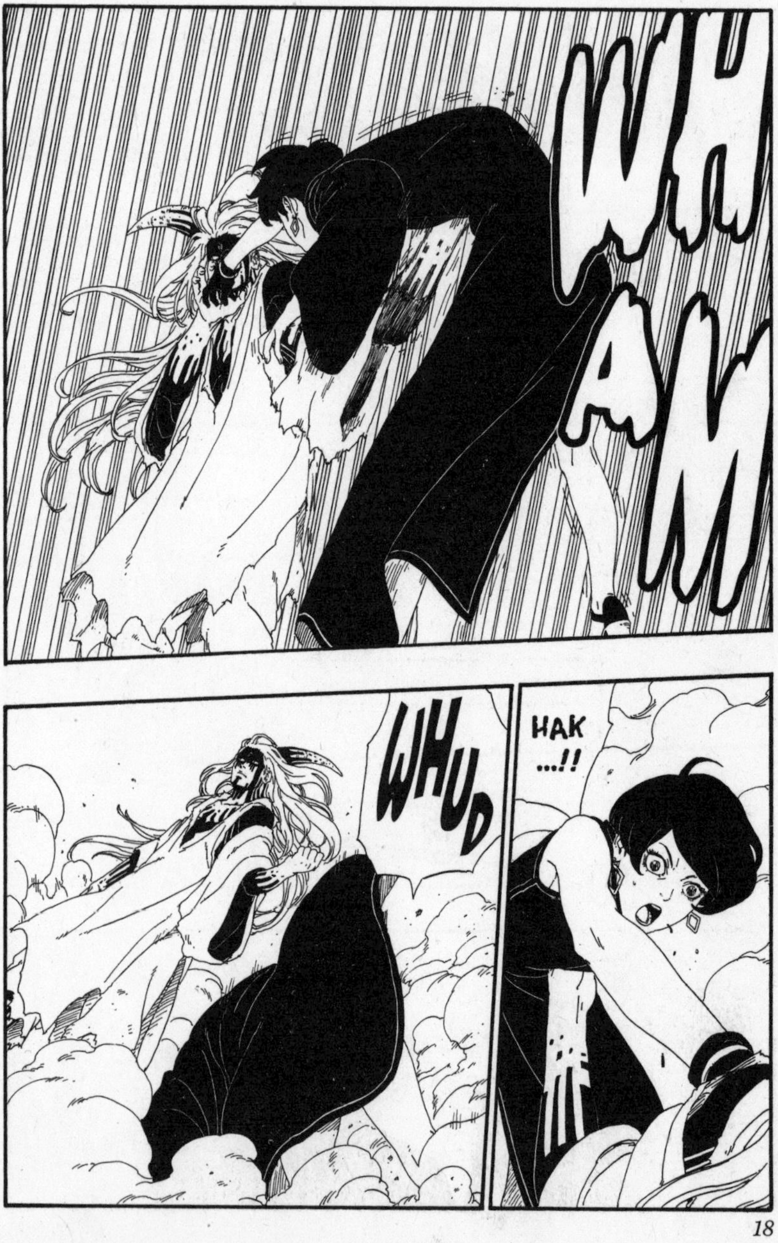
WHAM
HAK ...!!
WHUD

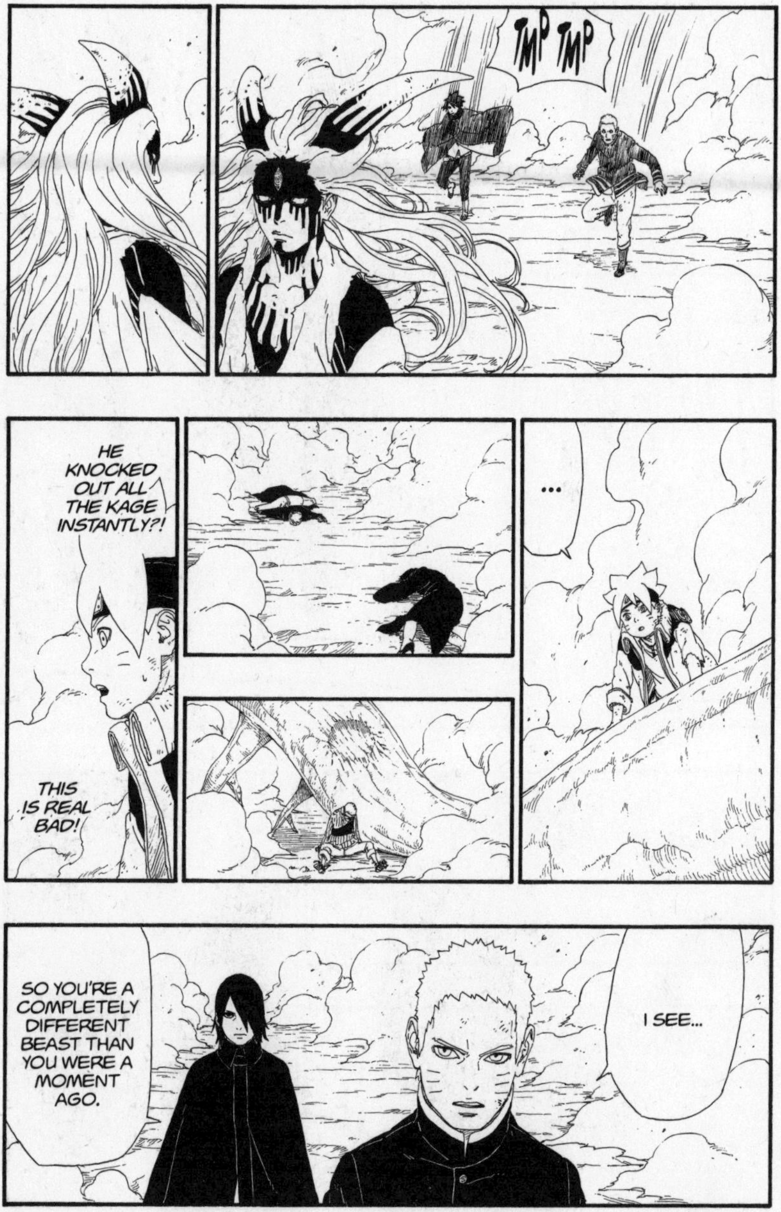
TMP TMP
...
HE KNOCKED OUT ALL THE KAGE INSTANTLY?!
THIS IS REAL BAD!
I SEE...
SO YOU'RE A COMPLETELY DIFFERENT BEAST THAN YOU WERE A MOMENT AGO.

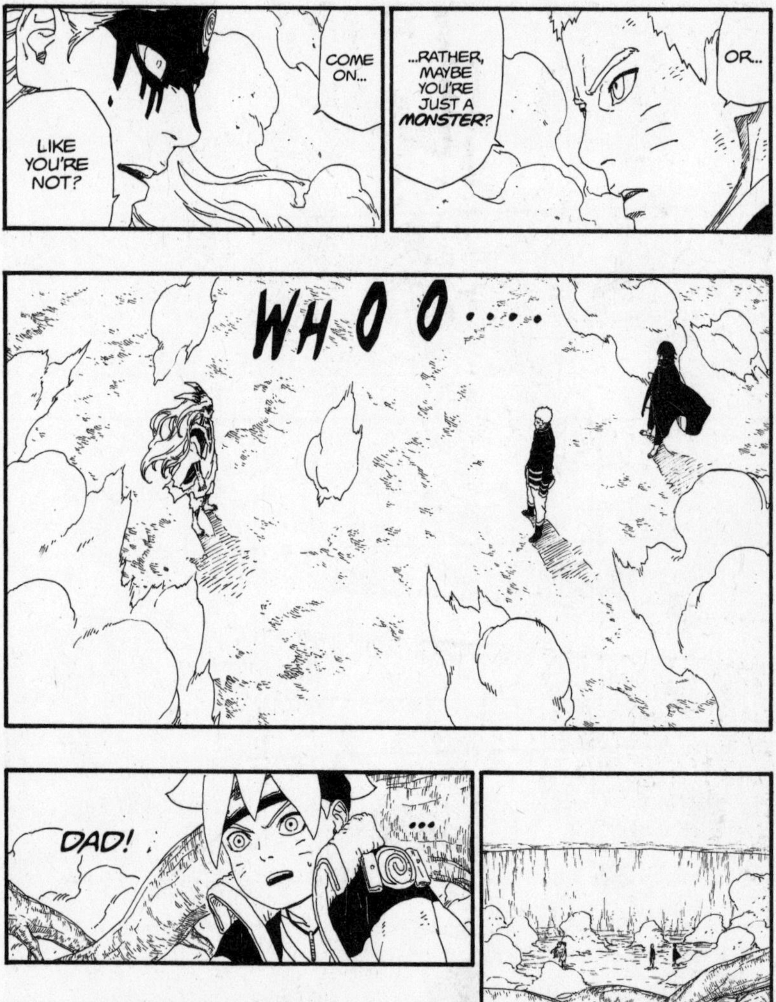
OR..
...RATHER, MAYBE YOU'RE JUST A MONSTER?
COME ON...
LIKE YOU'RE NOT?
WHO O....
...
DAD!
...

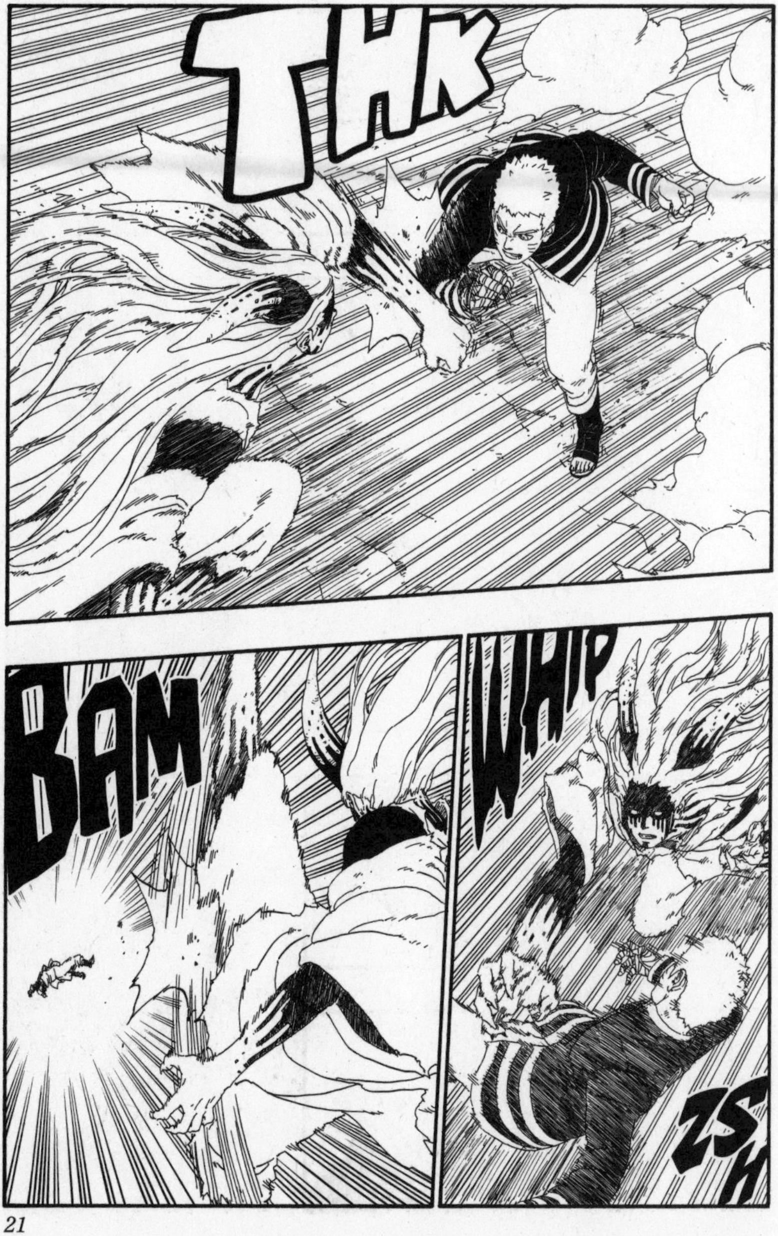
THK
WHIP
ZSH
BAM

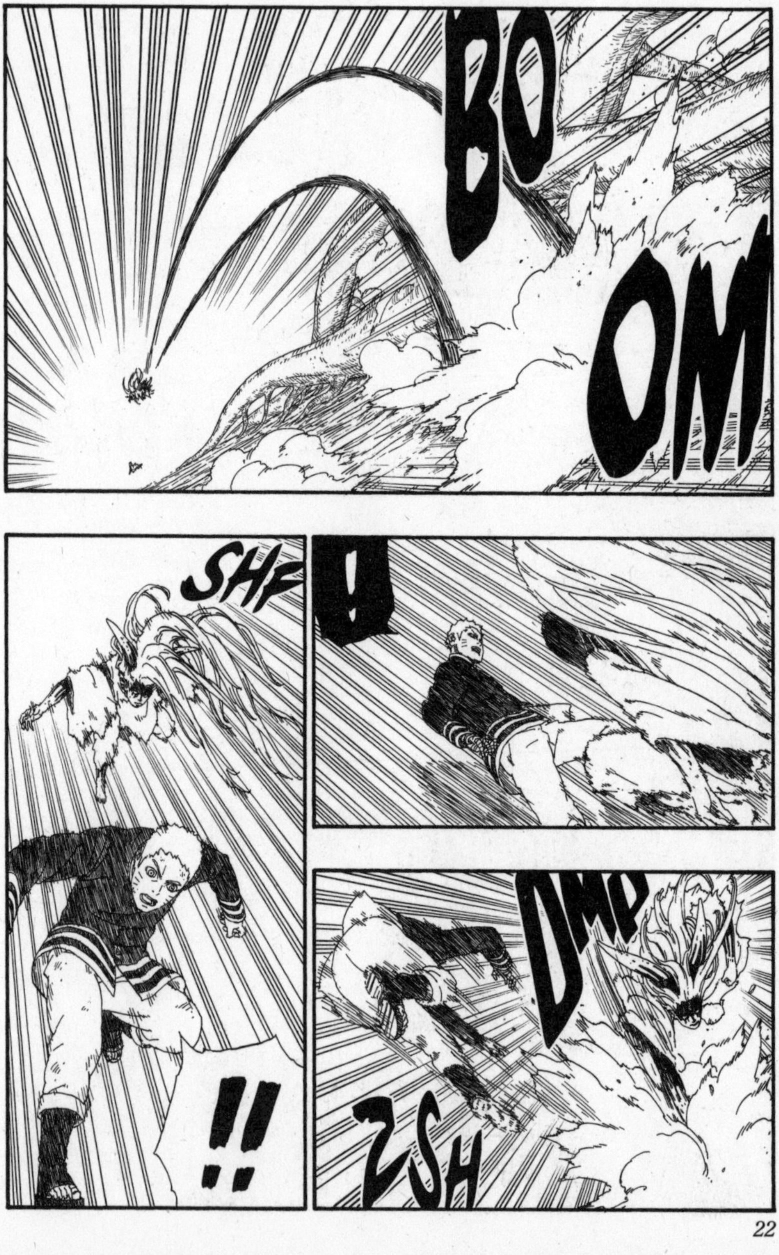
BOOM
!
DMD
ZSH
SHF
!!

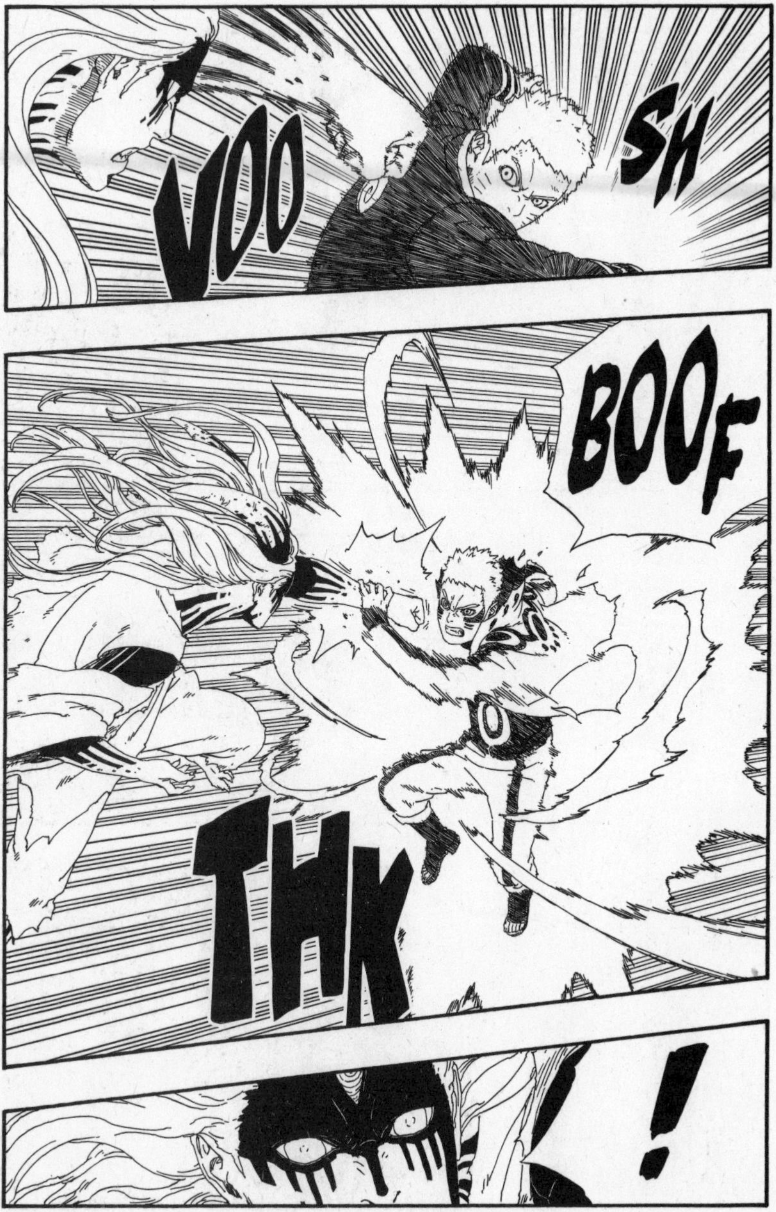
VOO
SH
BOOF
THK
!

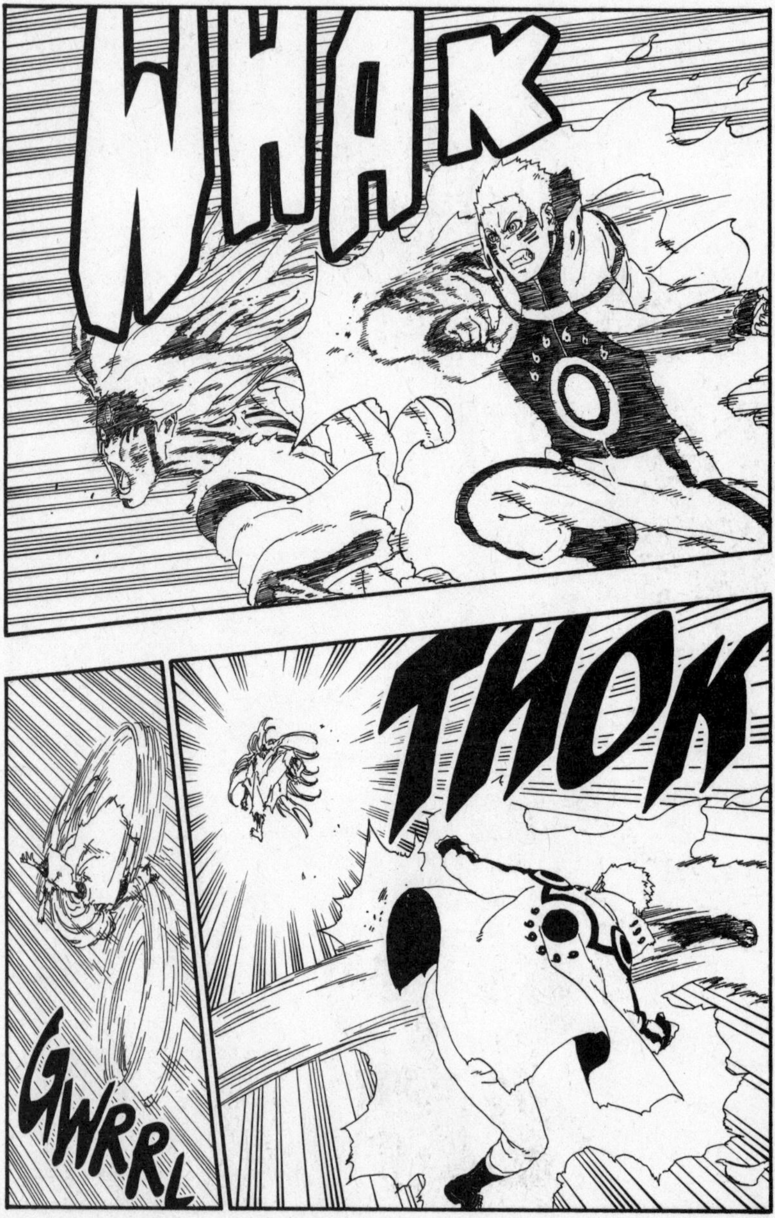
WHAK
THOK
GWRRL

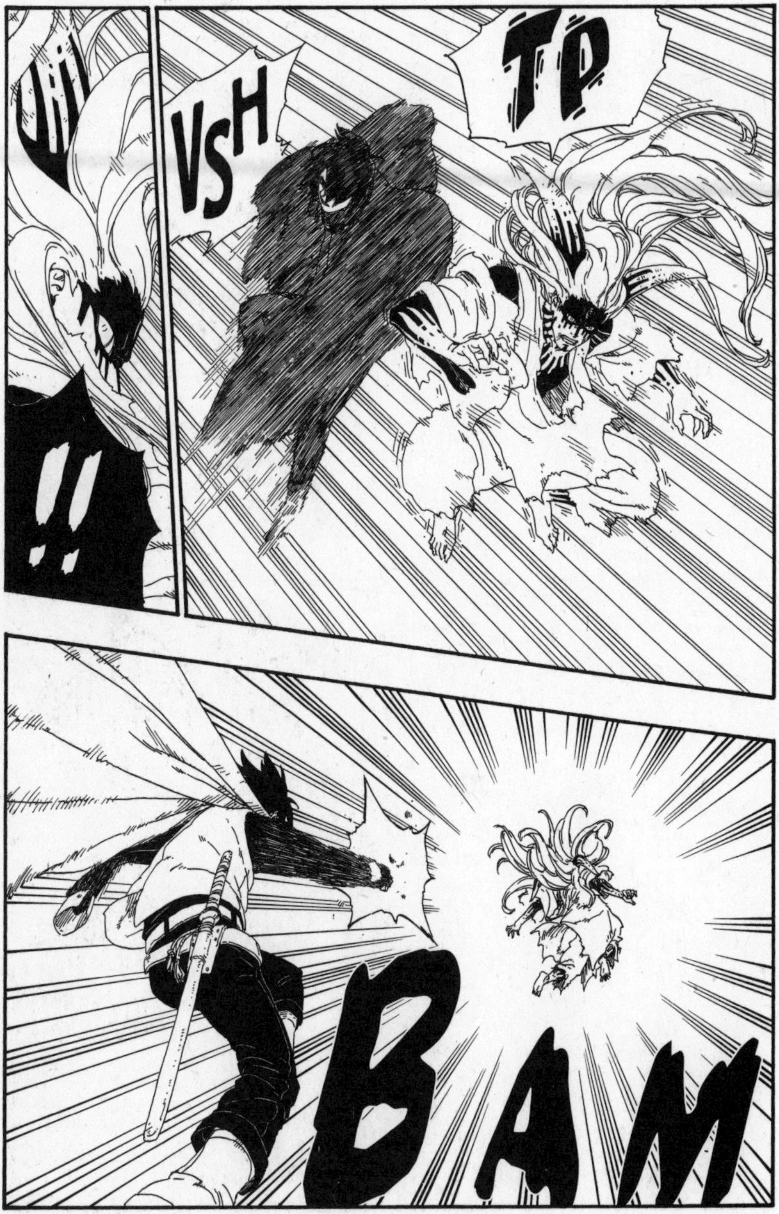
TP
VSH
!!
BAM

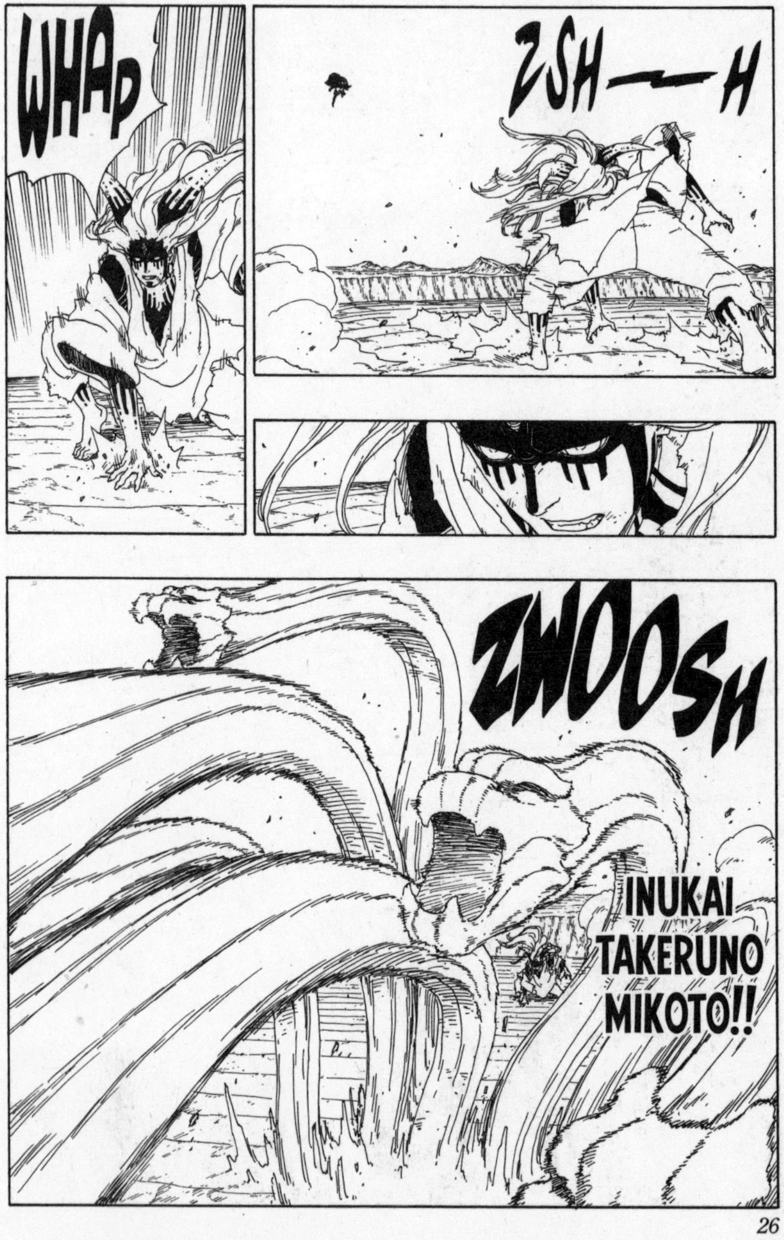
ZSH—H
WHAP
ZWOOSH
INUKAI TAKERUNO MIKOTO!!

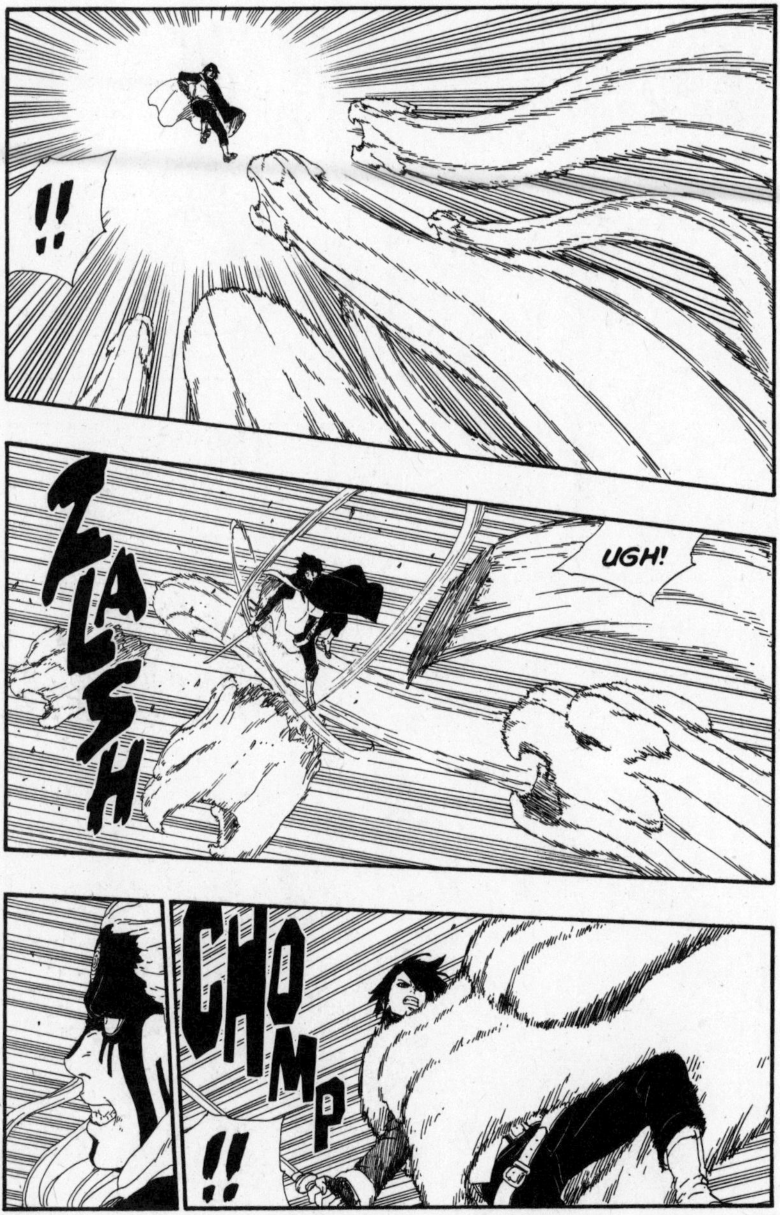
!!
UGH!
FLASH
CHOMP
!!

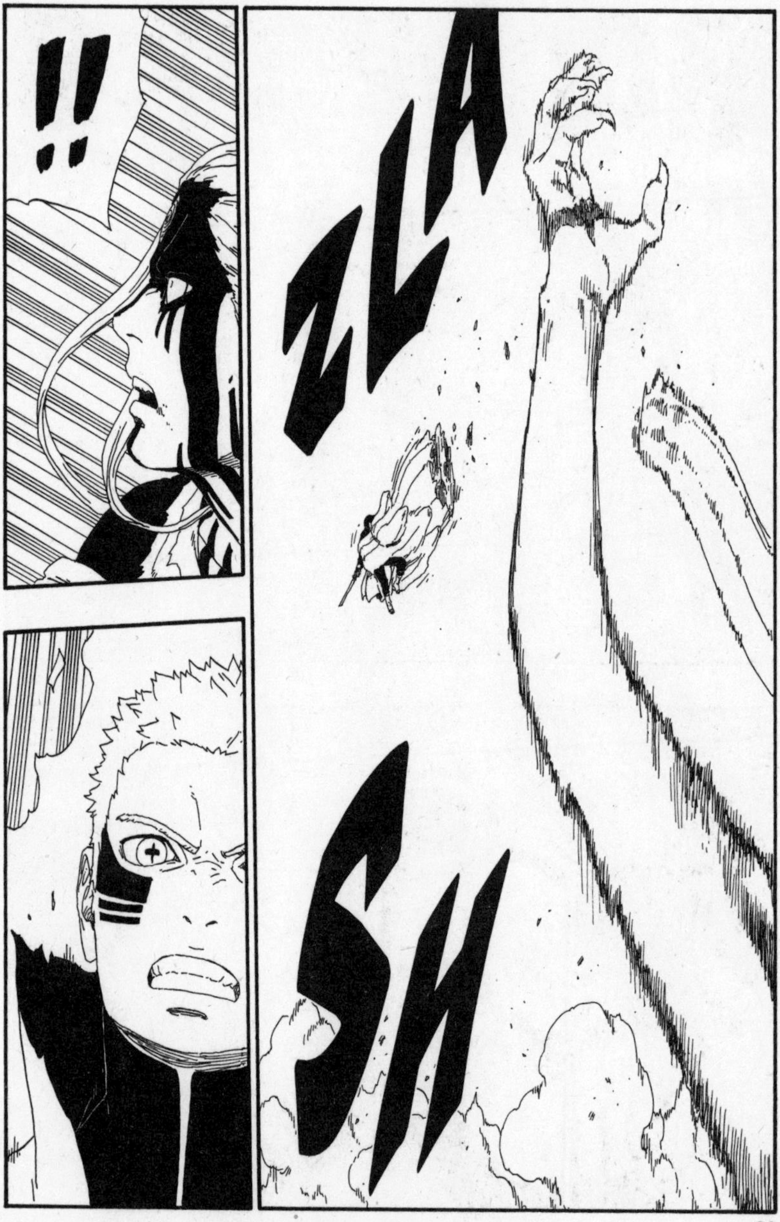
ZZA
SH
!!

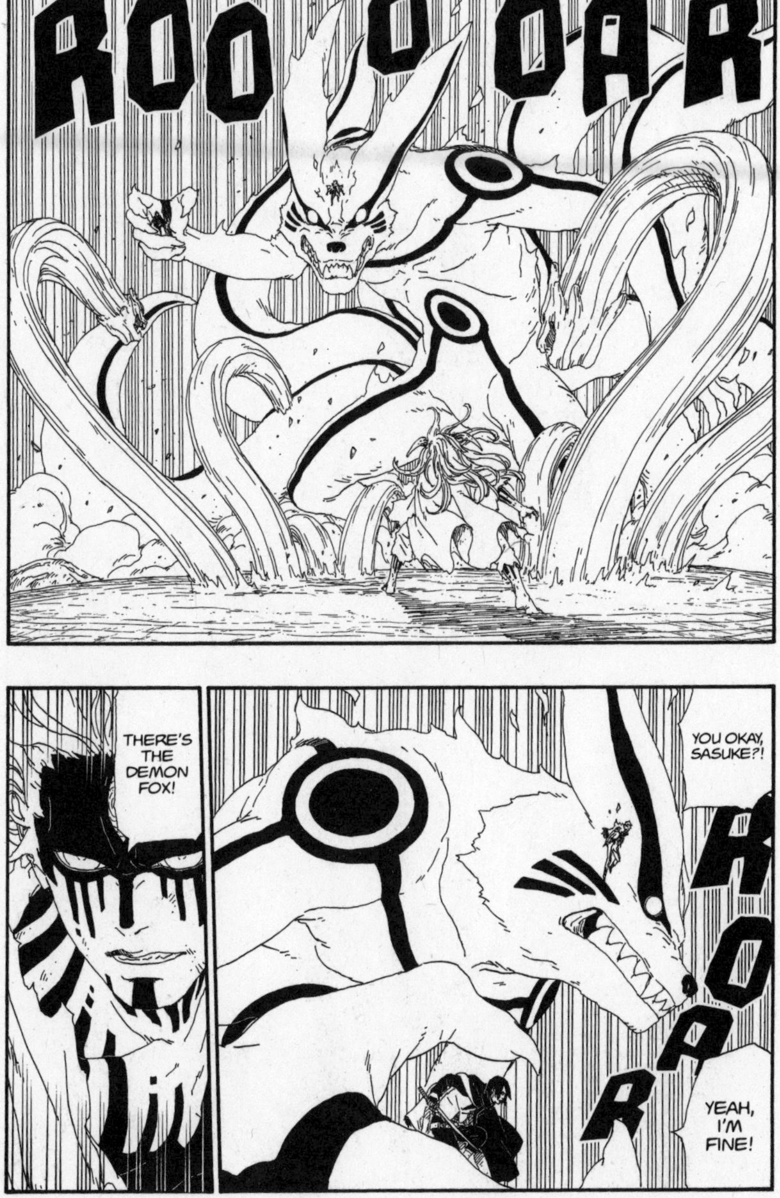
ROOOOAR
YOU OKAY, SASUKE?!
ROAR
YEAH, I'M FINE!
THERE'S THE DEMON FOX!

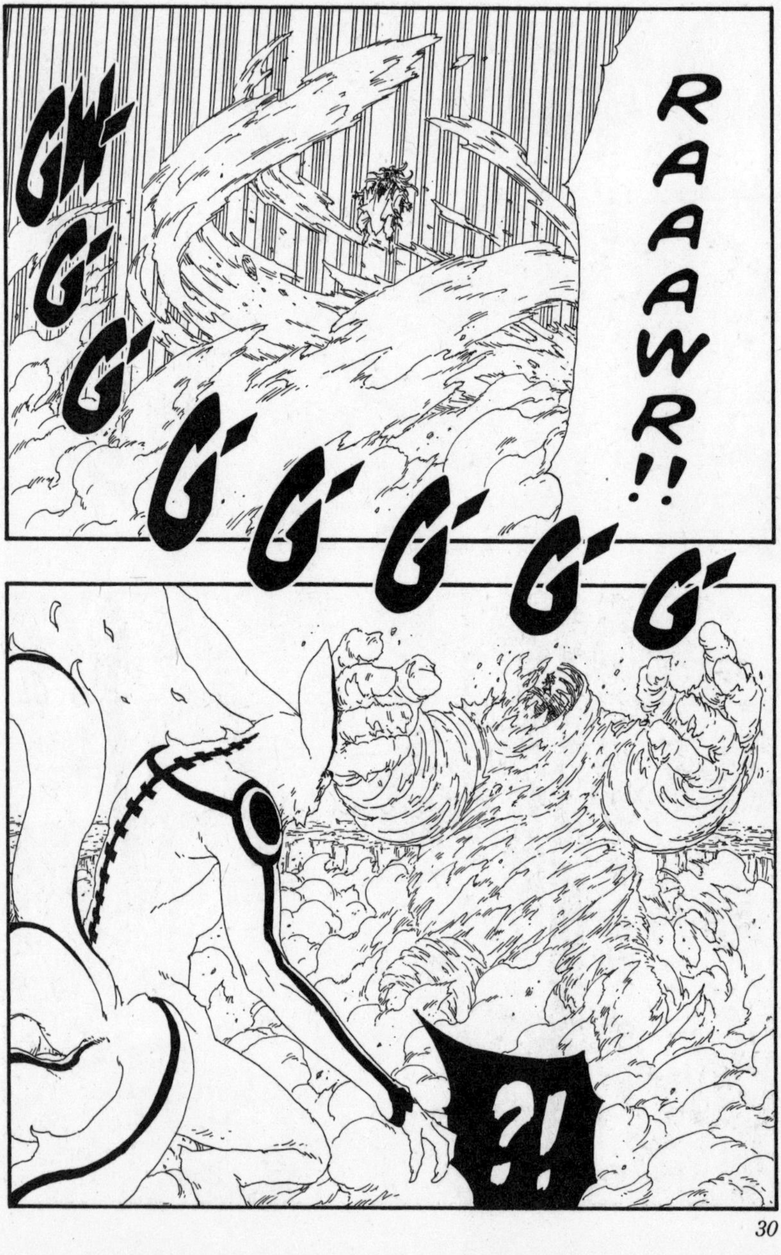
RAAAWR!!
GH-G-G-G-G-G-G-G
?!

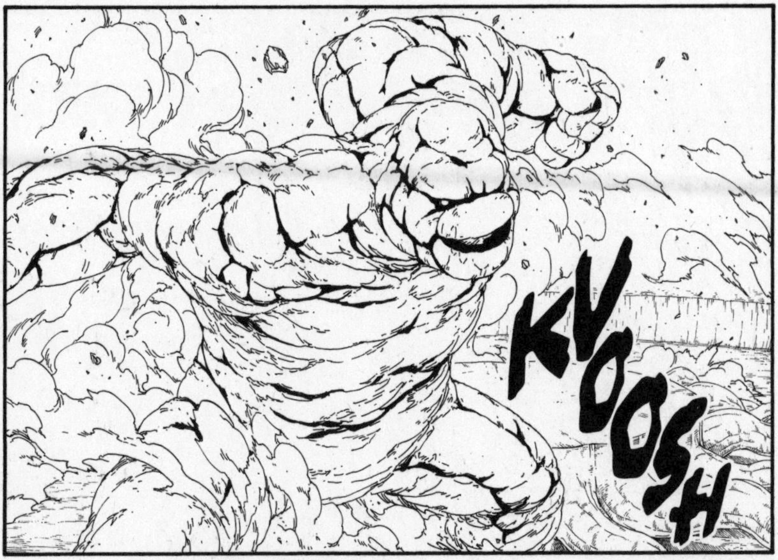
KVOOSH

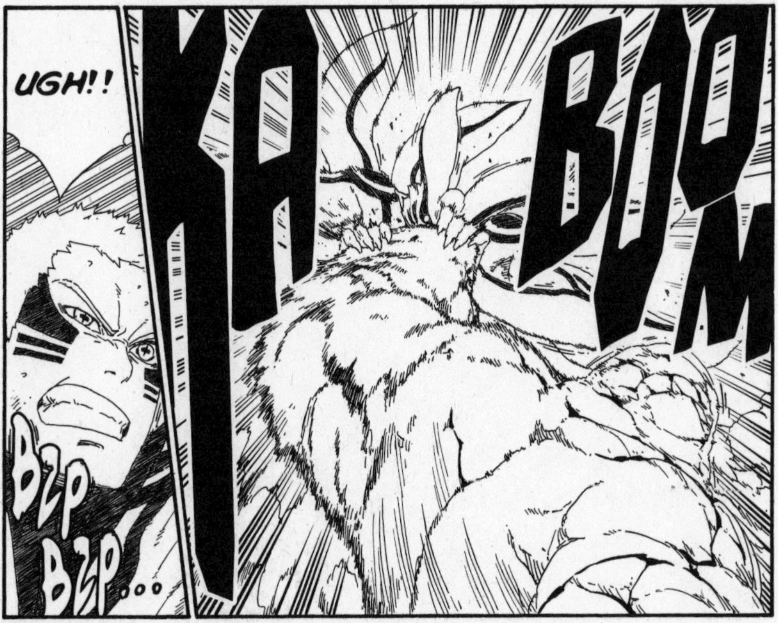
KA BOOM
UGH!!
BZP
BZP...

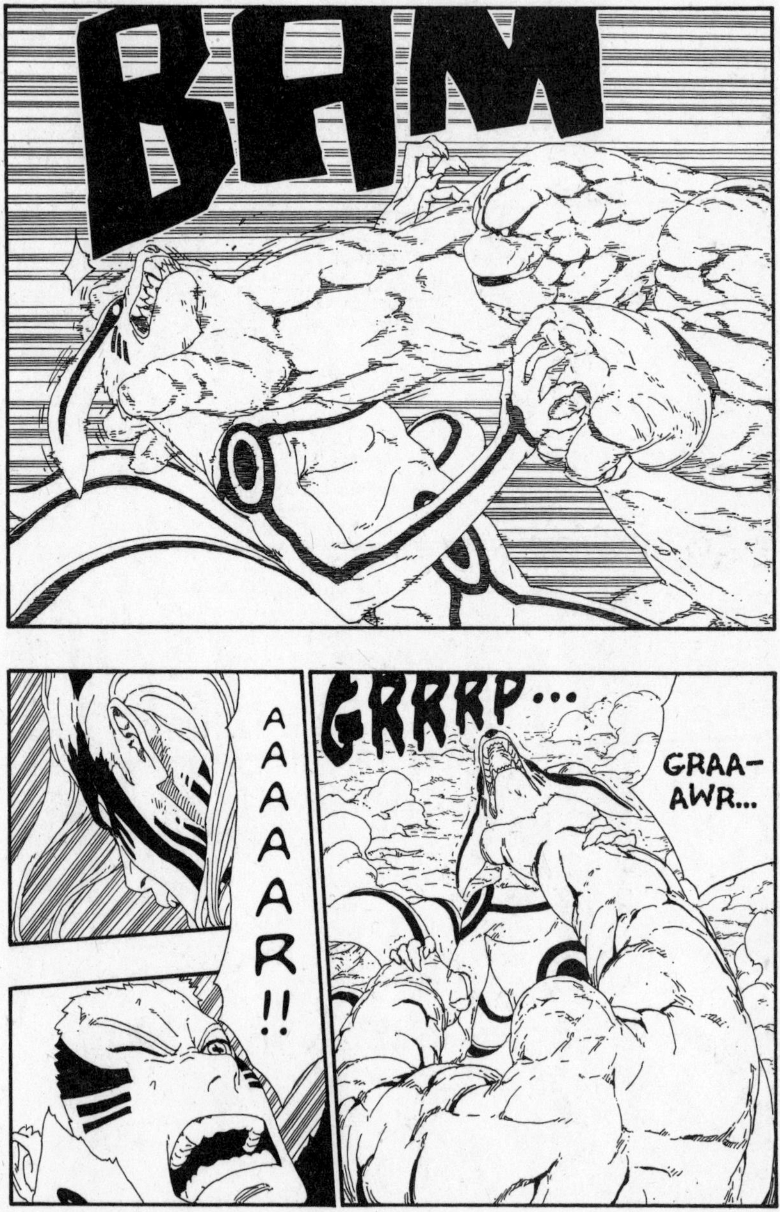
BAM
GRRRP...
GRAA-AWR...
AAAAAR!!

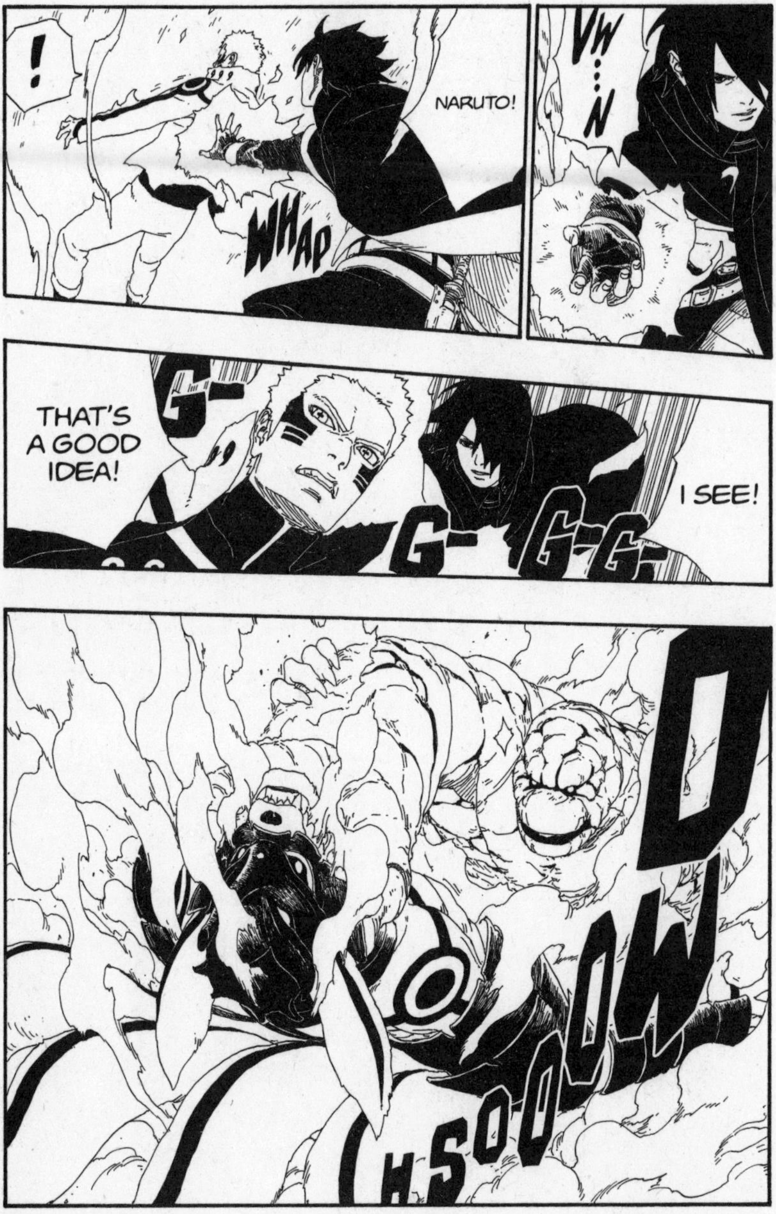
VW...N
NARUTO!
!
WHAP
I SEE!
G-G-G-
G-
THAT'S A GOOD IDEA!
G-
DWOOOOSH

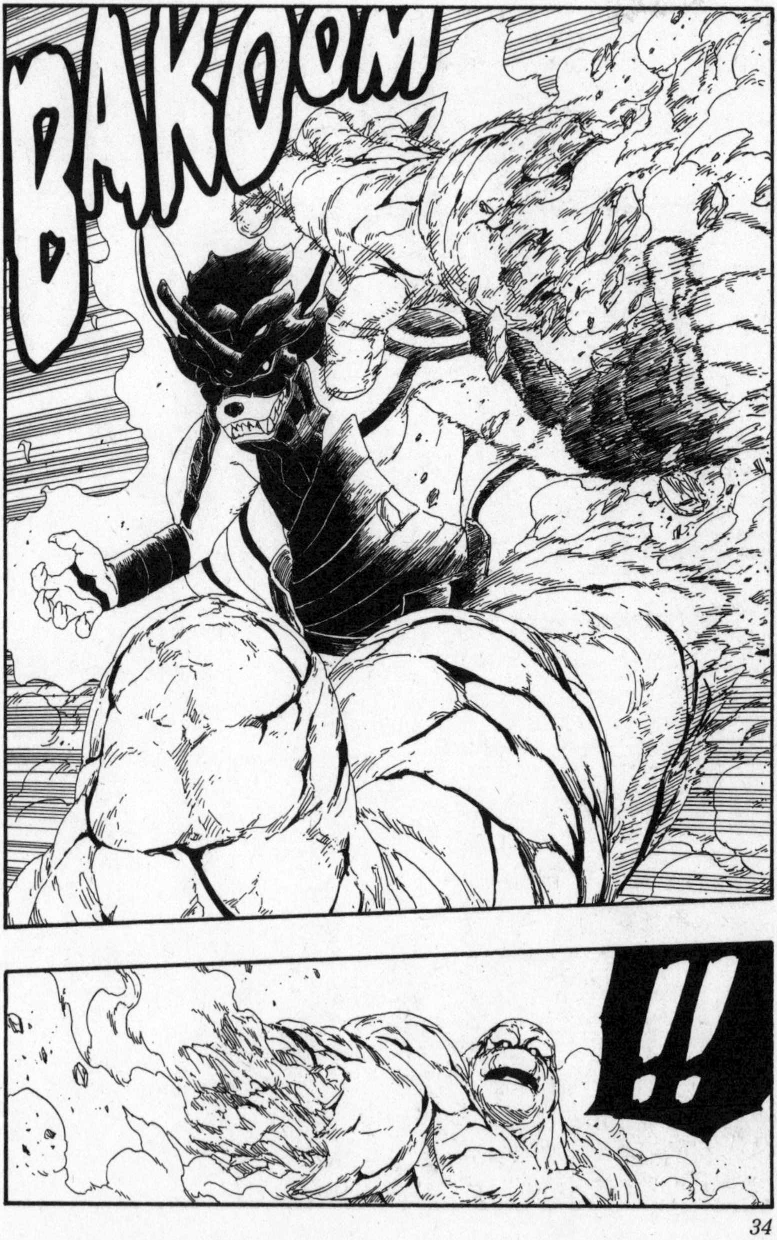
BAKOOM
!!

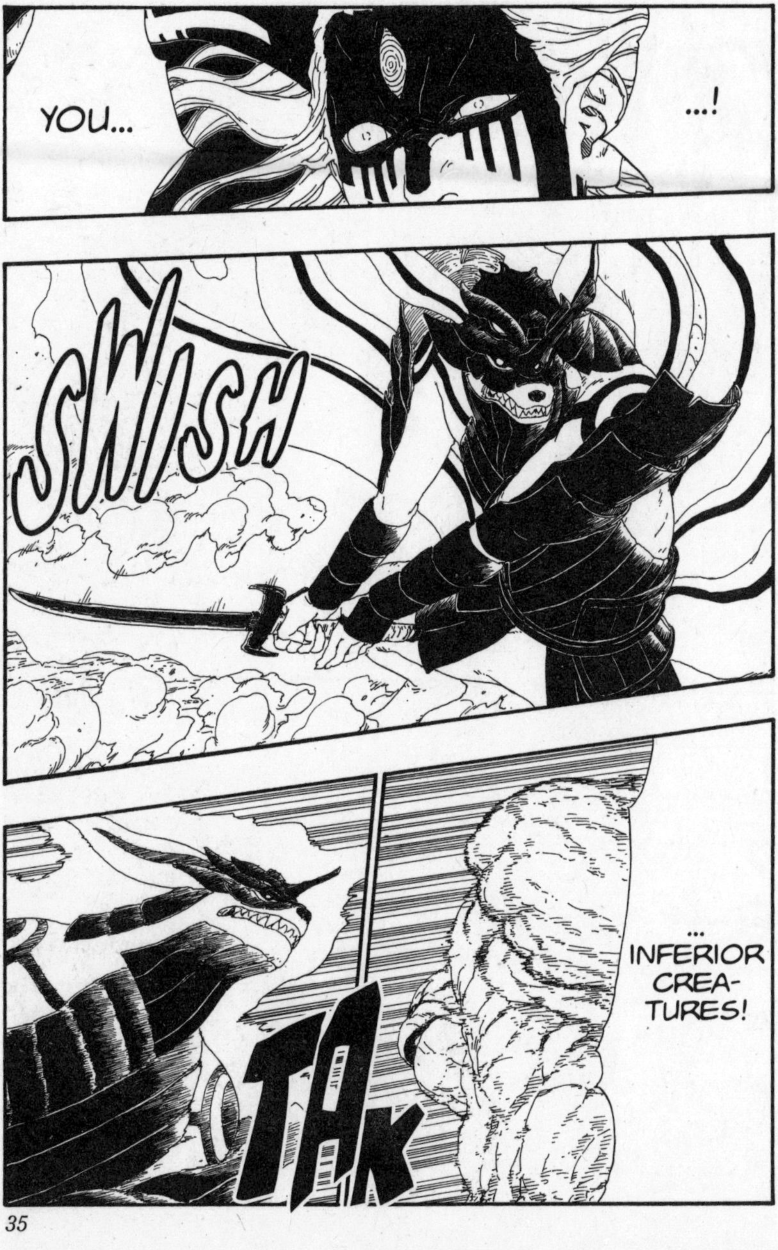
...!
YOU...
SWISH
... INFERIOR CREA-TURES!
TAK

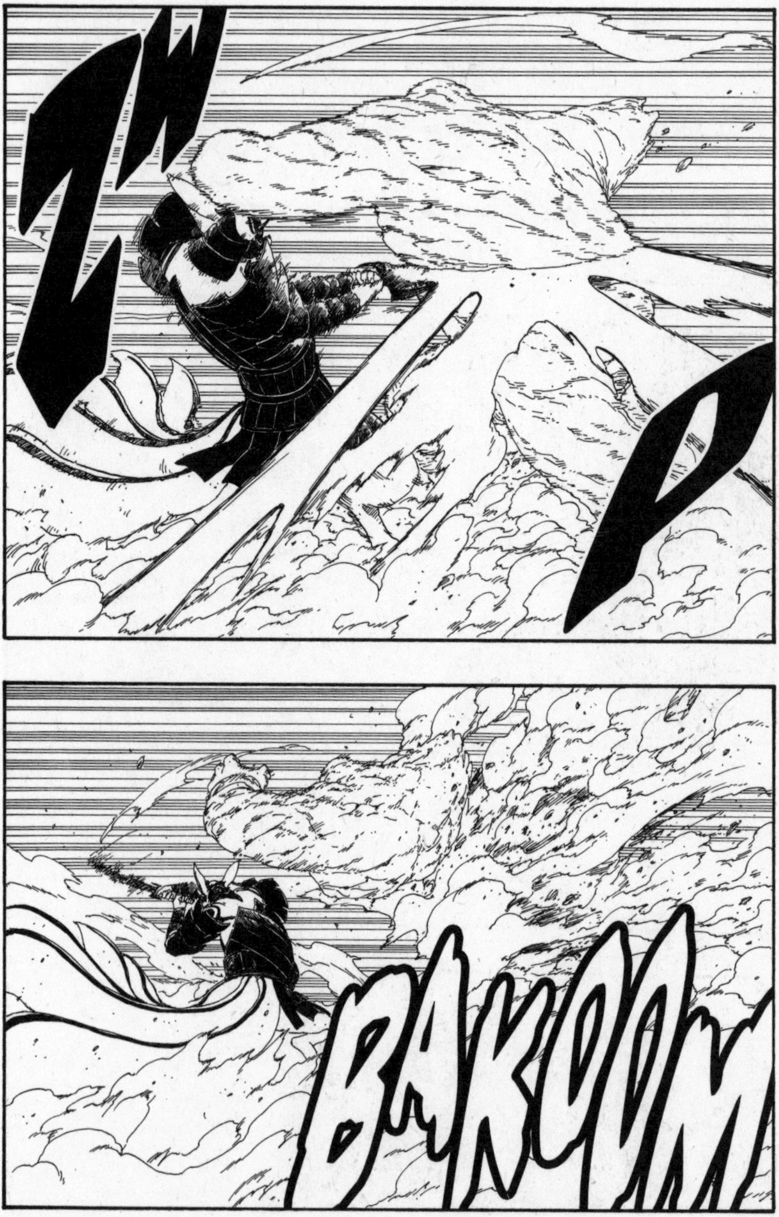
BAKOOM

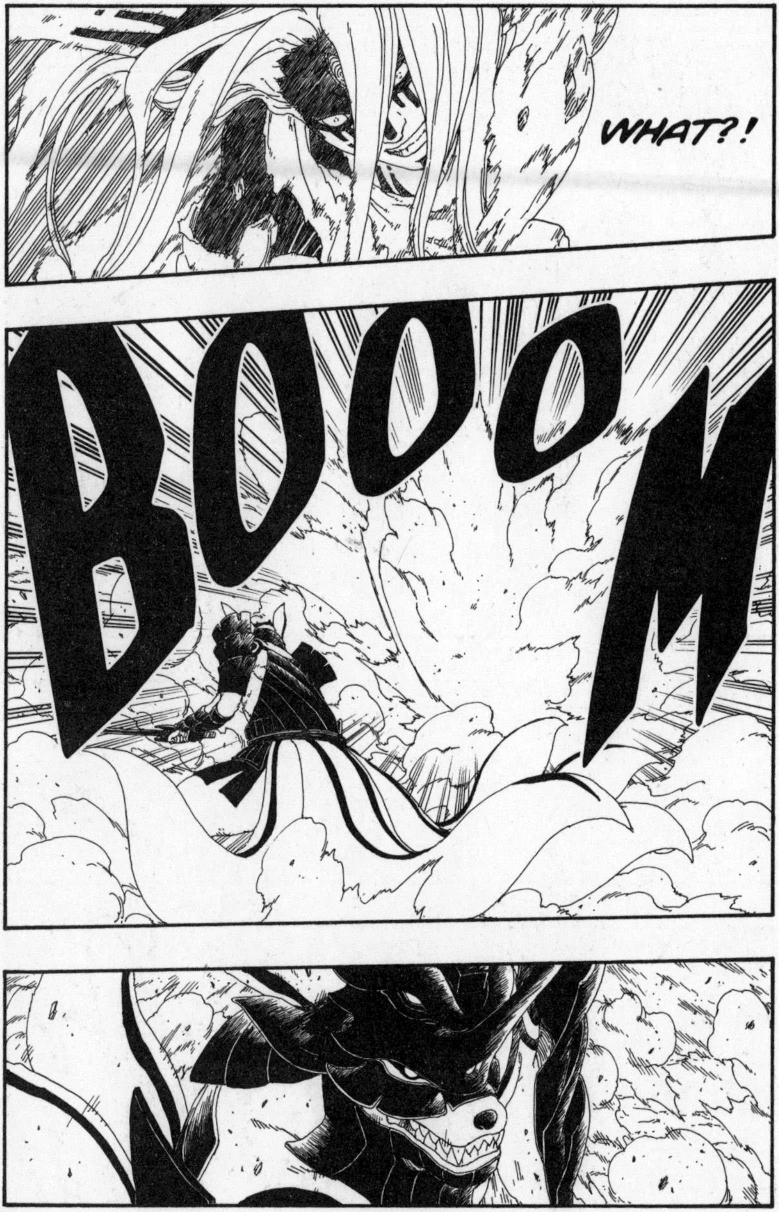
WHAT?!
BOOOM

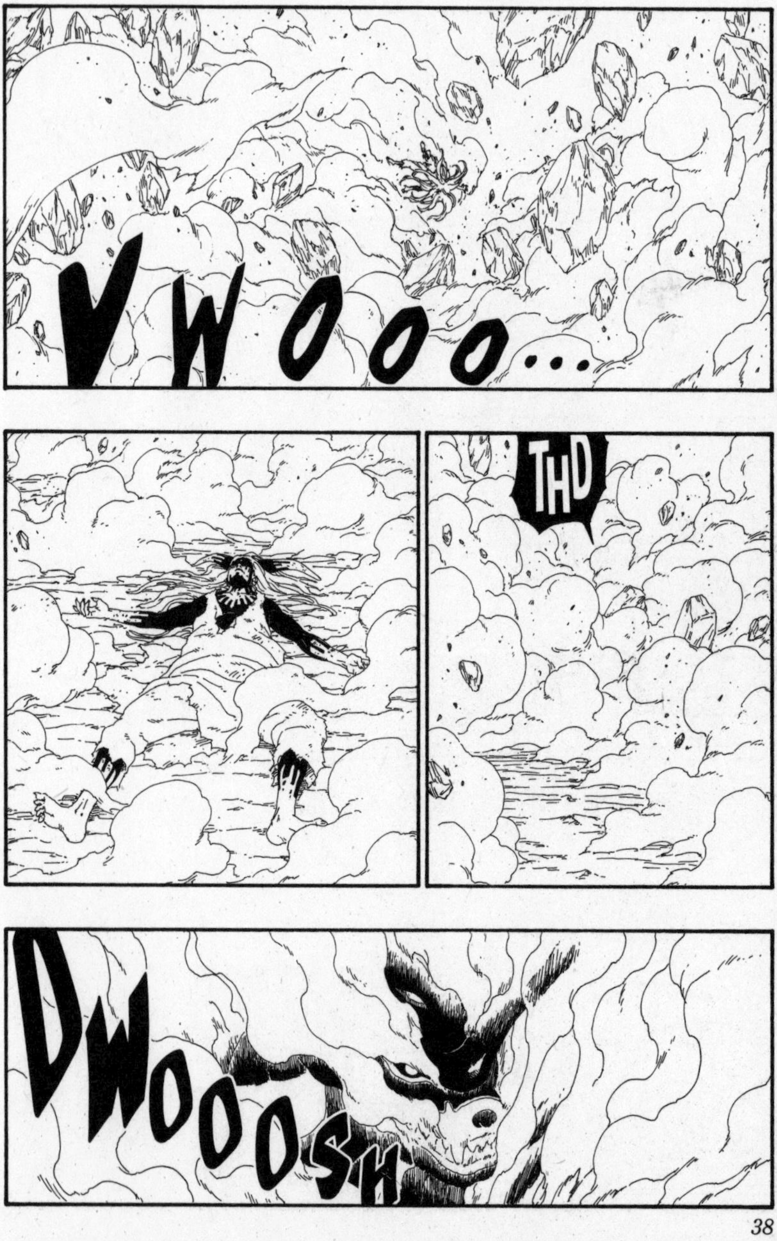
VWOOO...
THD
DWOOOSH

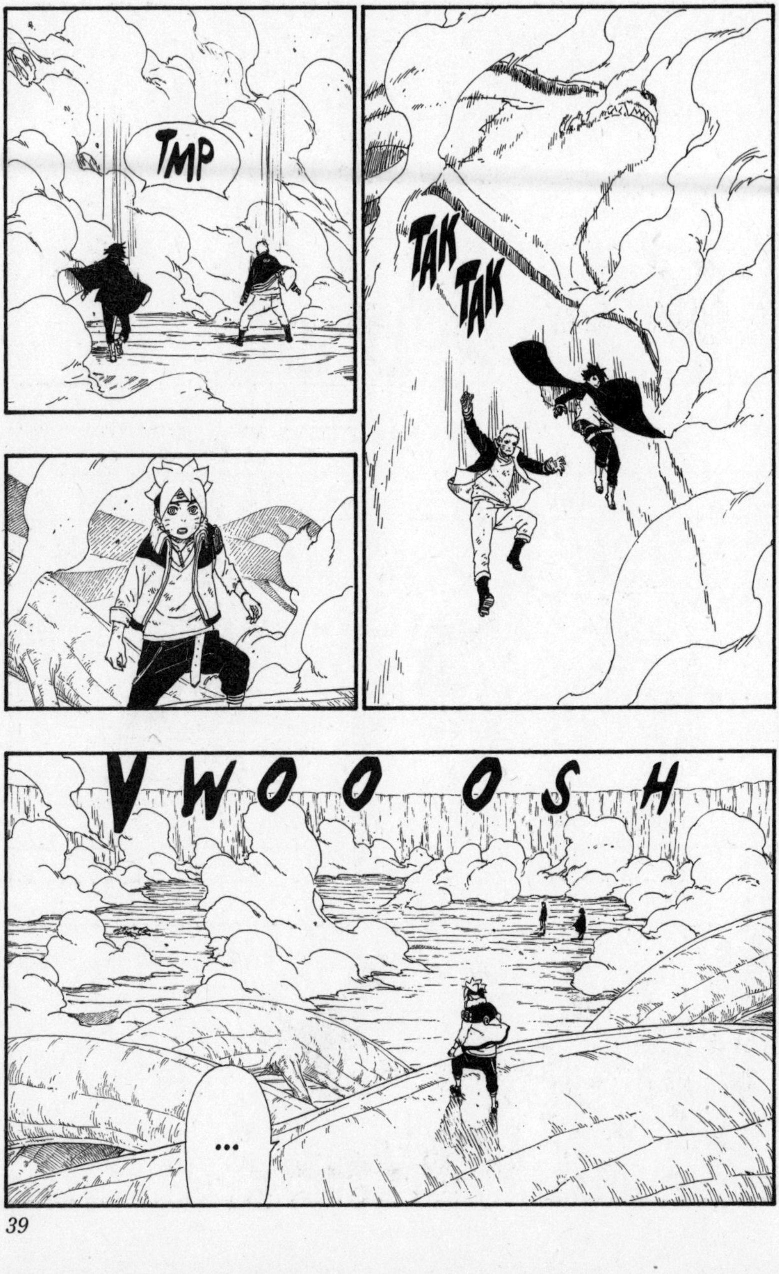
TAK TAK
TMP
VWOOOSH
...

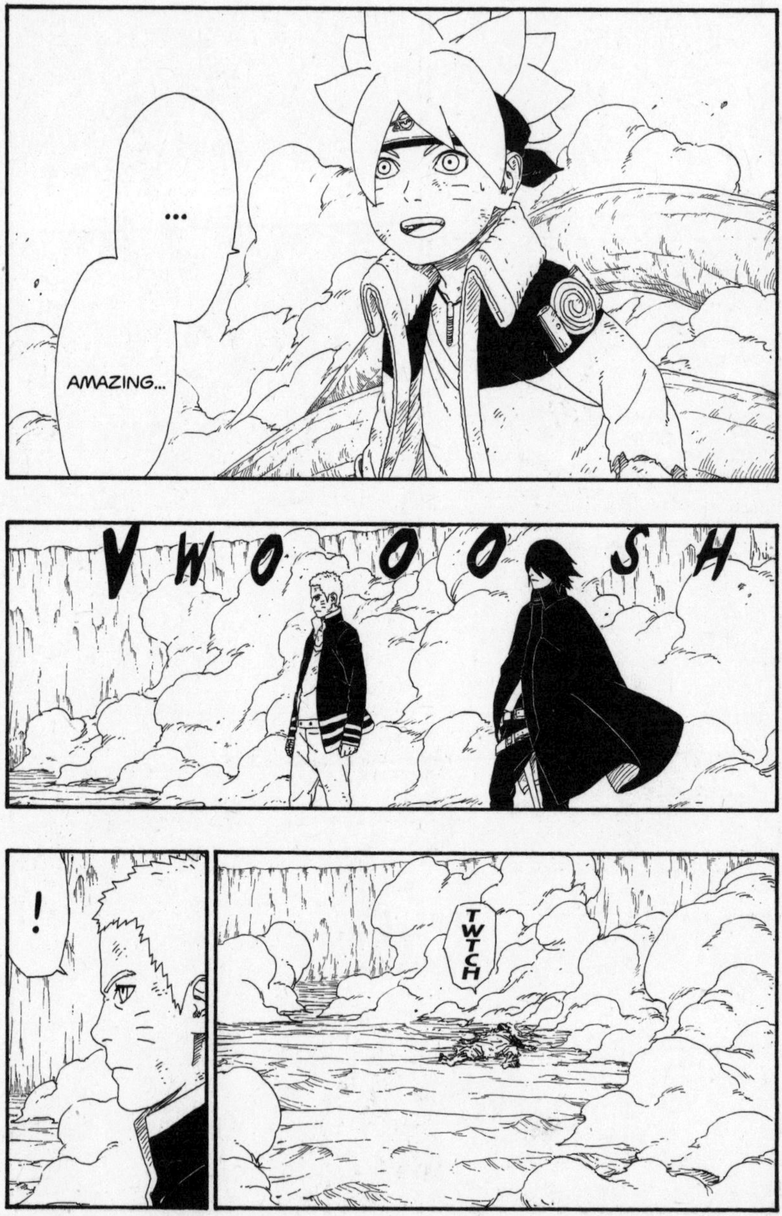
...
AMAZING...
VWOOOSH
TWTCH
!

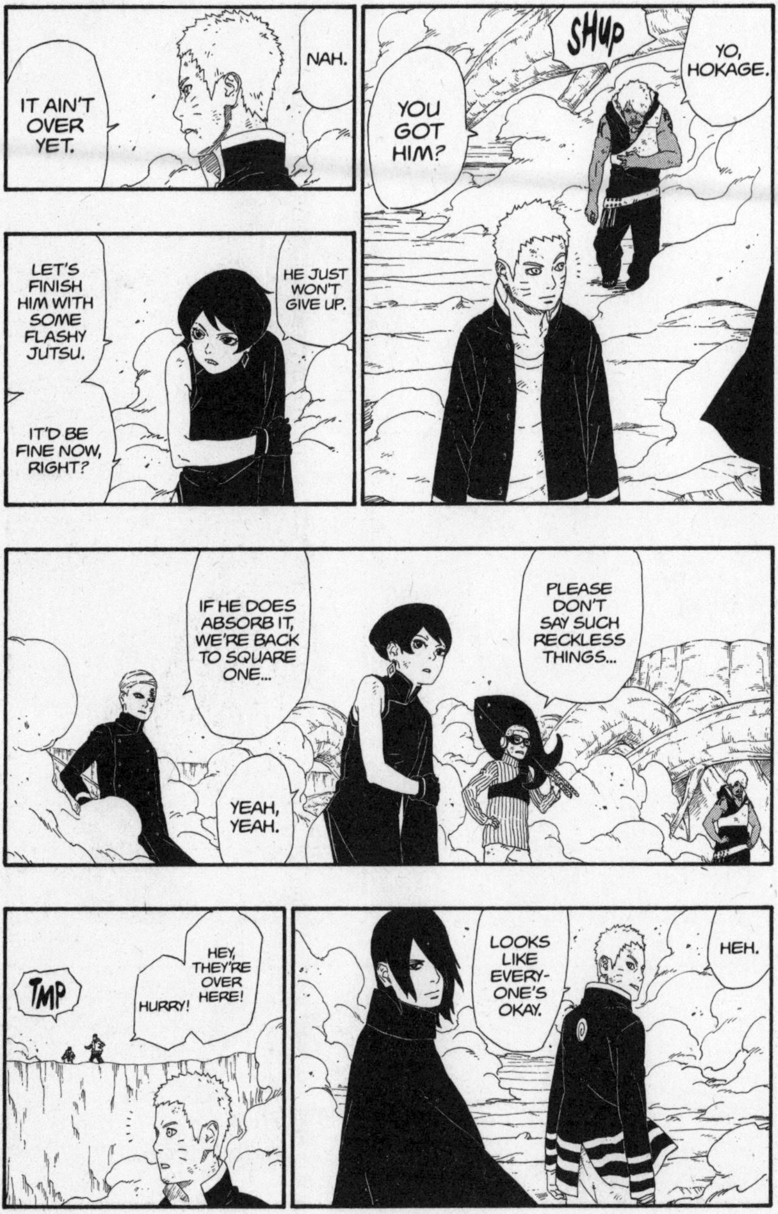
SHUP
YO, HOKAGE.
YOU GOT HIM?
NAH.
IT AIN'T OVER YET.
HE JUST WON'T GIVE UP.
LET'S FINISH HIM WITH SOME FLASHY JUTSU.
IT'D BE FINE NOW, RIGHT?
PLEASE DON'T SAY SUCH RECKLESS THINGS...
IF HE DOES ABSORB IT, WE'RE BACK TO SQUARE ONE...
YEAH, YEAH.
HEH.
LOOKS LIKE EVERY-ONE'S OKAY.
HEY, THEY'RE OVER HERE!
HURRY!
TMP

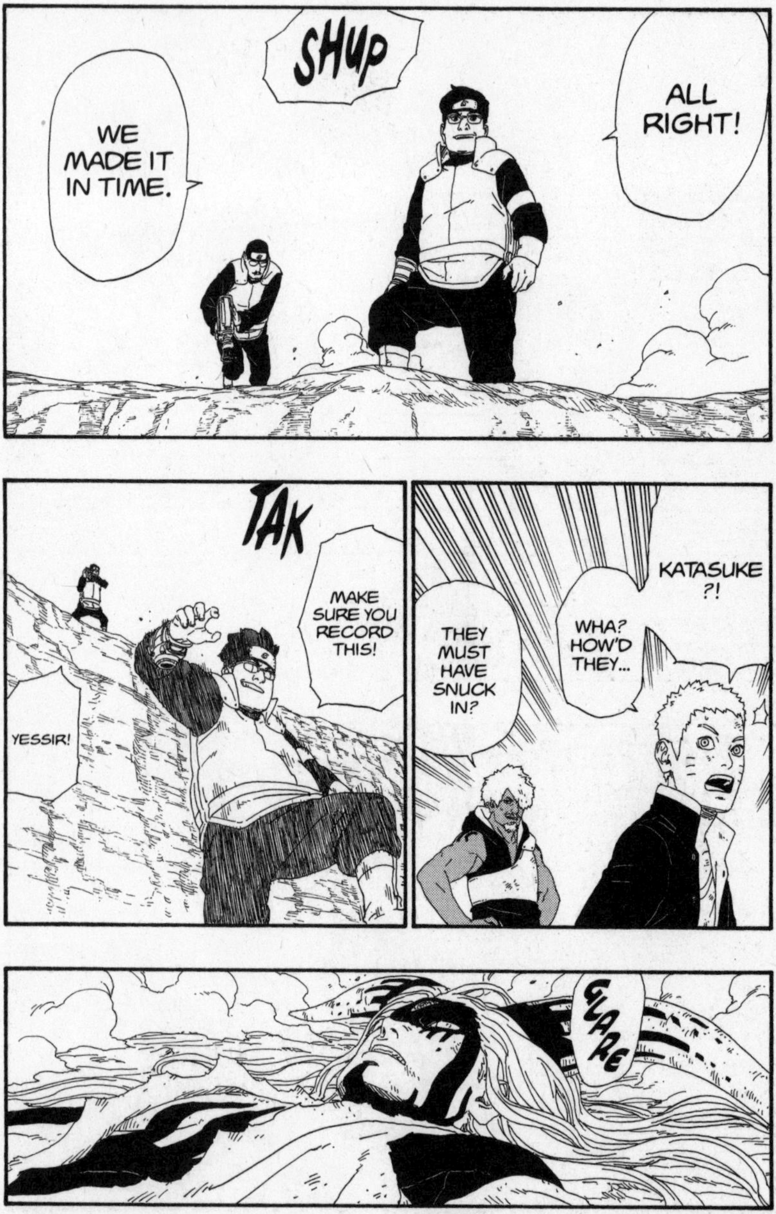
ALL RIGHT!
SHUP
WE MADE IT IN TIME.
KATASUKE ?!
WHA? HOW'D THEY...
THEY MUST HAVE SNUCK IN?
TAK
MAKE SURE YOU RECORD THIS!
YESSIR!
GLARE

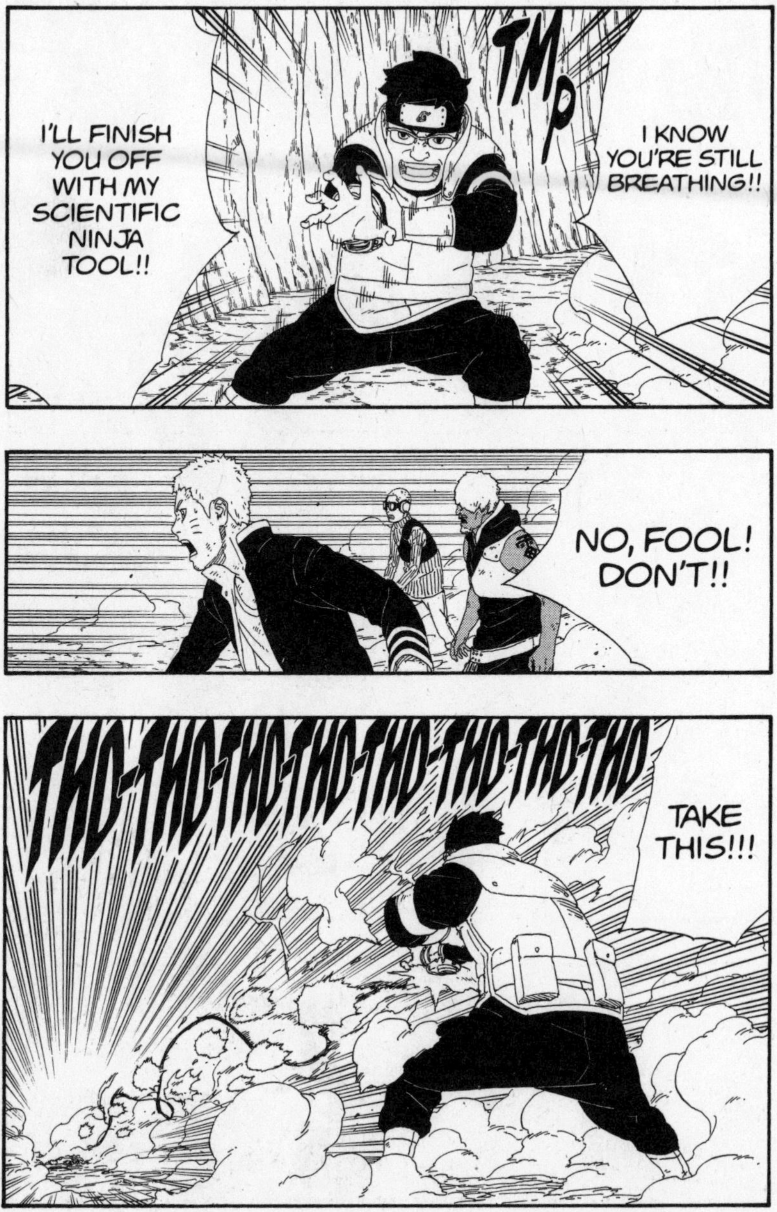
TMP
I KNOW YOU'RE STILL BREATHING!!
I'LL FINISH YOU OFF WITH MY SCIENTIFIC NINJA TOOL!!
NO, FOOL! DON'T!!
THD-THD-THD-THD-THD-THD-THD-THD
TAKE THIS!!!

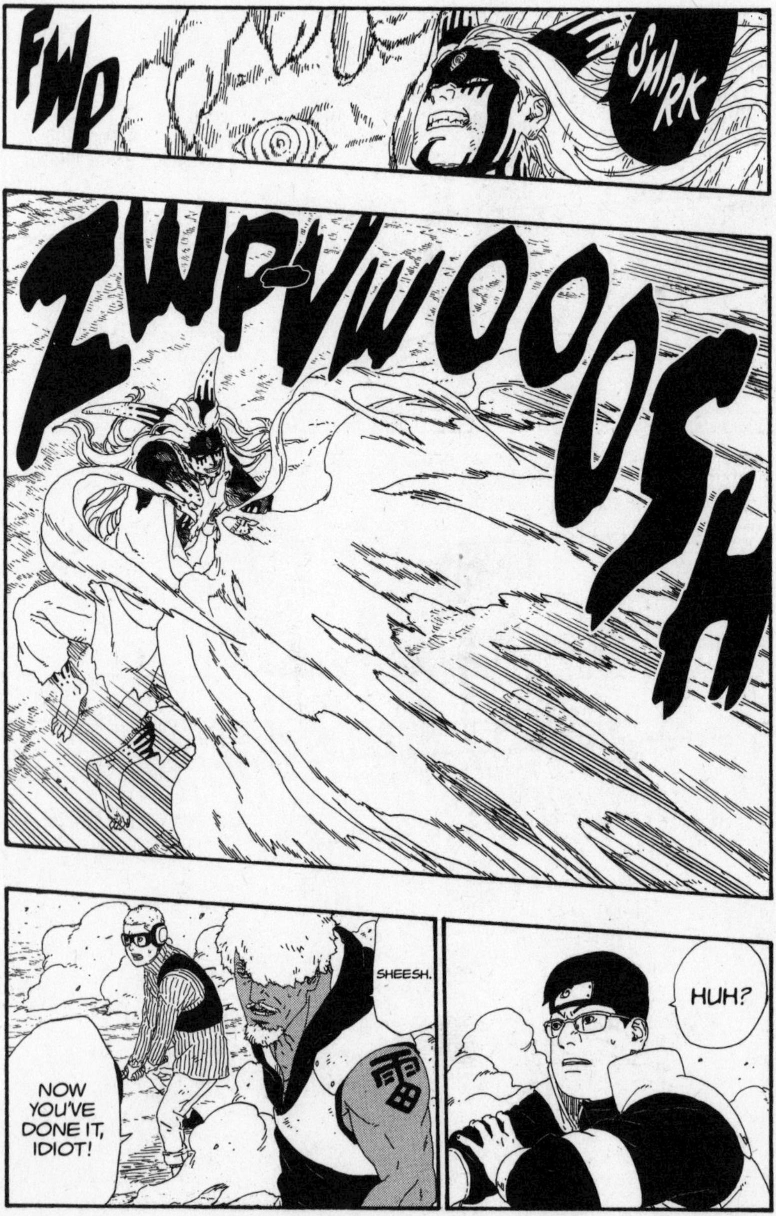
SMIRK
FWP
ZWP-VWOOOSH
HUH?
SHEESH.
NOW YOU'VE DONE IT, IDIOT!

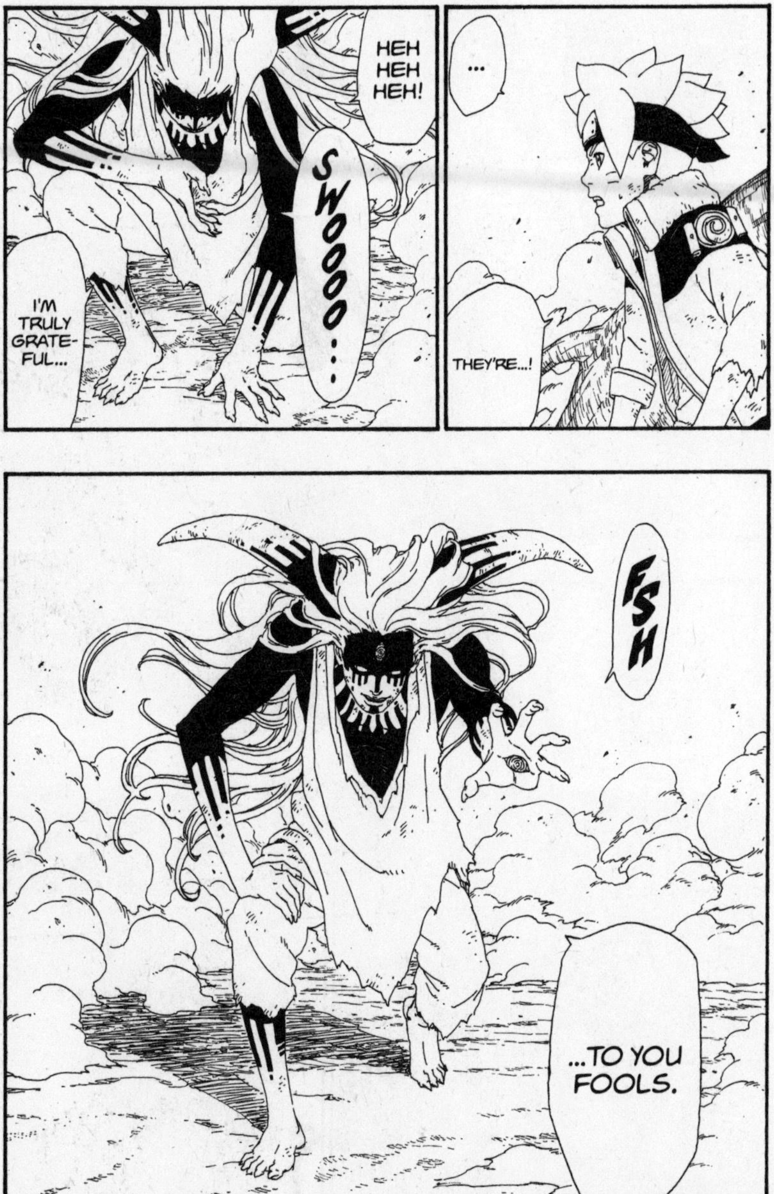
...
THEY'RE...!
HEH HEH HEH!
SWOOOO...
I'M TRULY GRATEFUL...
FSH
...TO YOU FOOLS.

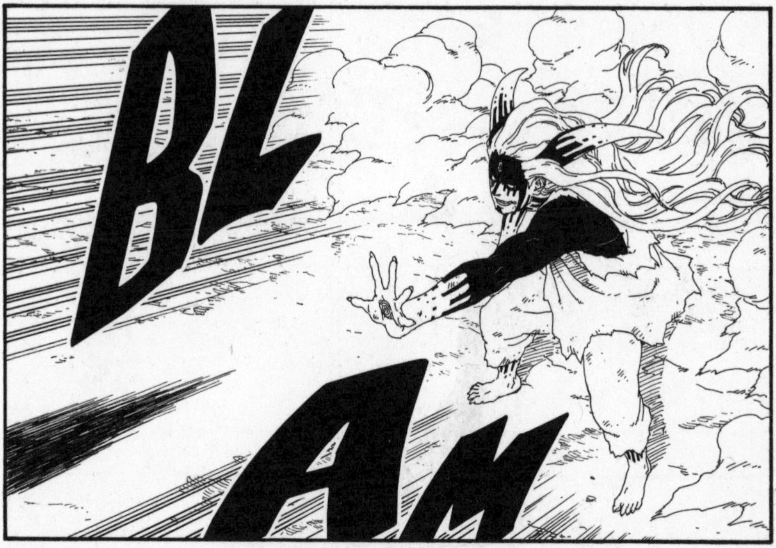
BLAM
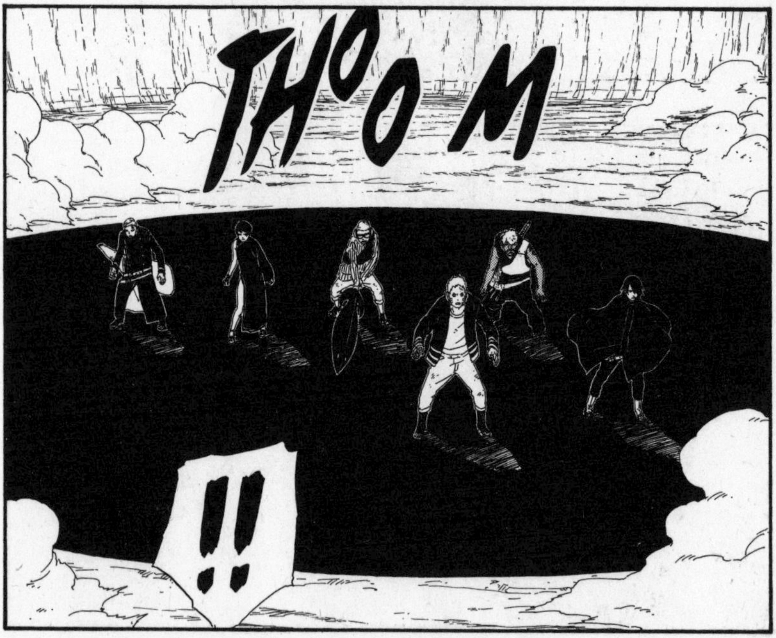
THOOM
!!

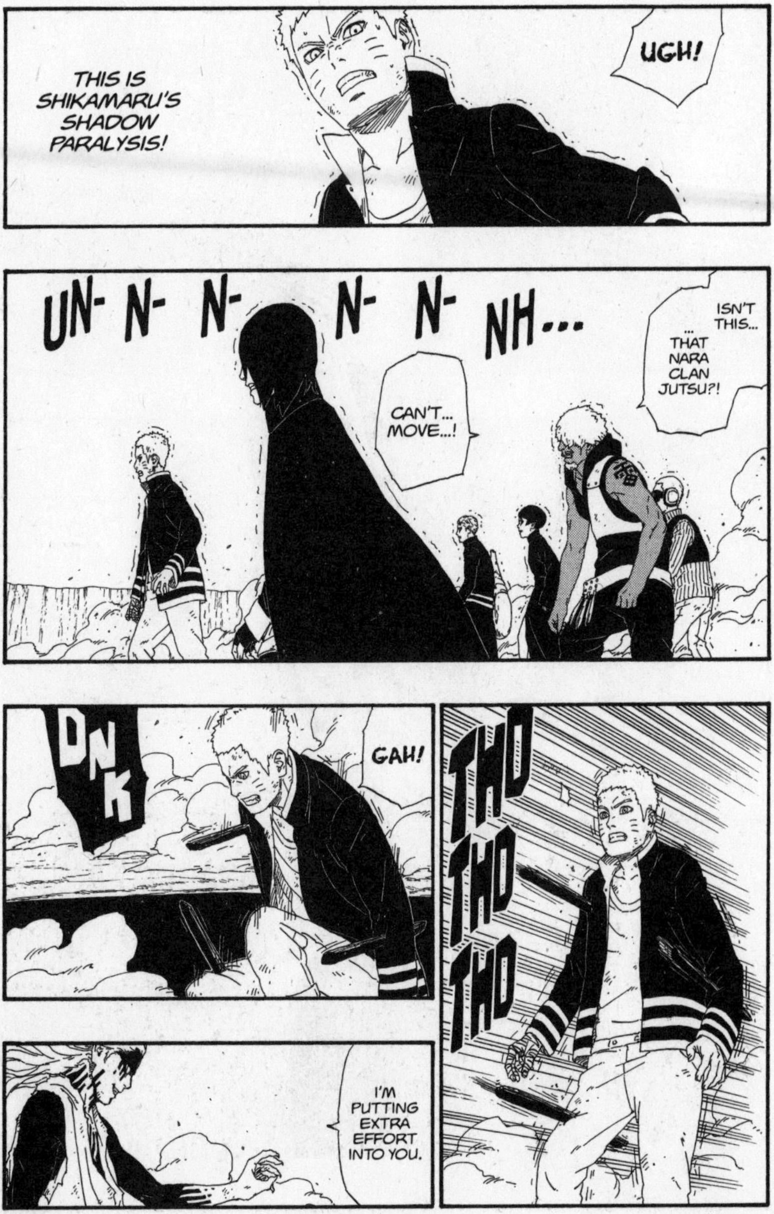
UGH!
THIS IS SHIKAMARU'S SHADOW PARALYSIS!
ISN'T THIS... ...THAT NARA CLAN JUTSU?!
UN- N- N- N- N- NH...
CAN'T... MOVE...!
THO THO THO THO
GAH!
DNK
I'M PUTTING EXTRA EFFORT INTO YOU.

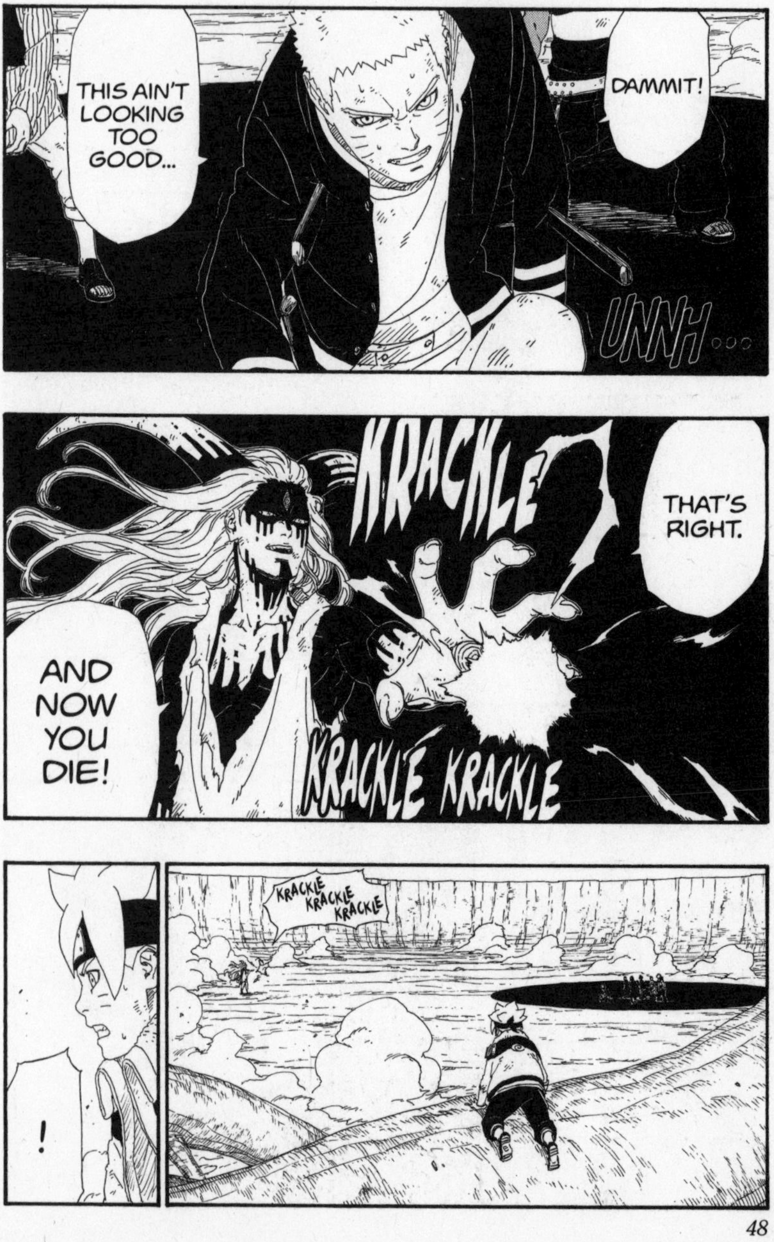
DAMMIT!
THIS AIN'T LOOKING TOO GOOD...
UNNH...
KRACKLE
THAT'S RIGHT.
AND NOW YOU DIE!
KRACKLE KRACKLE
KRACKLE KRACKLE KRACKLE
!

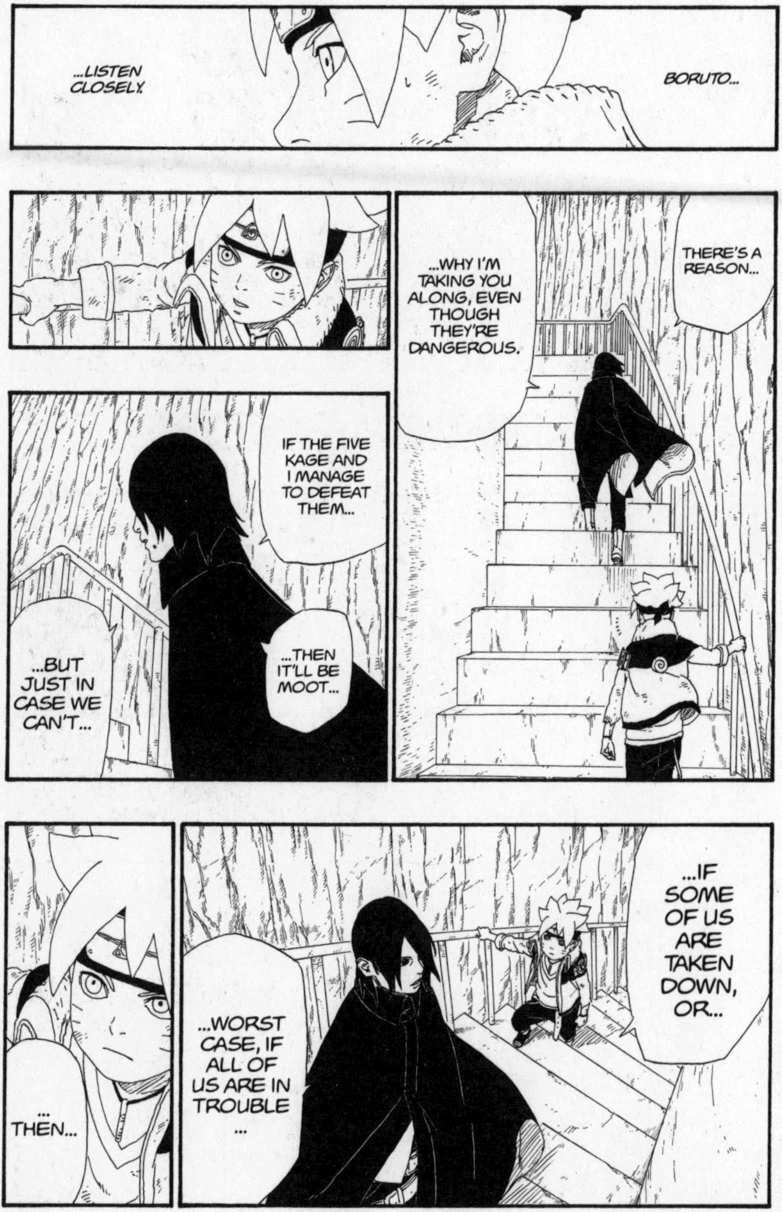
BORUTO...
...LISTEN CLOSELY.
THERE'S A REASON...
...WHY I'M TAKING YOU ALONG, EVEN THOUGH THEY'RE DANGEROUS.
IF THE FIVE KAGE AND I MANAGE TO DEFEAT THEM...
...THEN IT'LL BE MOOT...
...BUT JUST IN CASE WE CAN'T...
...IF SOME OF US ARE TAKEN DOWN, OR...
...WORST CASE, IF ALL OF US ARE IN TROUBLE ...
... THEN...

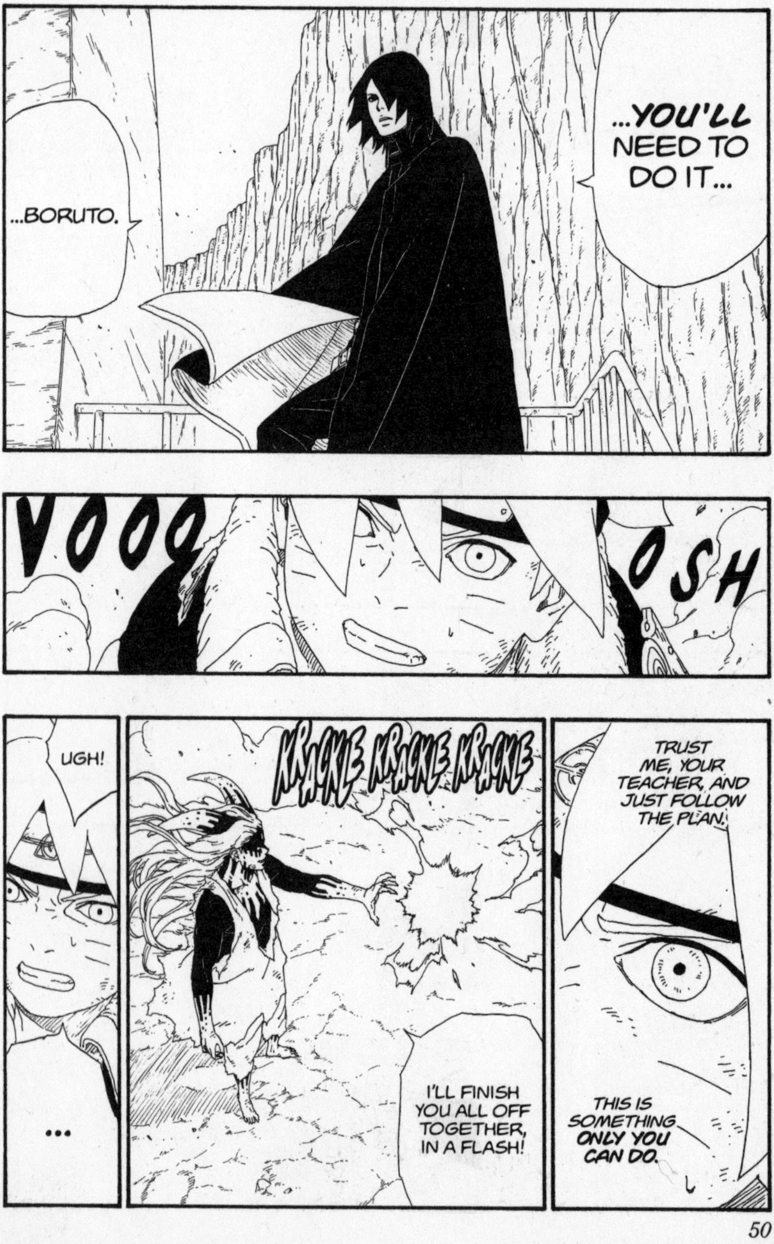
...YOU'LL NEED TO DO IT...
...BORUTO.
VOOOOSH
TRUST ME, YOUR TEACHER, AND JUST FOLLOW THE PLAN.
THIS IS SOMETHING ONLY YOU CAN DO.
KRACKLE KRACKLE KRACKLE
I'LL FINISH YOU ALL OFF TOGETHER, IN A FLASH!
UGH!
...

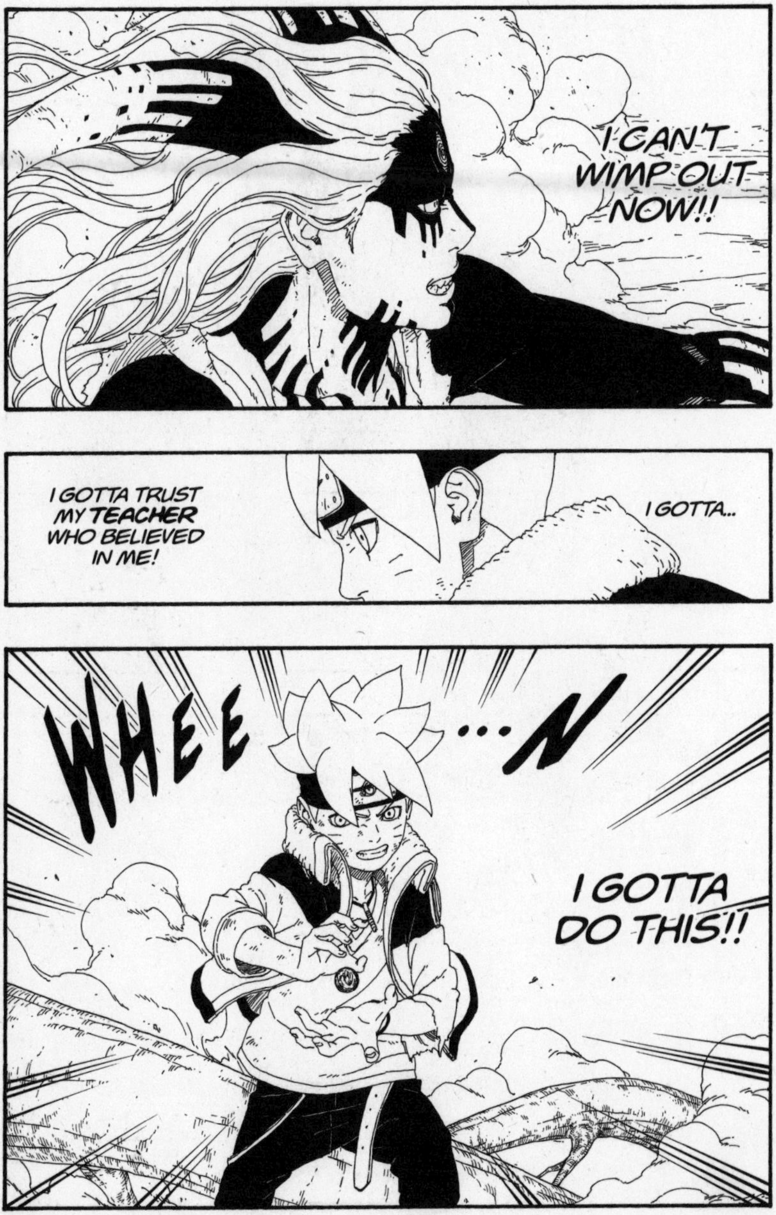
I CAN'T WIMP OUT NOW!!
I GOTTA...
I GOTTA TRUST MY TEACHER WHO BELIEVED IN ME!
WHEE...N
I GOTTA DO THIS!!

NINJA ENCYCLOPEDIA • ENTRY 7

UZUMAKI NARUTO

"What's most important to a ninja is teamwork."

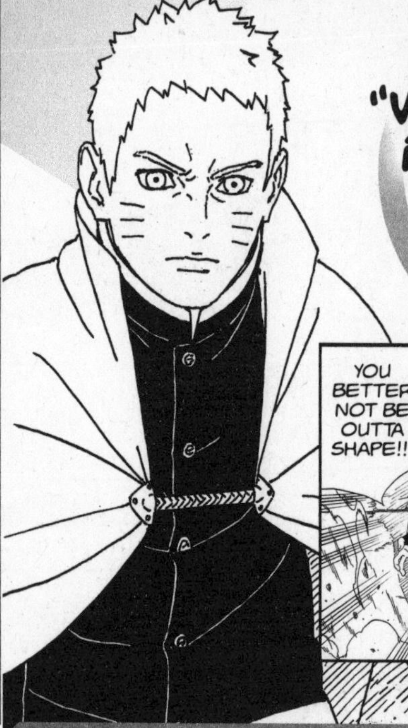

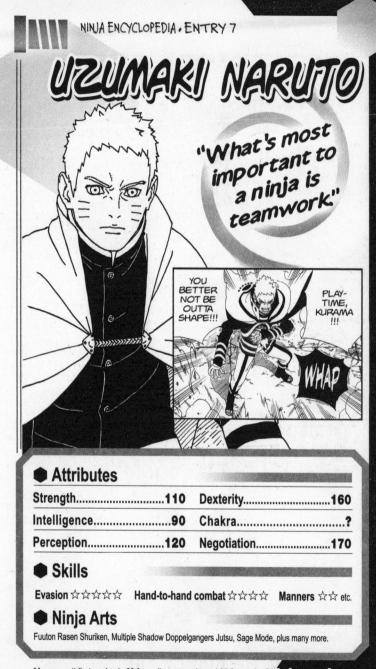

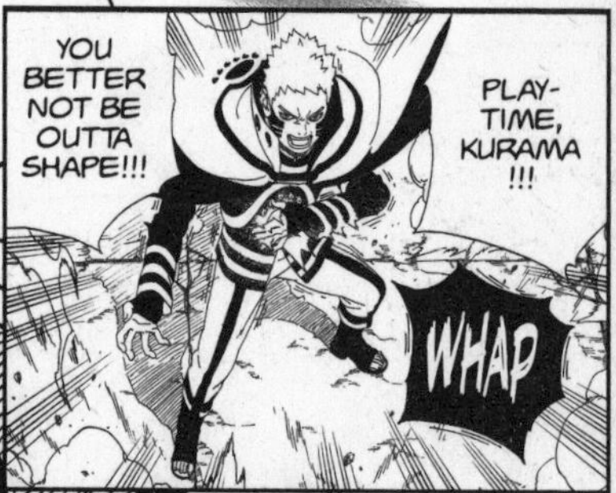
PLAY-TIME, KURAMA!!!
YOU BETTER NOT BE OUTTA SHAPE!!!
WHAP

Attributes

Strength	110	Dexterity	160
Intelligence	90	Chakra	?
Perception	120	Negotiation	170

Skills

Evasion ☆☆☆☆☆ Hand-to-hand combat ☆☆☆☆ Manners ☆☆ etc.

Ninja Arts

Fuuton Rasen Shuriken, Multiple Shadow Doppelgangers Jutsu, Sage Mode, plus many more.

*Average attribute value is 60 for ordinary people and 90 for genin. Skill values range from 1 to 5☆ with 5☆ signifying super top-notch. *These are non-Sage Mode values.

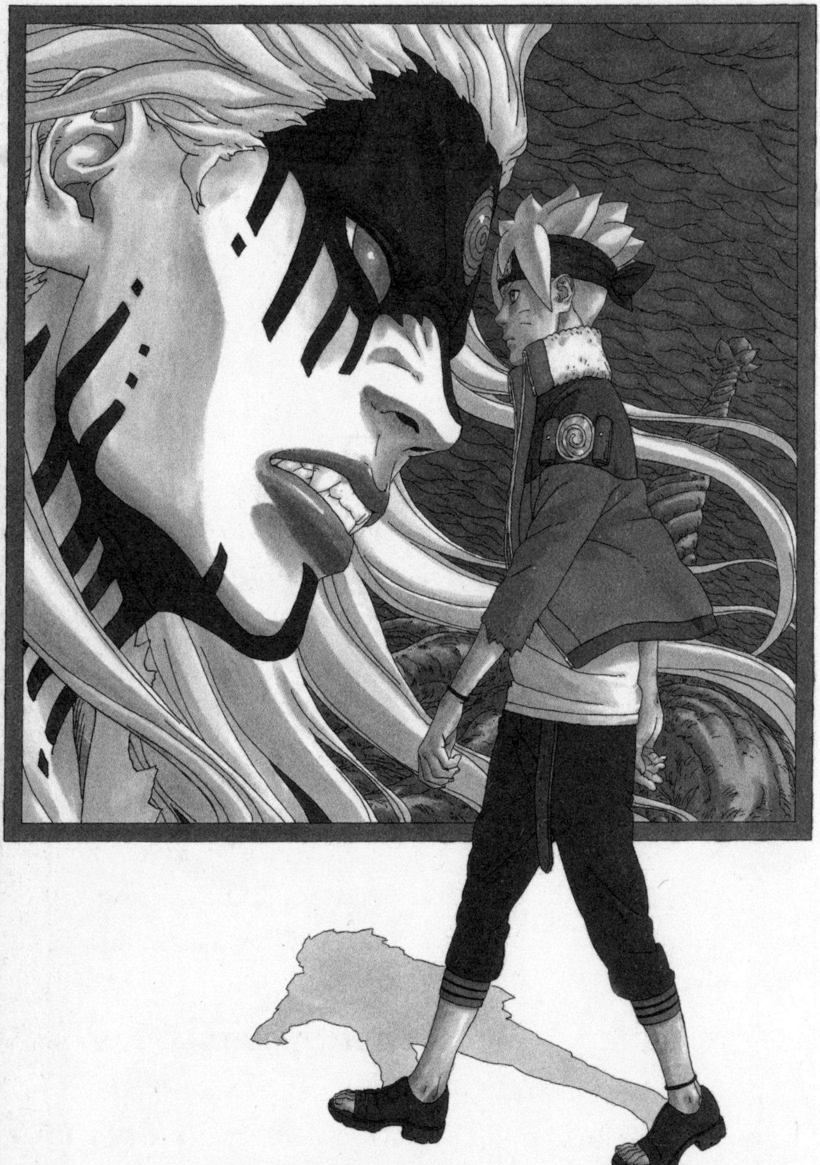

Number 9: You Remind Me Of...

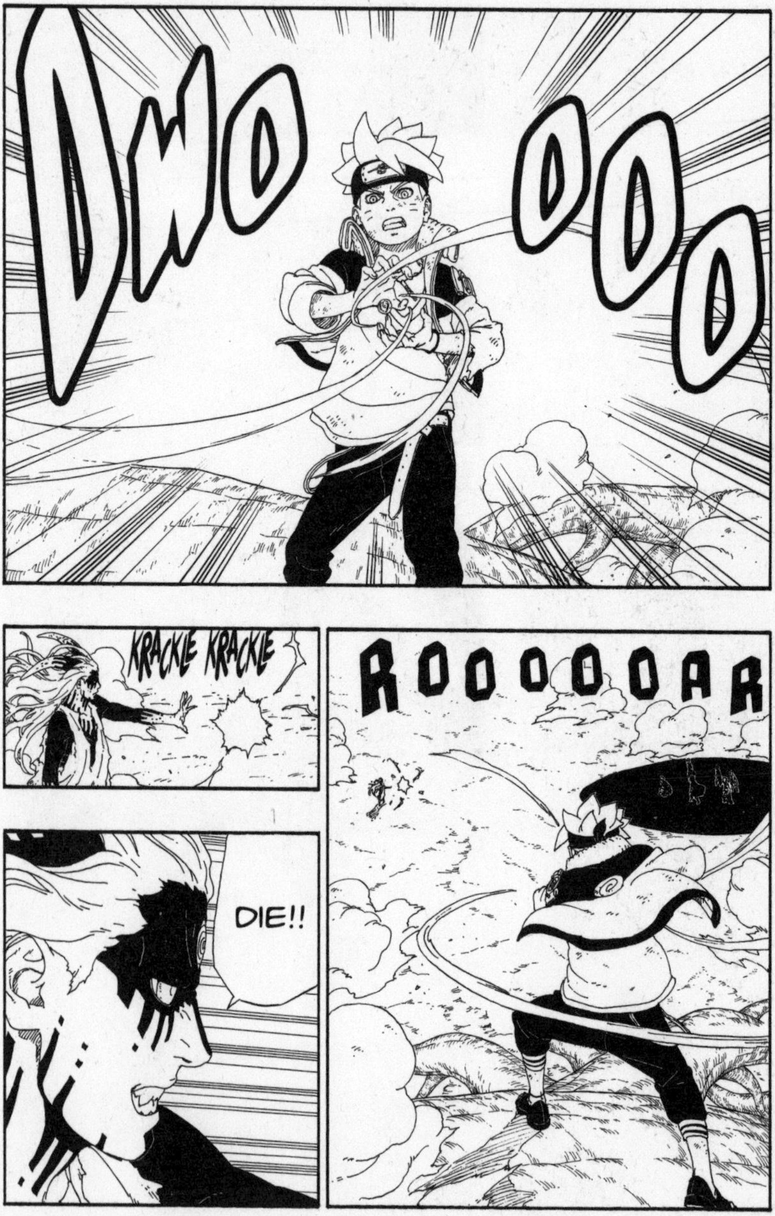
DWOOOOO
ROOOOOAR
KRACKLE KRACKLE
DIE!!

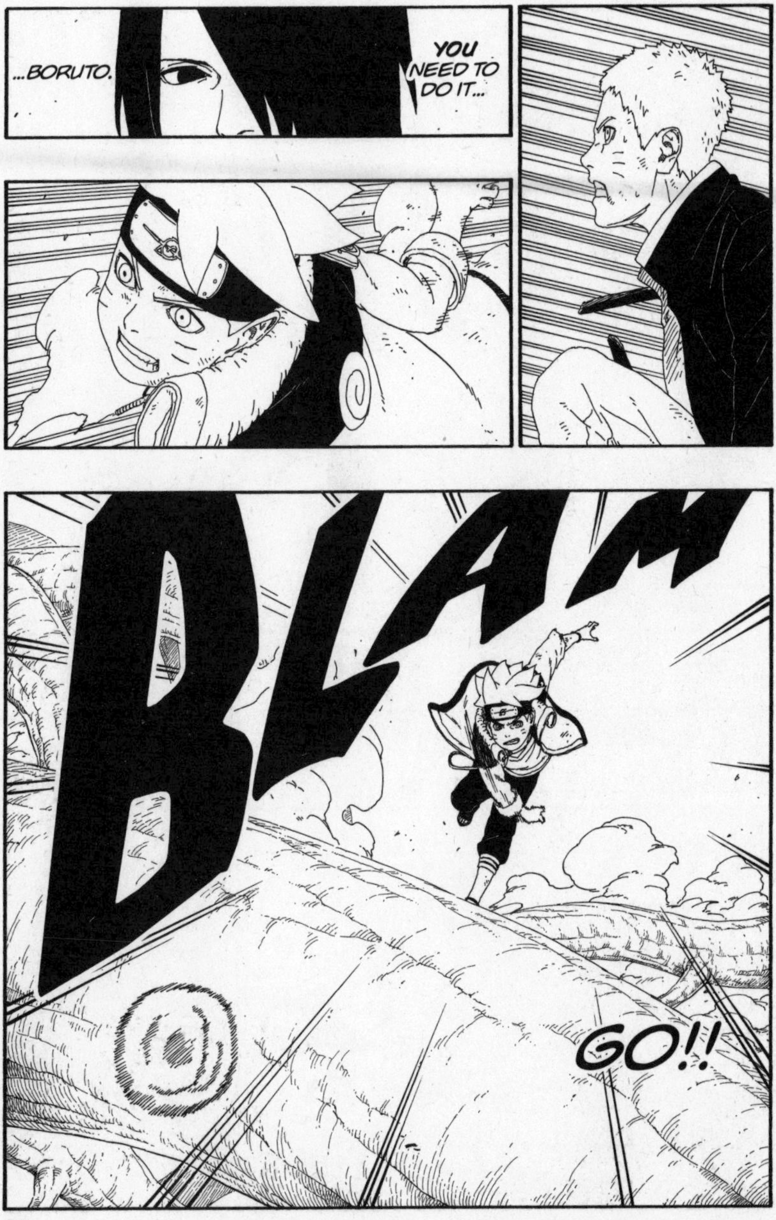
YOU NEED TO DO IT...
...BORUTO.
BLAM
GO!!

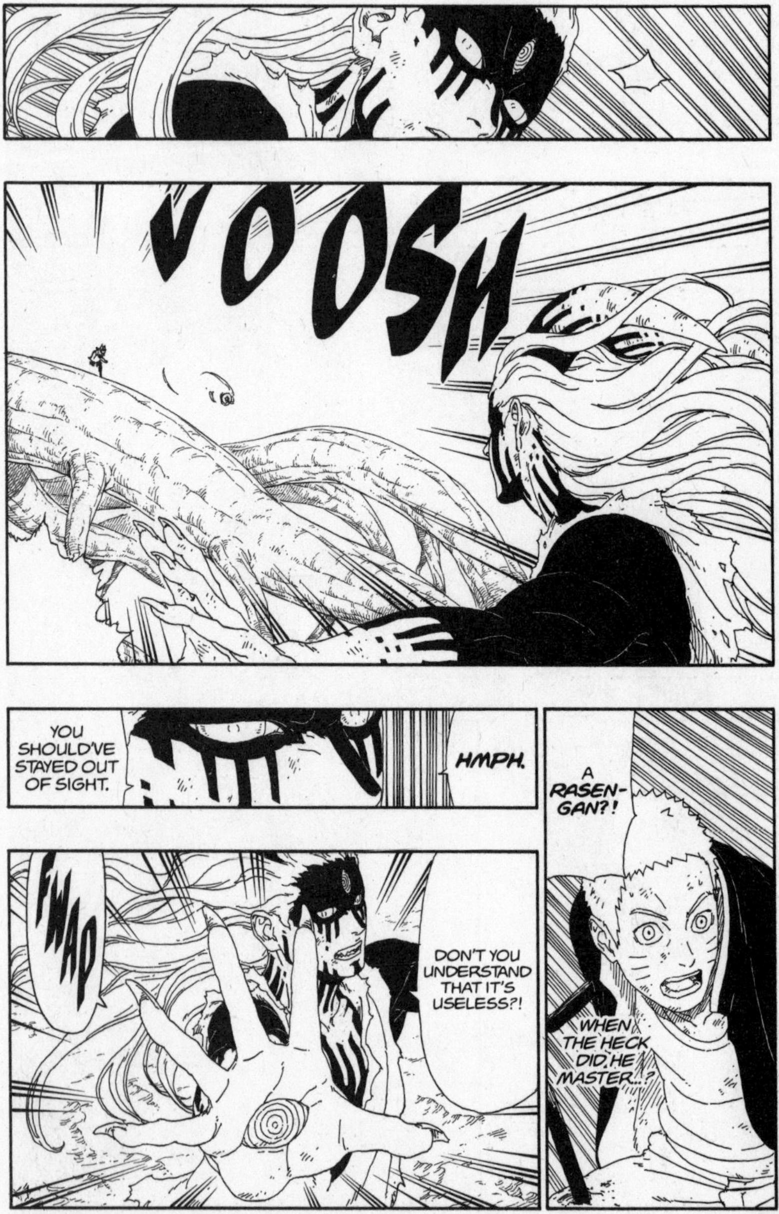
VOOSH
A RASEN-GAN?!
WHEN THE HECK DID HE MASTER...?
HMPH.
YOU SHOULD'VE STAYED OUT OF SIGHT.
DON'T YOU UNDERSTAND THAT IT'S USELESS?!
FWAP

WOOOOOO
EEEEEE...
POOF
!
?!
WHAT THE?!
IT FIZZLED OUT WELL BEFORE-HAND.
IT--
IT DIDN'T REACH!
...
WHAT A JOKE. IT DIDN'T EVEN GET CLOSE TO ME.
WELL, DON'T WORRY.
YOU'RE ALL GOING TO THE SAME PLACE...

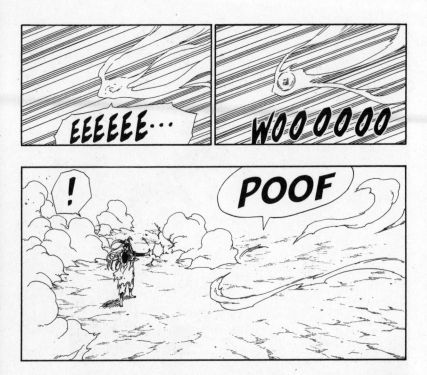

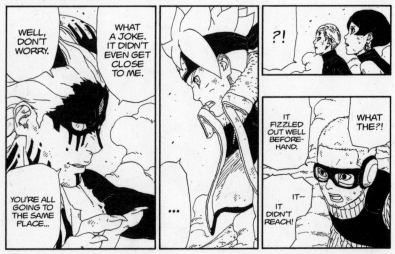

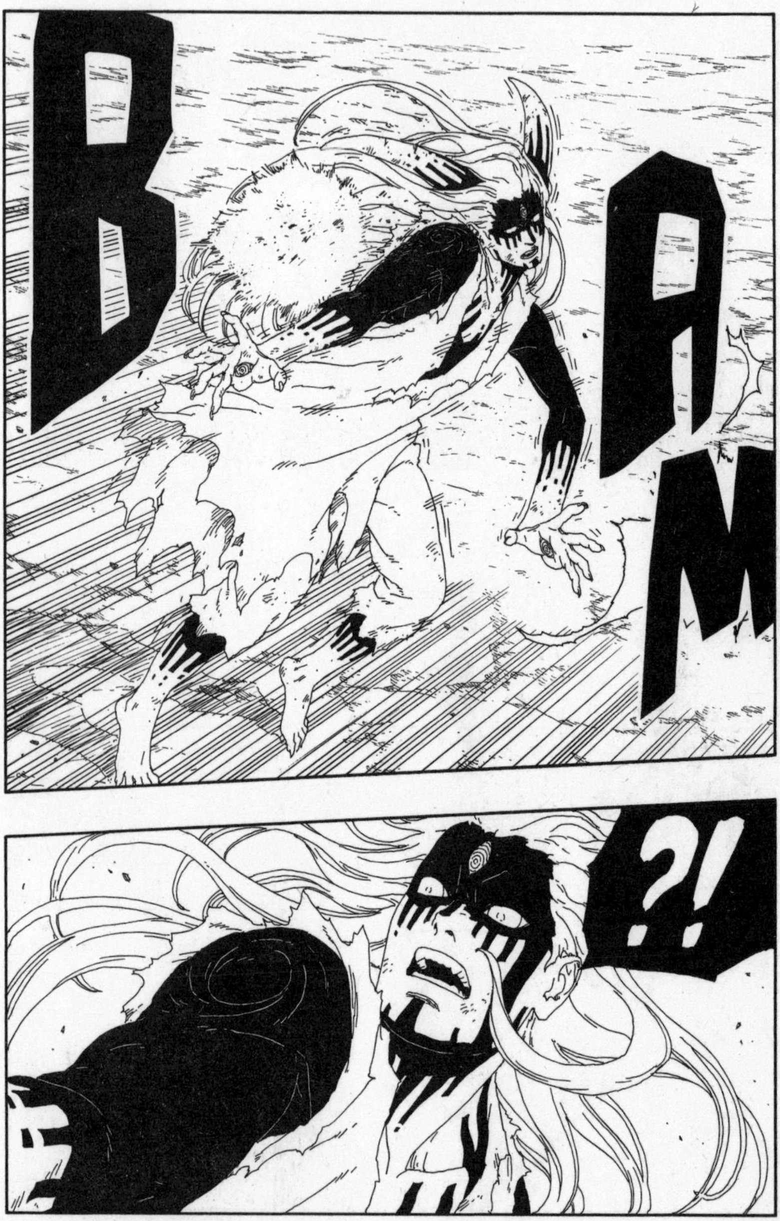
BAM
?!

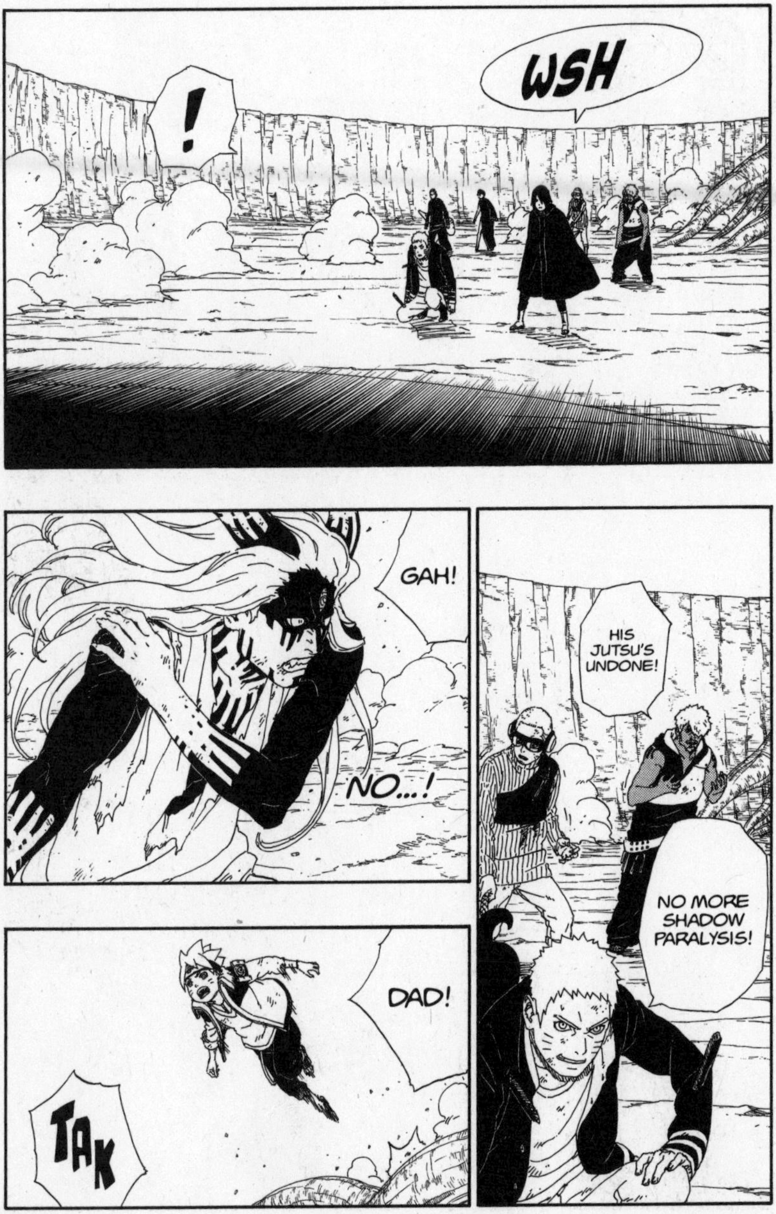
WSH
!
HIS JUTSU'S UNDONE!
NO MORE SHADOW PARALYSIS!
GAH!
NO...!
DAD!
TAK

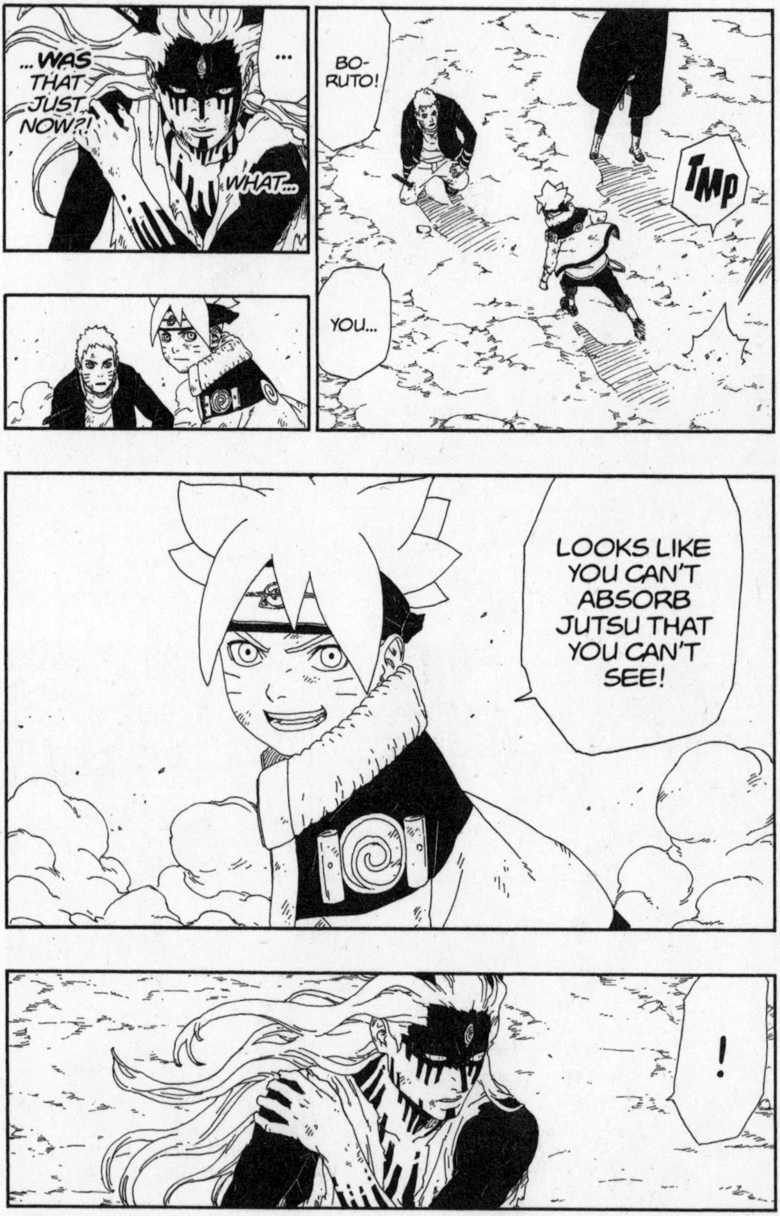

BO-RUTO!
TMP
YOU...
...
WHAT...
...WAS THAT JUST NOW?!
LOOKS LIKE YOU CAN'T ABSORB JUTSU THAT YOU CAN'T SEE!
!

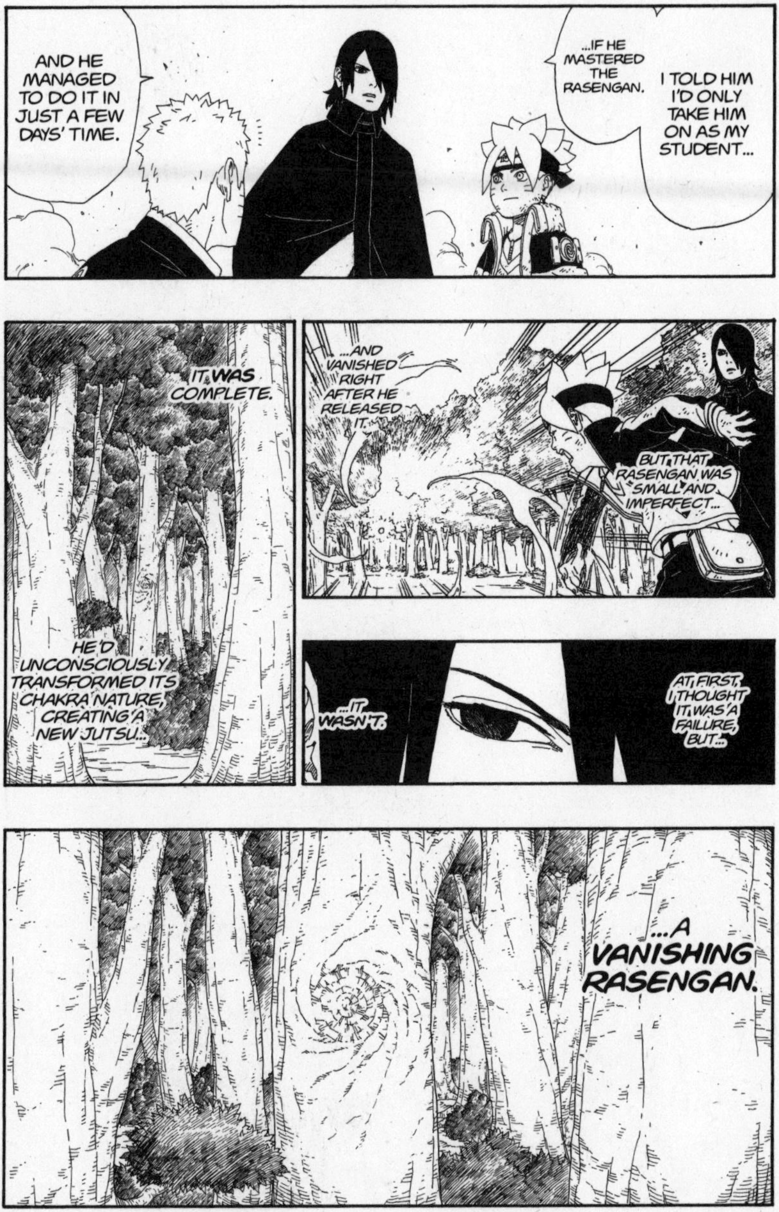
I TOLD HIM I'D ONLY TAKE HIM ON AS MY STUDENT...
...IF HE MASTERED THE RASENGAN.
AND HE MANAGED TO DO IT IN JUST A FEW DAYS' TIME.
BUT THAT RASENGAN WAS SMALL AND IMPERFECT...
...AND VANISHED RIGHT AFTER HE RELEASED IT.
AT FIRST, I THOUGHT IT WAS A FAILURE, BUT...
...IT WASN'T.
IT WAS COMPLETE.
HE'D UNCONSCIOUSLY TRANSFORMED ITS CHAKRA NATURE, CREATING A NEW JUTSU...
...A VANISHING RASENGAN.

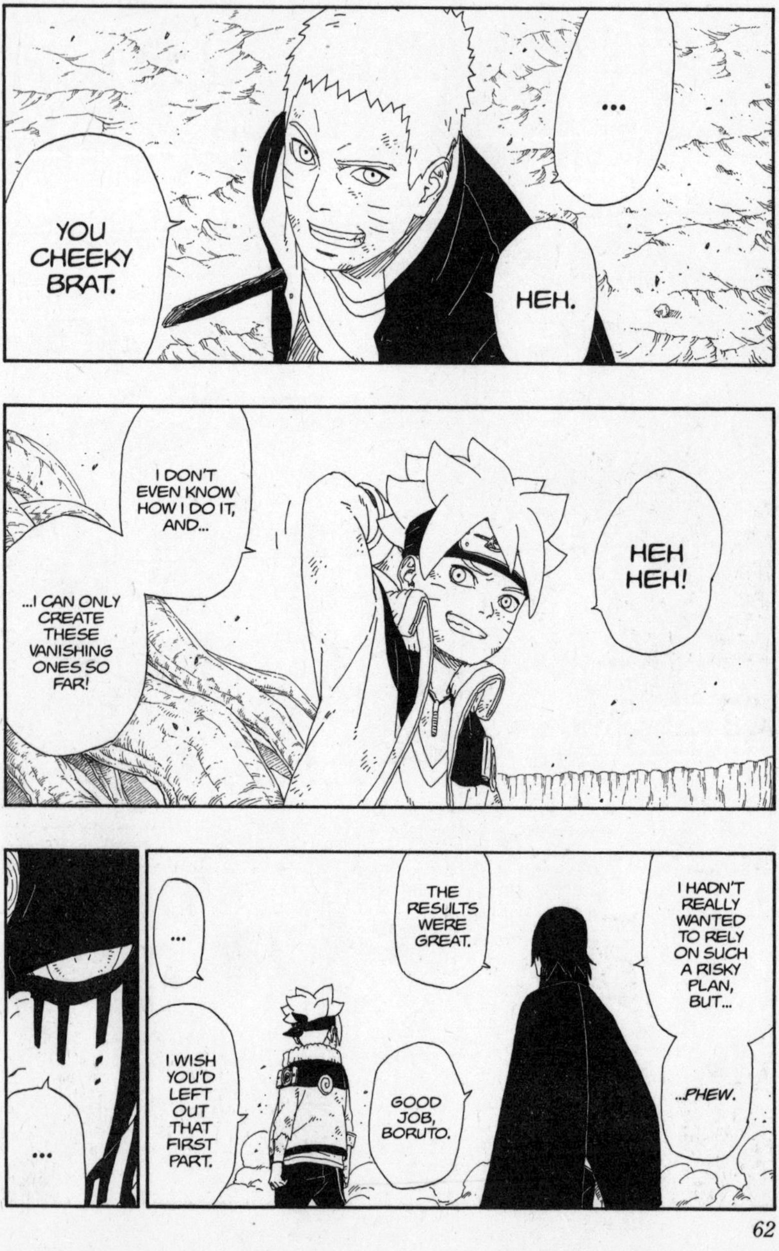
...
HEH.
YOU CHEEKY BRAT.
HEH HEH!
I DON'T EVEN KNOW HOW I DO IT, AND...
...I CAN ONLY CREATE THESE VANISHING ONES SO FAR!
I HADN'T REALLY WANTED TO RELY ON SUCH A RISKY PLAN, BUT...
...PHEW.
THE RESULTS WERE GREAT.
GOOD JOB, BORUTO.
...
I WISH YOU'D LEFT OUT THAT FIRST PART.
...

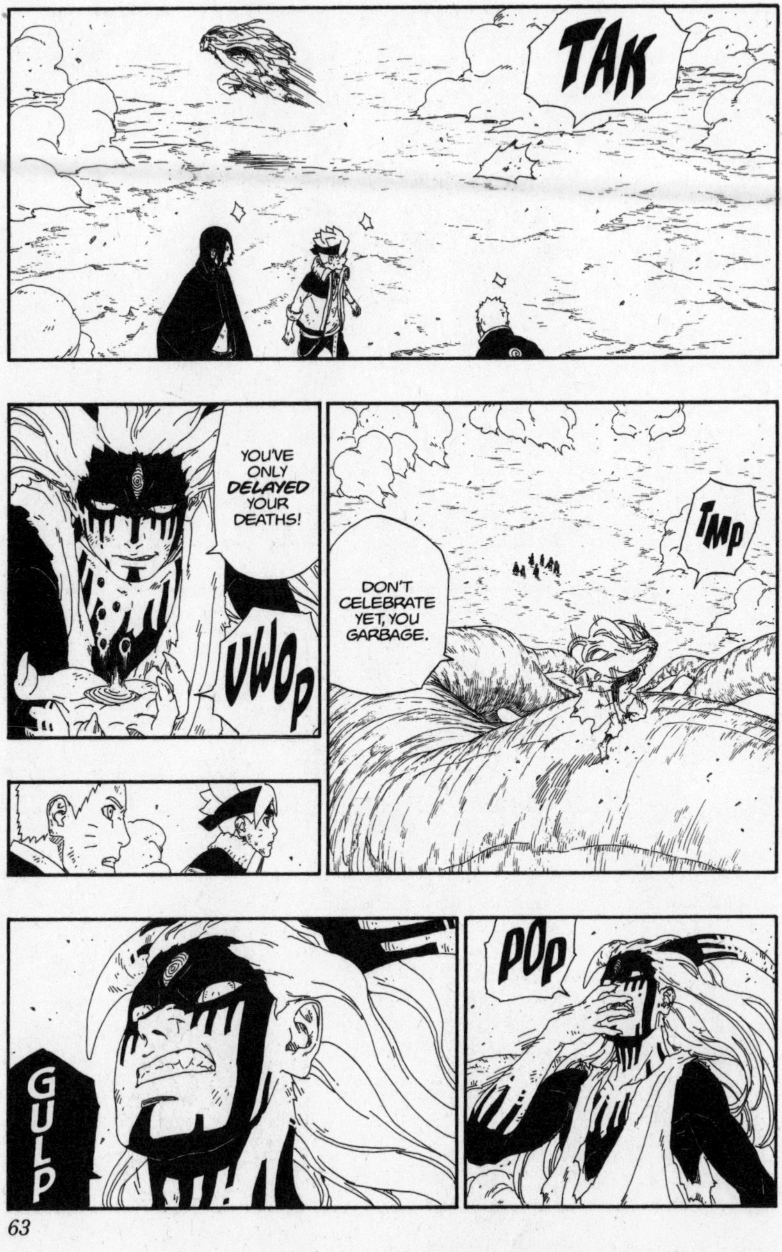
TAK
TMP
DON'T CELEBRATE YET, YOU GARBAGE.
YOU'VE ONLY *DELAYED* YOUR DEATHS!
UWOP
POP
GULP

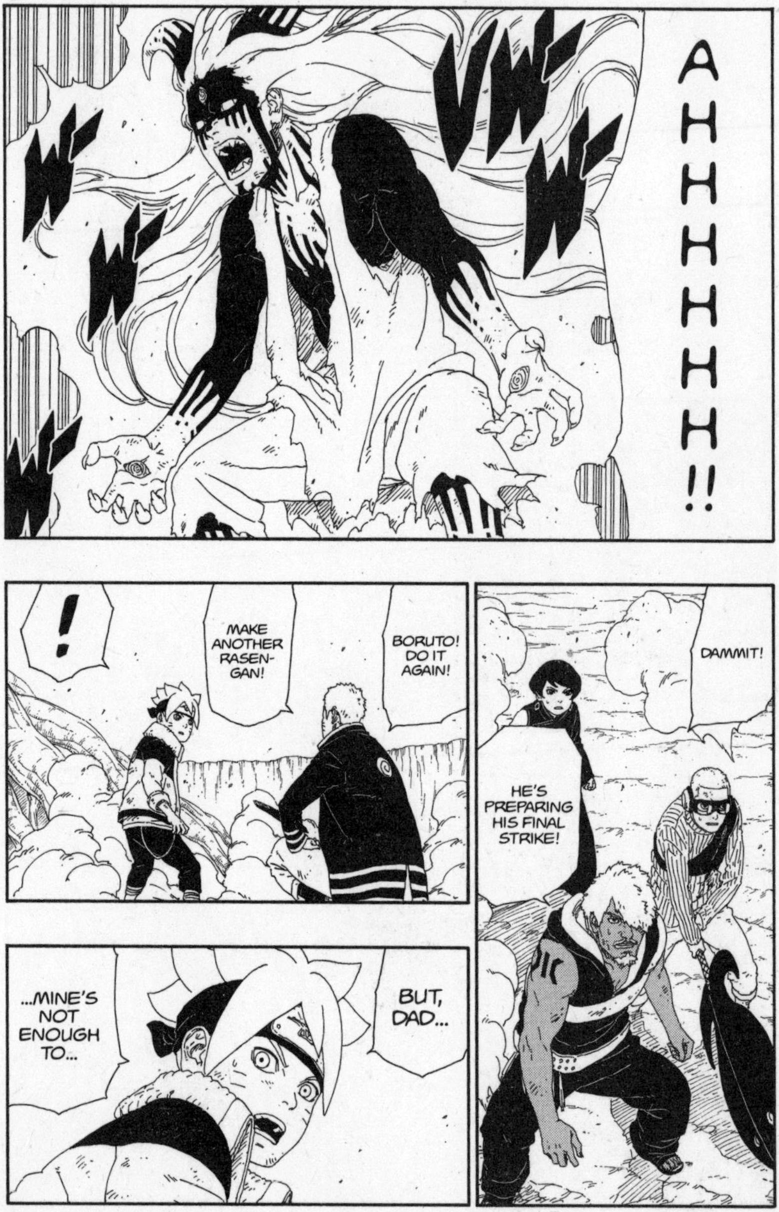
AHHHHH!!
VWF
WF
WF
WF
BORUTO! DO IT AGAIN!
MAKE ANOTHER RASEN-GAN!
!
DAMMIT!
HE'S PREPARING HIS FINAL STRIKE!
BUT, DAD...
...MINE'S NOT ENOUGH TO...

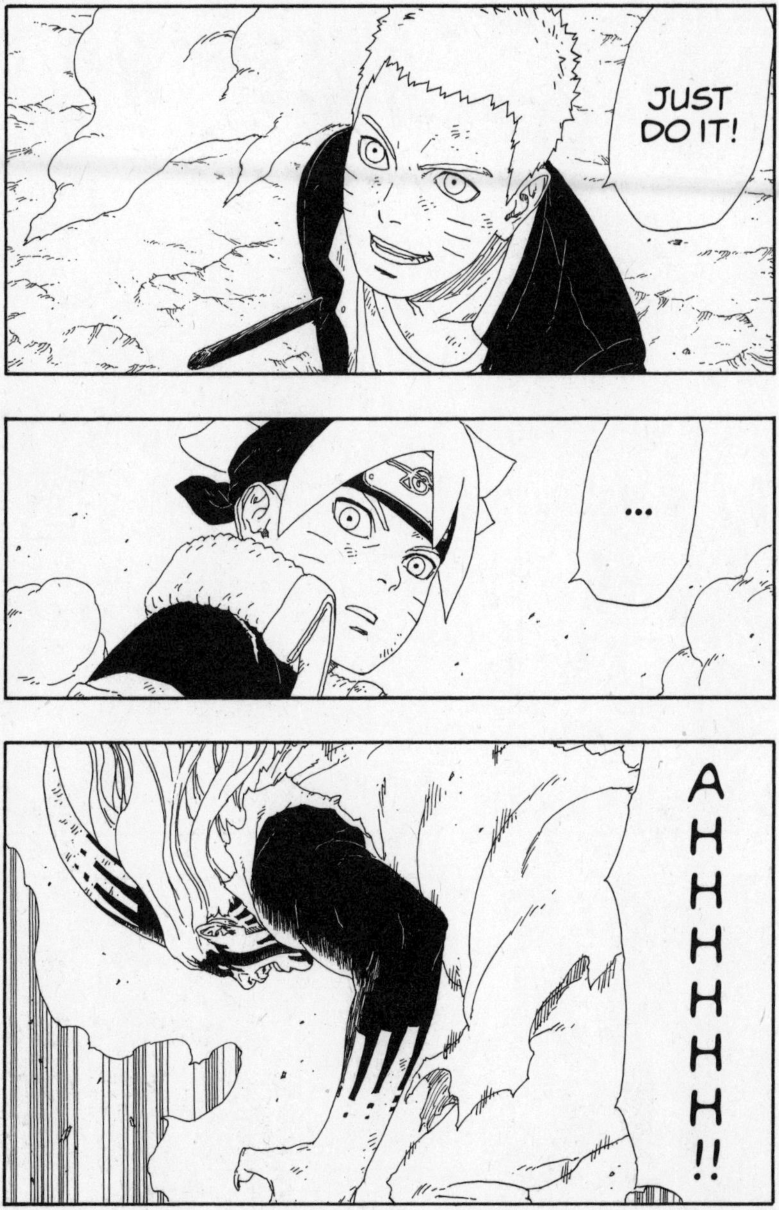
JUST DO IT!
...
AHHHHH!!

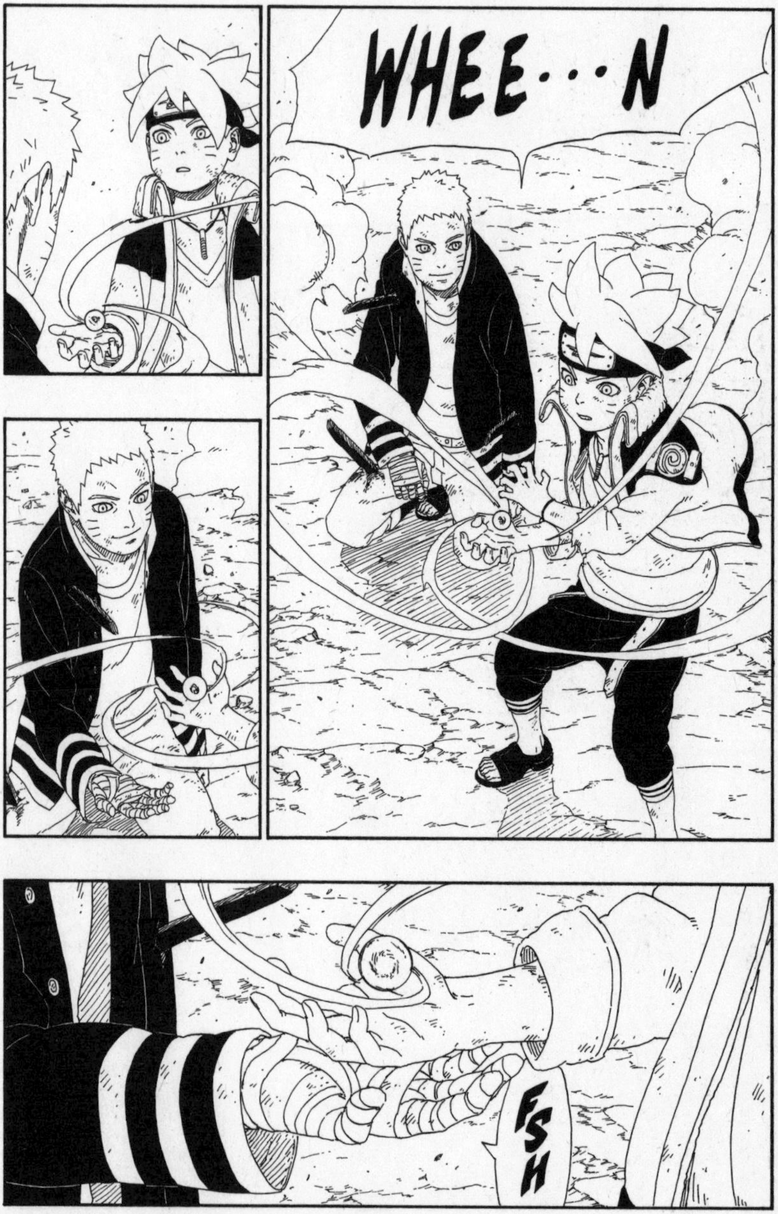
WHEE...N
FSH

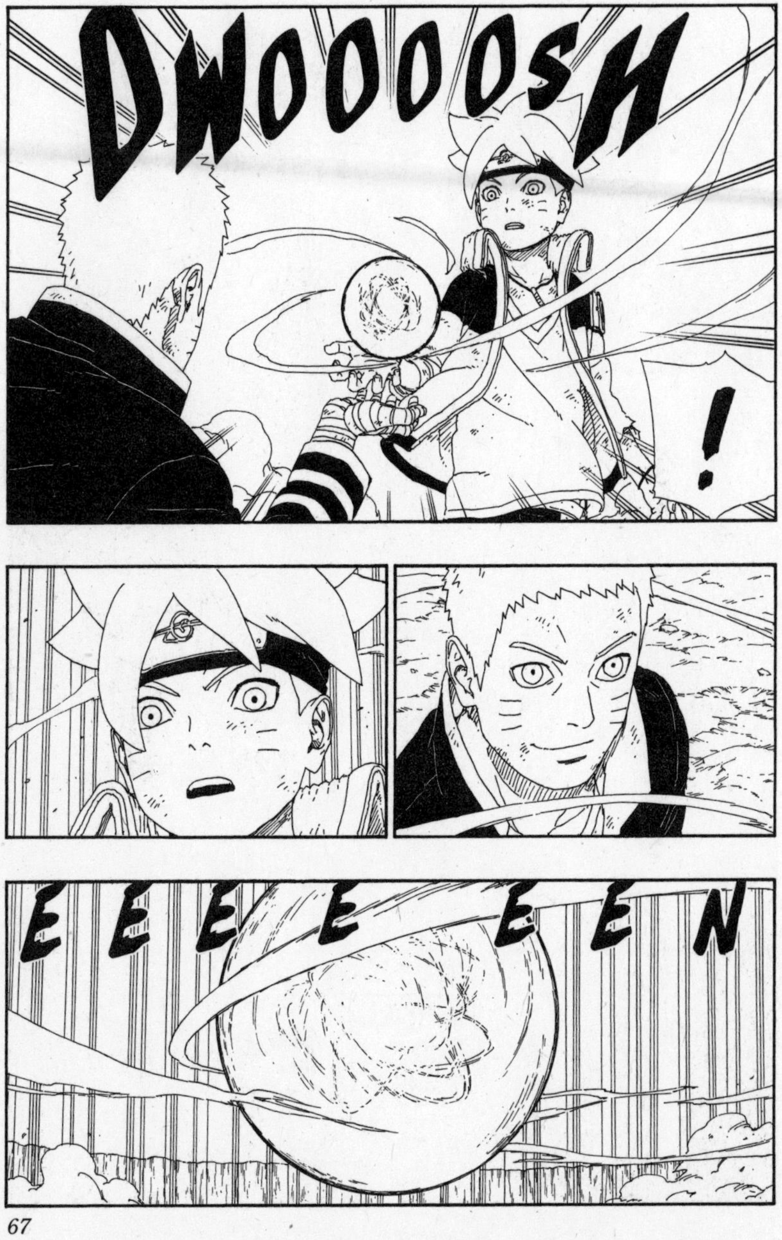
DWOOOOSH
!
EEEEEEN

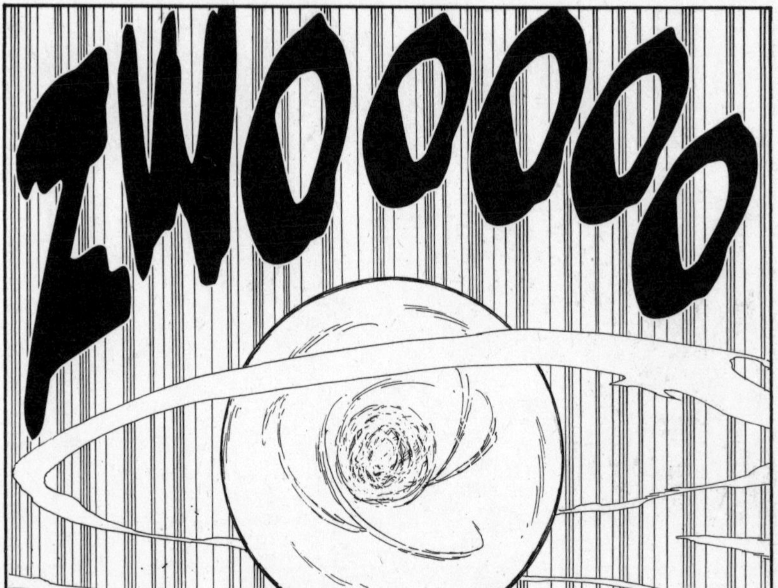
ZWOOOOO

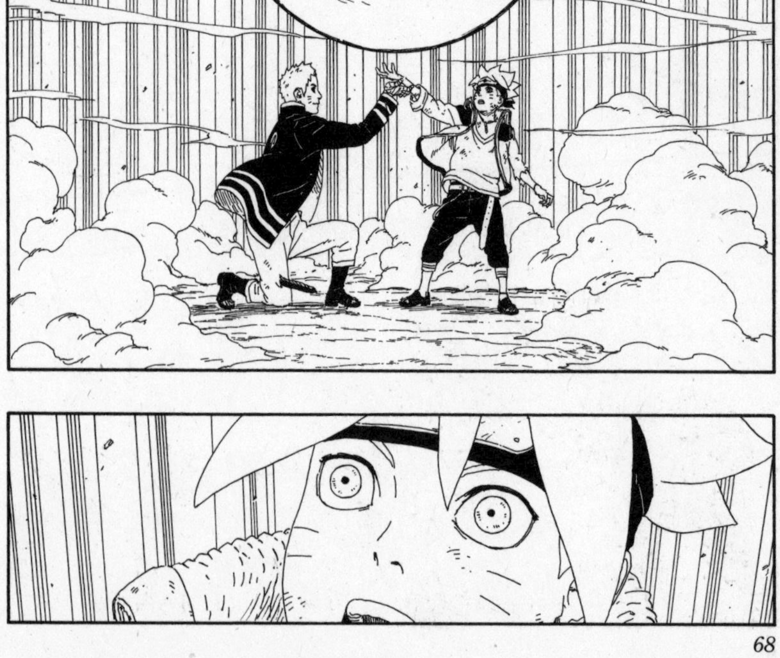

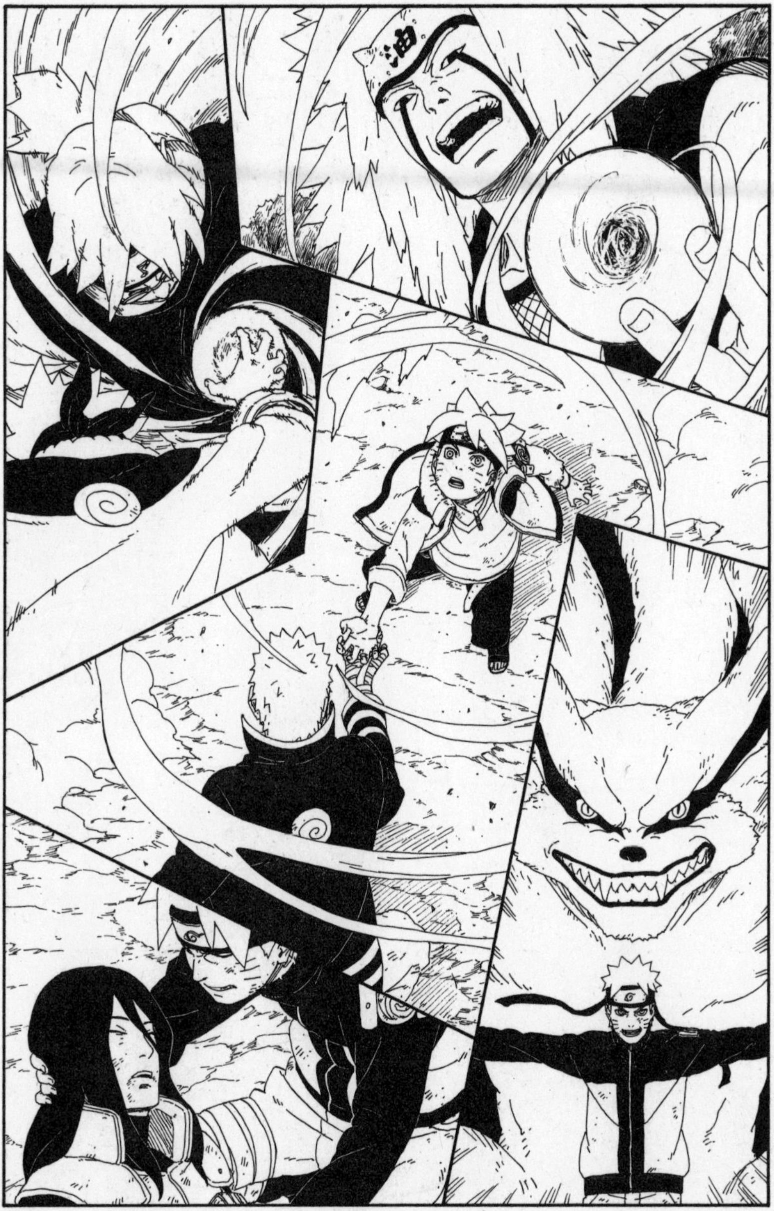
油

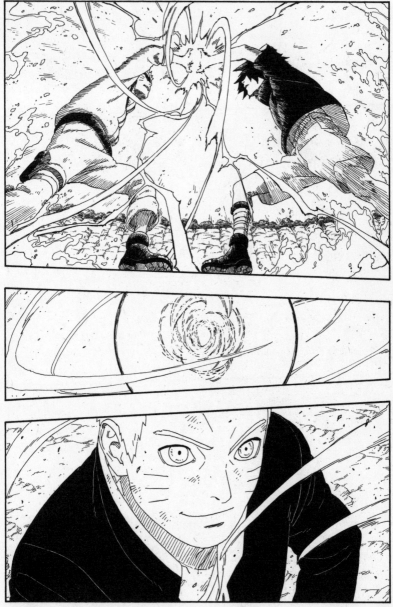

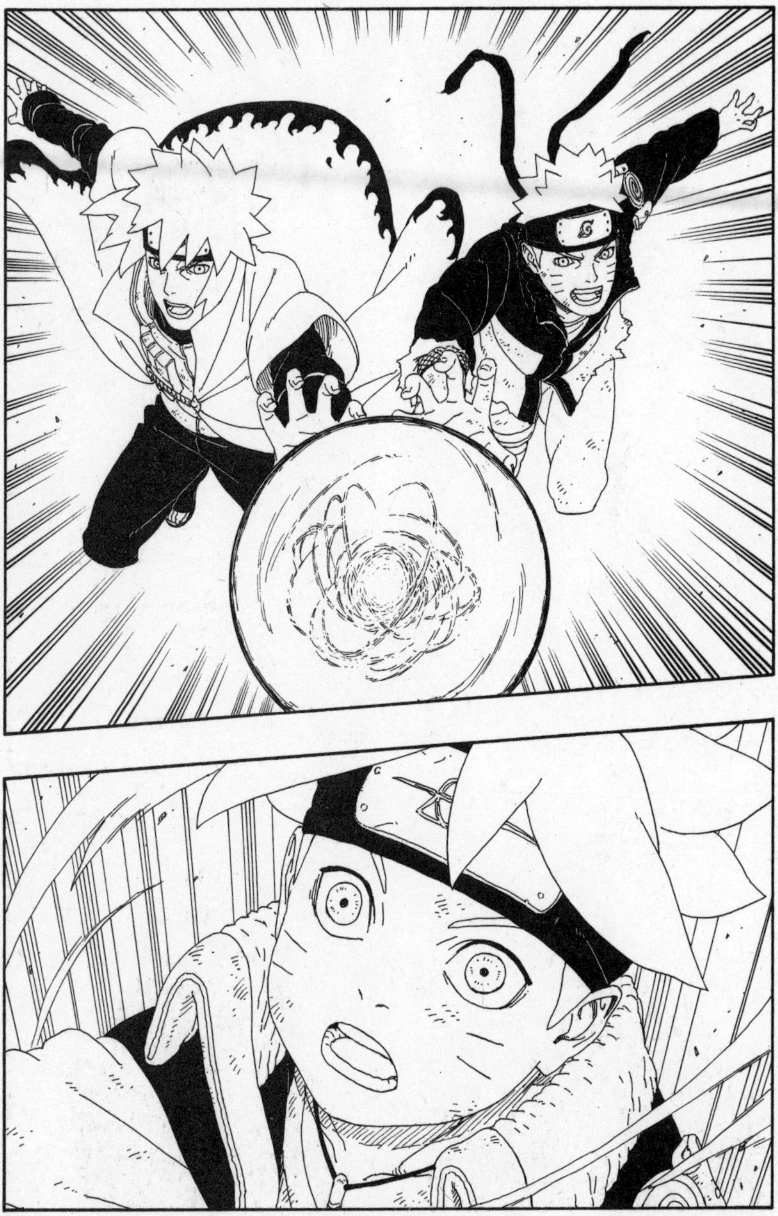

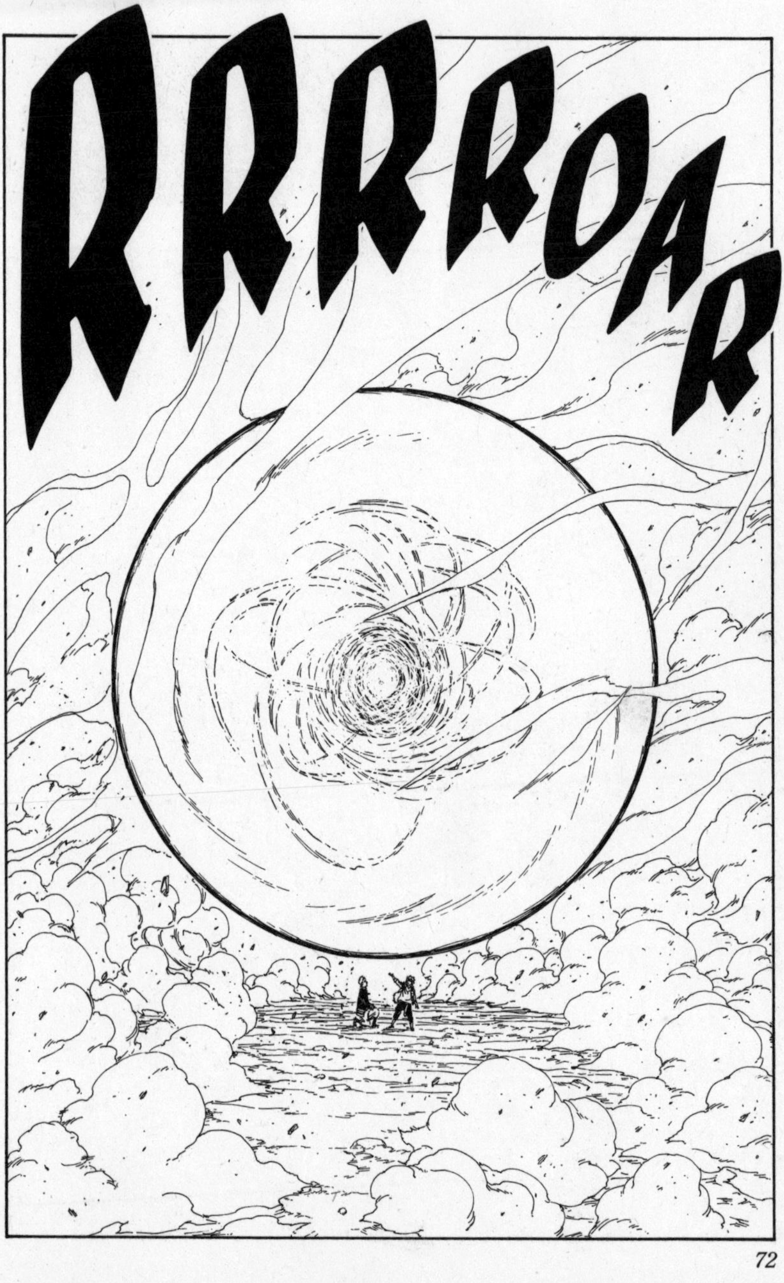
RRRROAR

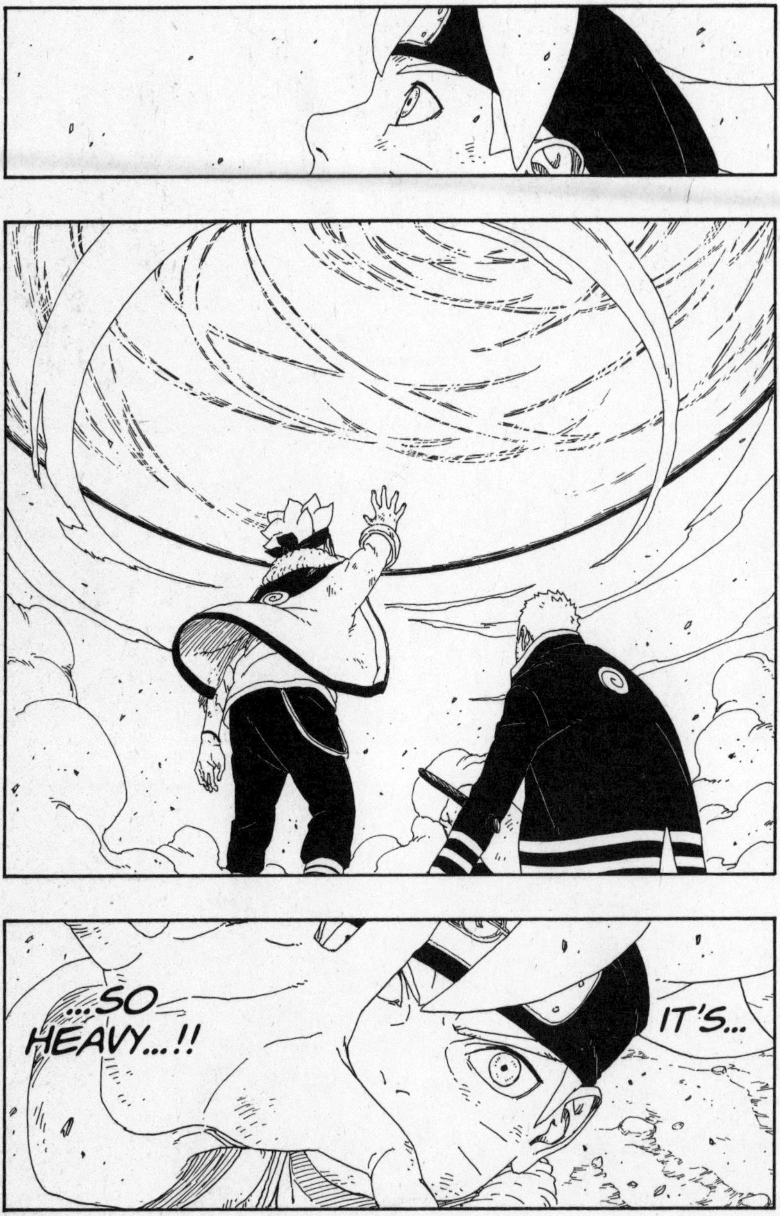
IT'S...
...SO HEAVY...!!

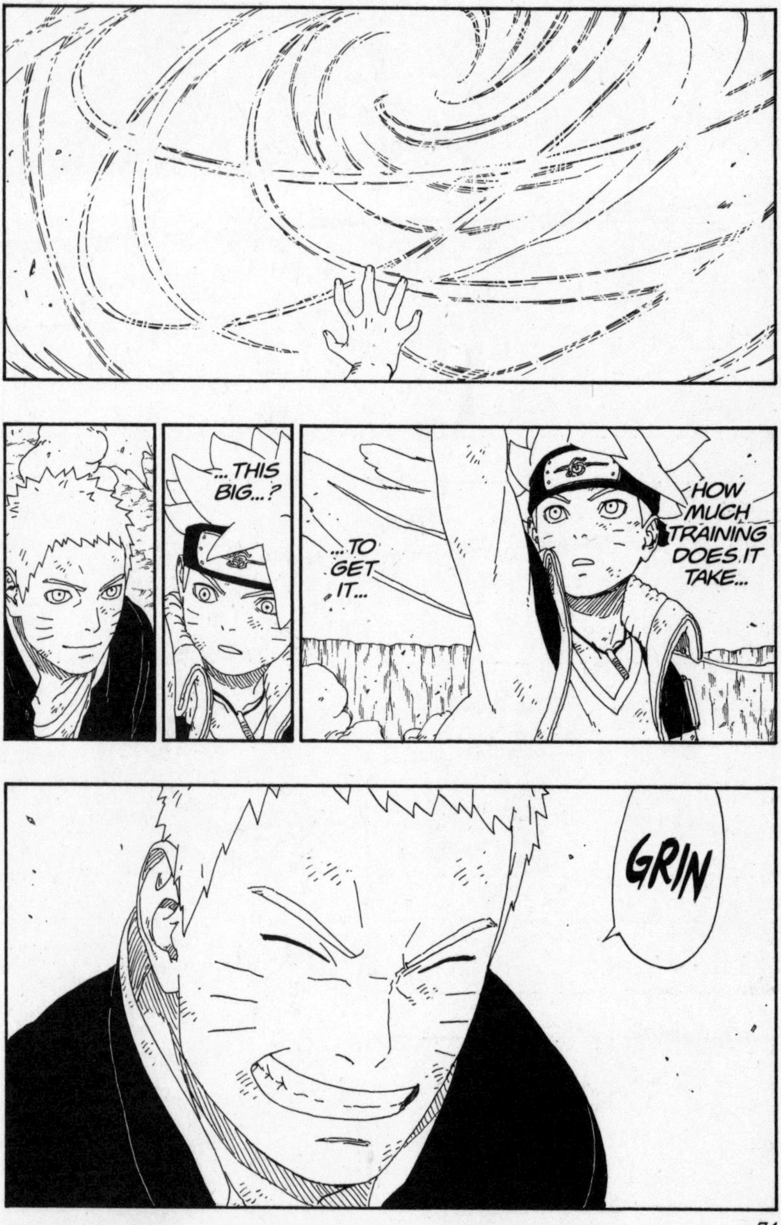
HOW MUCH TRAINING DOES IT TAKE...
...TO GET IT...
...THIS BIG...?
GRIN

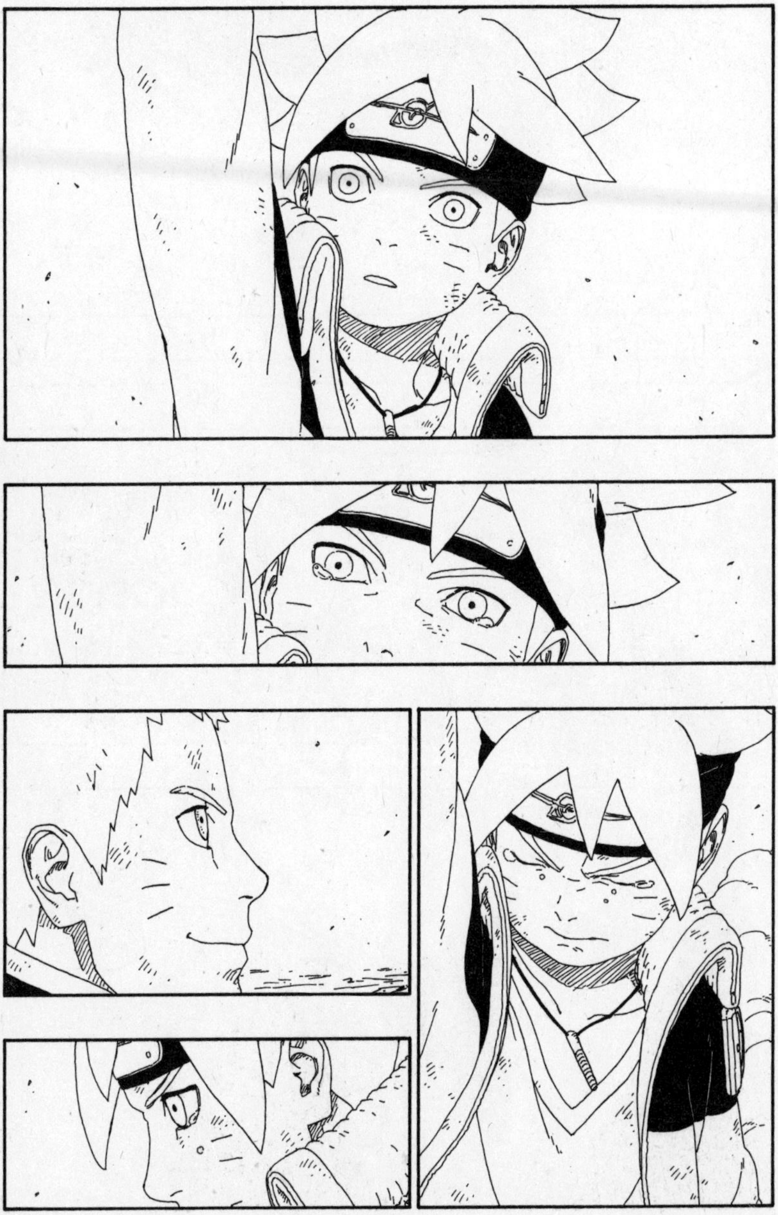

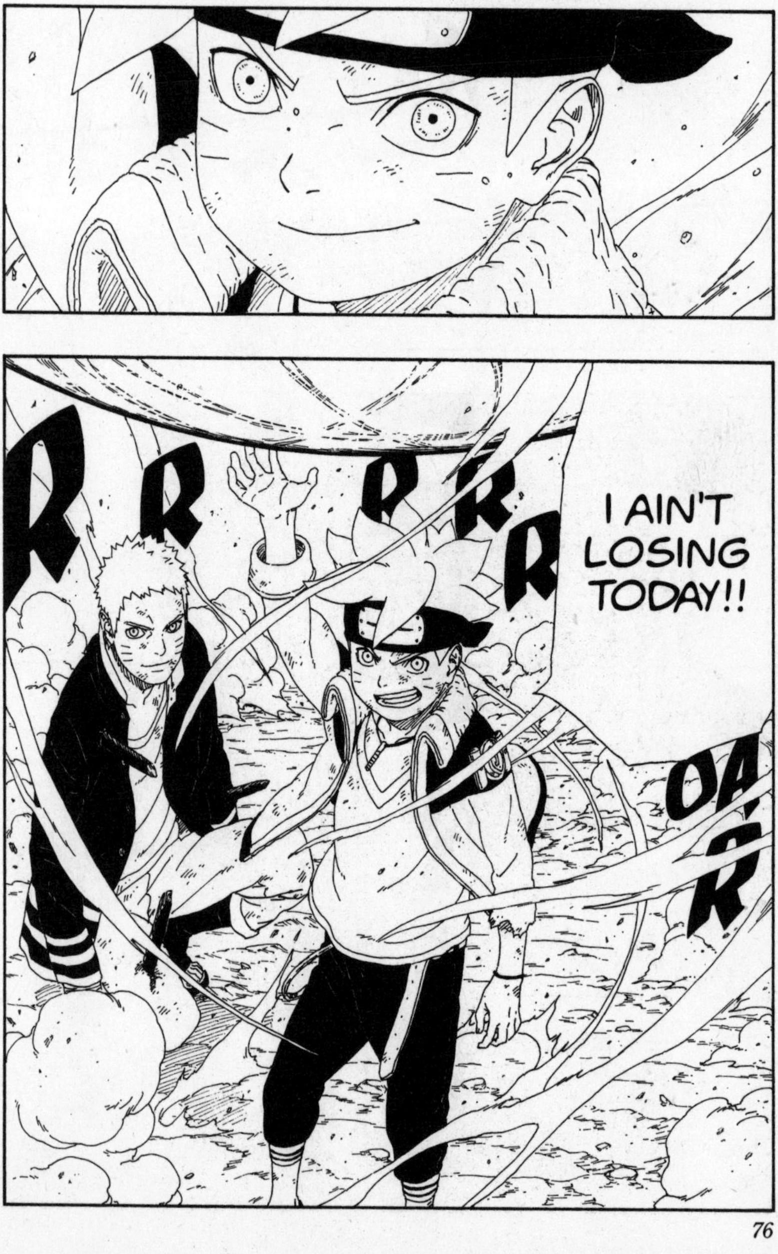
I AIN'T LOSING TODAY!!
RRRRR
OAR

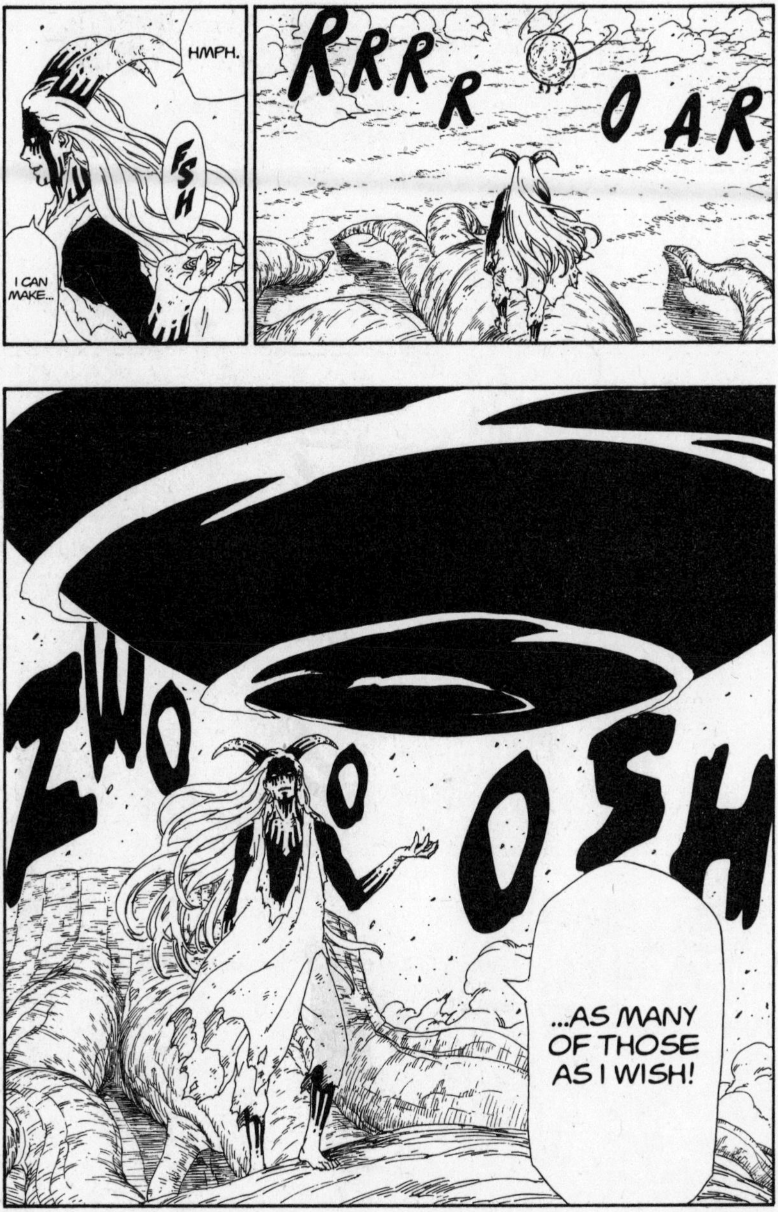
RRRROAR
HMPH.
FSH
I CAN MAKE...
ZWOOOSH
...AS MANY OF THOSE AS I WISH!

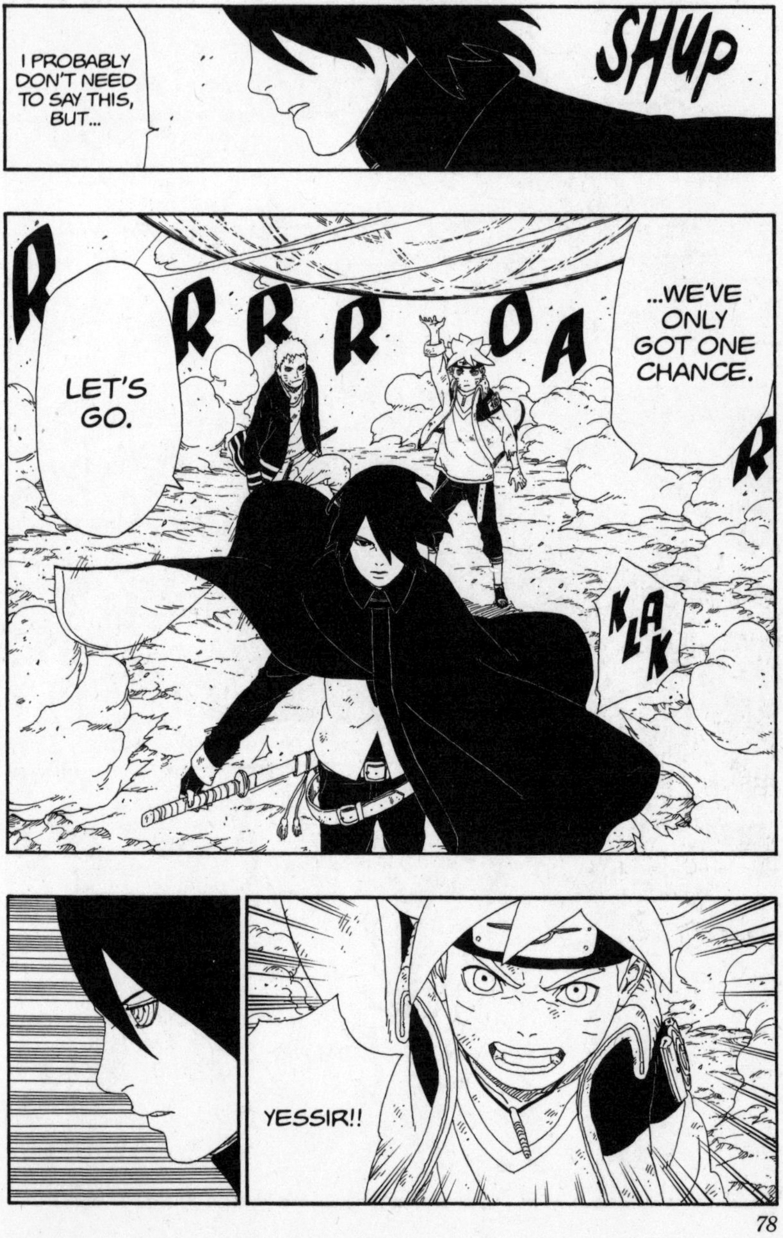
SHUP
I PROBABLY DON'T NEED TO SAY THIS, BUT...
...WE'VE ONLY GOT ONE CHANCE.
RRRROAR
LET'S GO.
KLAK
YESSIR!!

TAK TAK
ZAP
ZSH
BOOM

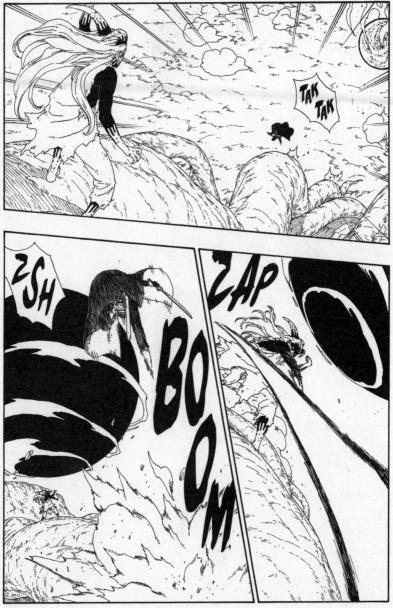

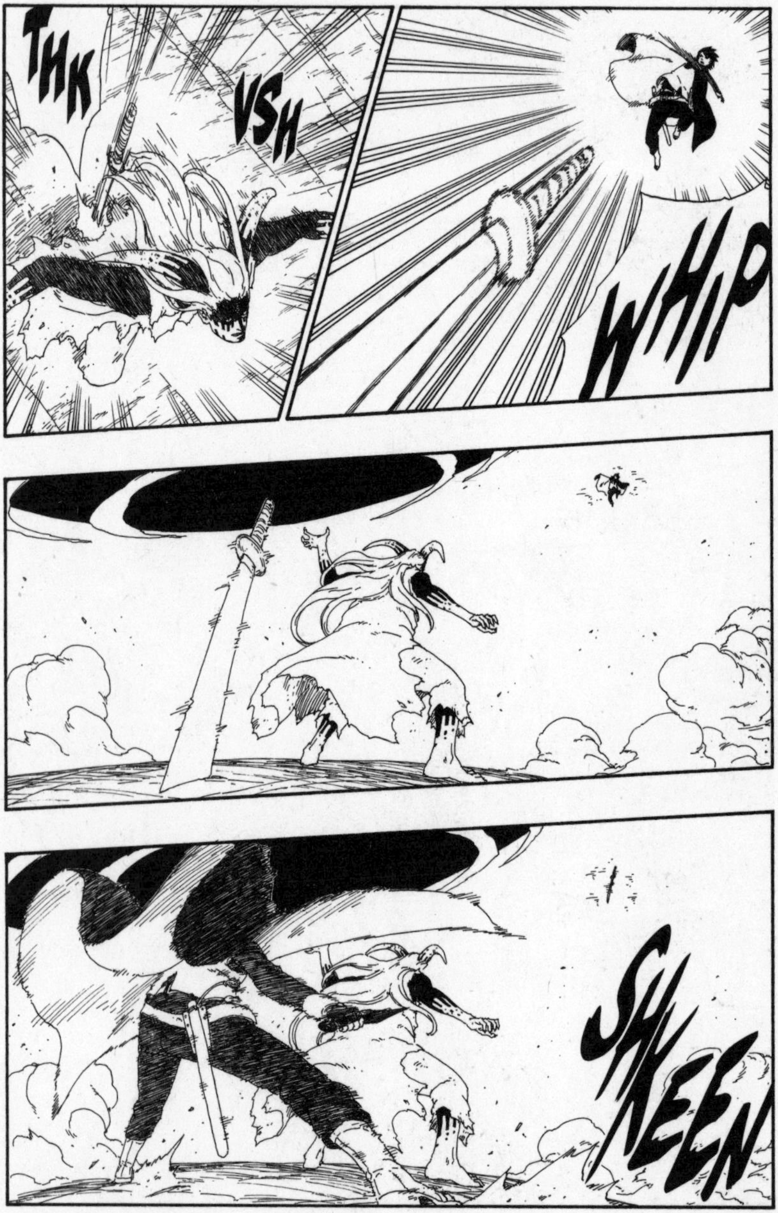
WHIP
VSH
THK
SHKEEN

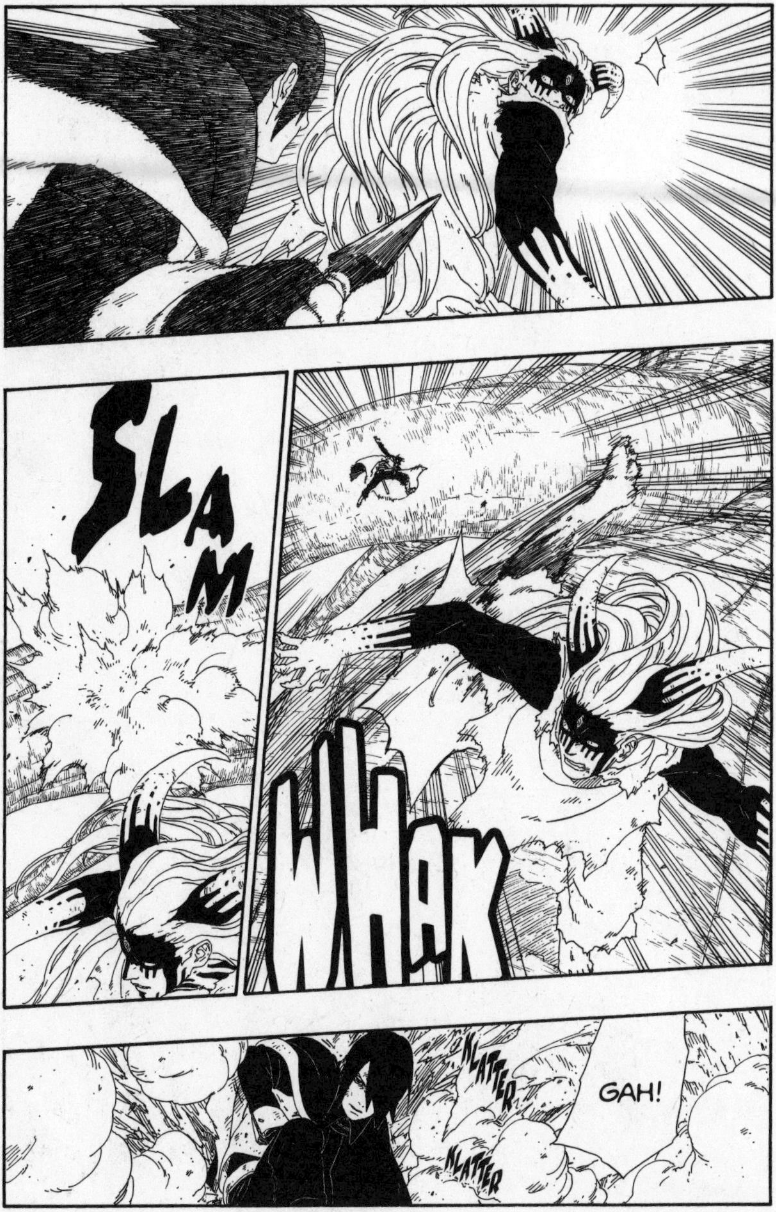
WHAK
SLAM
GAH!
KLATTER
KLATTER

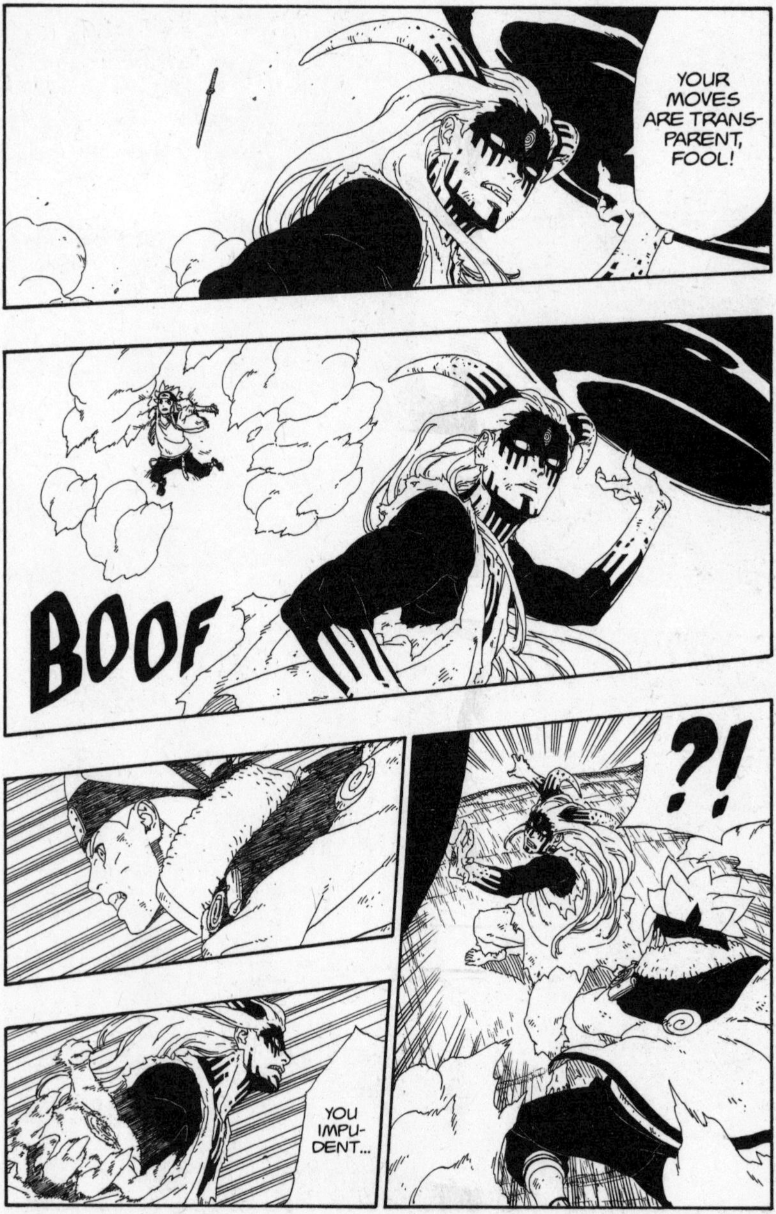
YOUR MOVES ARE TRANSPARENT, FOOL!
BOOF
?!
YOU IMPUDENT...

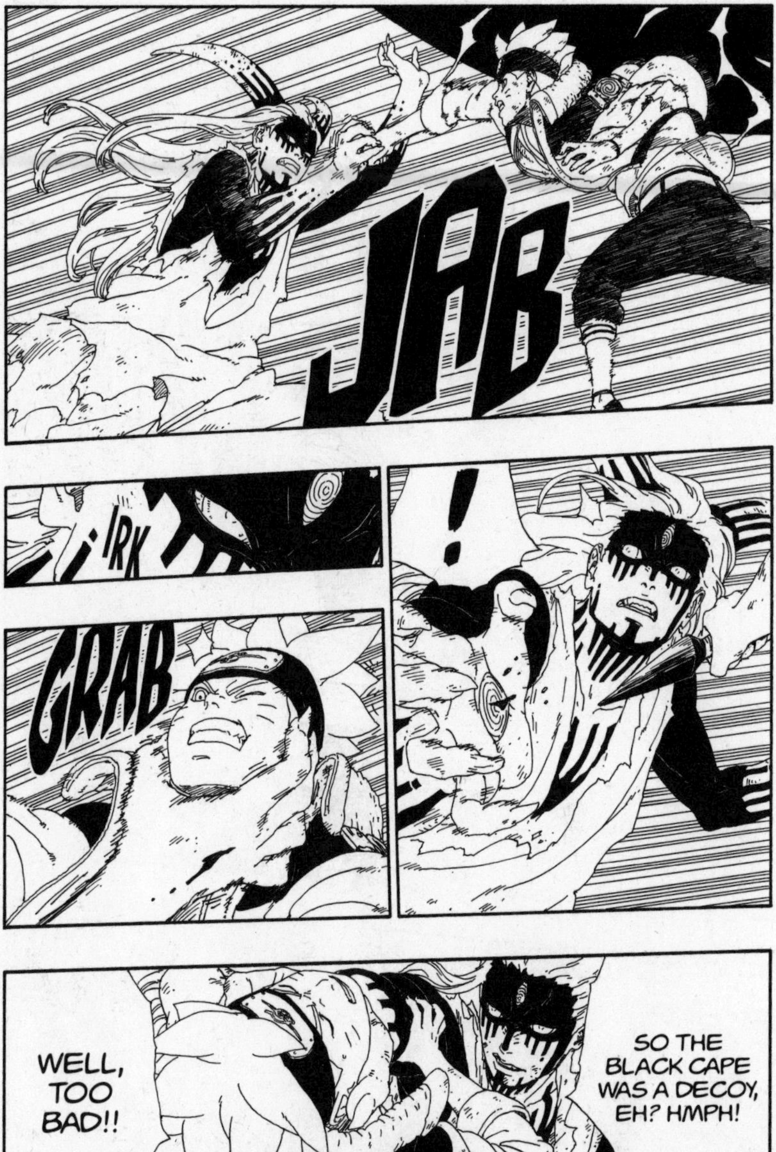
JAB
!
IRK
GRAB
SO THE BLACK CAPE WAS A DECOY, EH? HMPH!
WELL, TOO BAD!!
GRP...

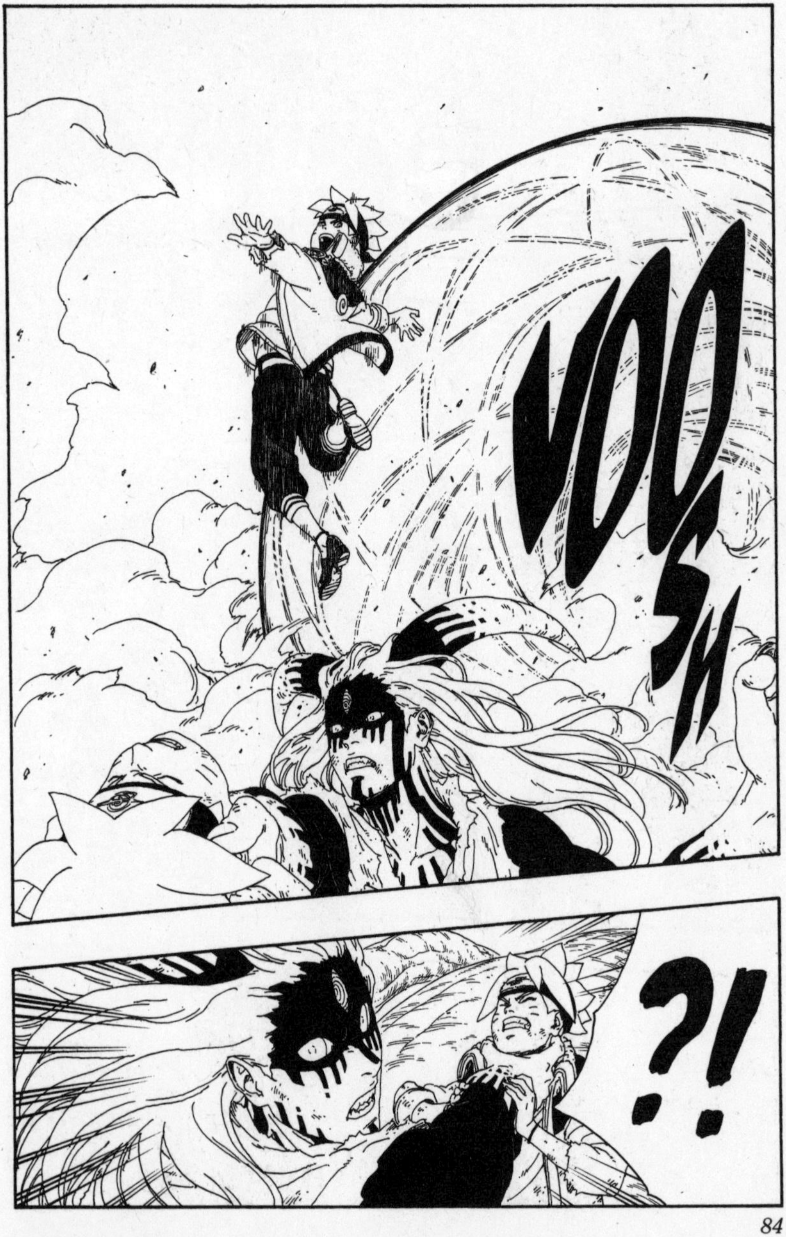
VOOSH
?!

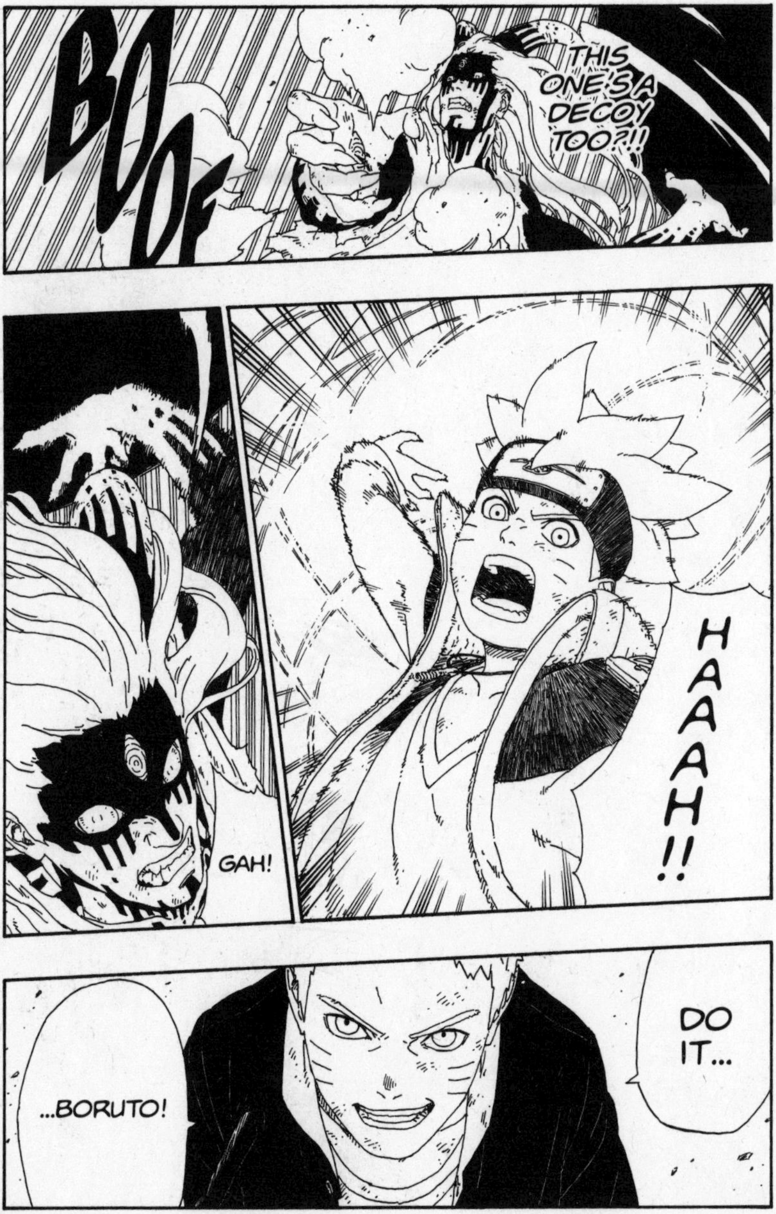
THIS ONE'S A DECOY TOO?!!
BOOF
HAAAAH!!
GAH!
DO IT...
...BORUTO!

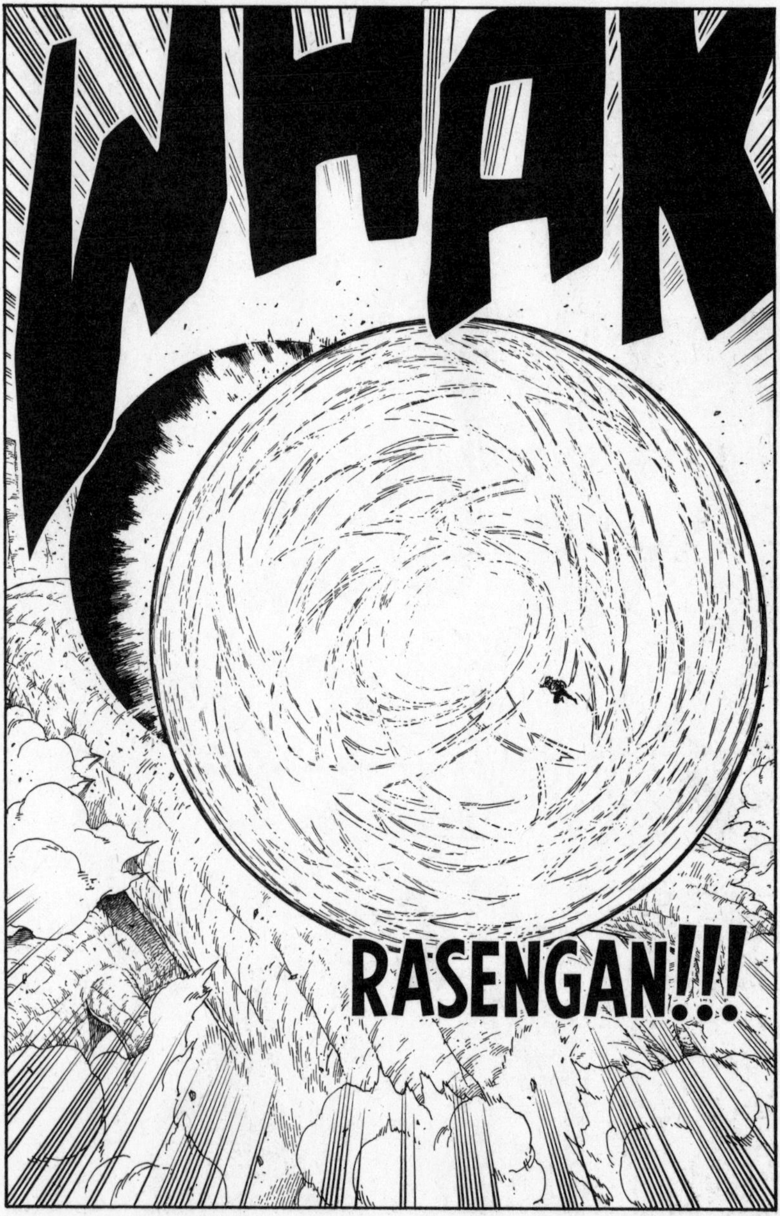
WHAK
RASENGAN!!!

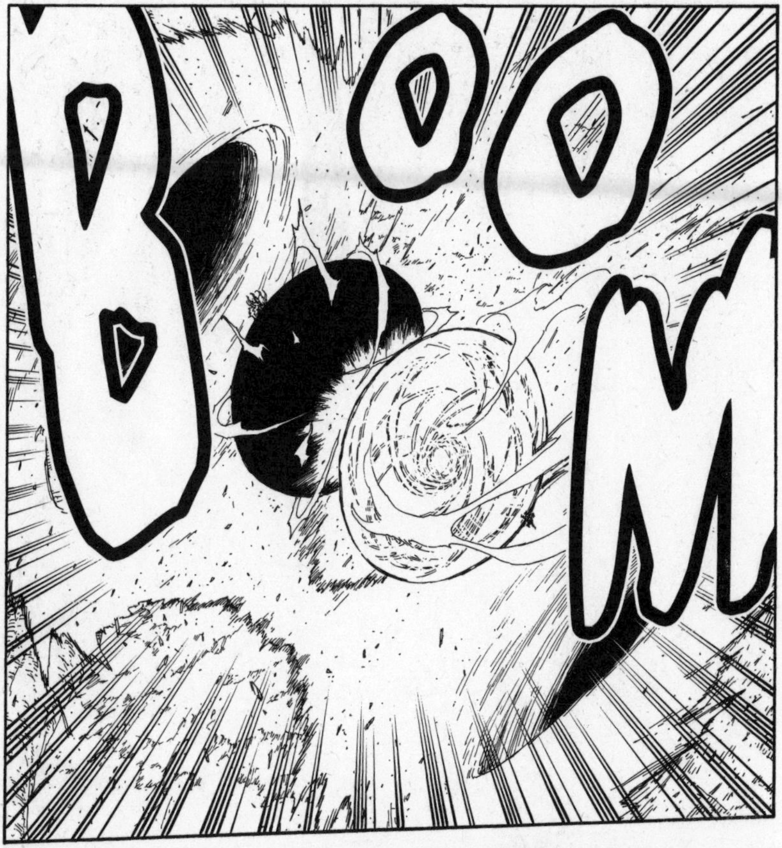
BOOOM

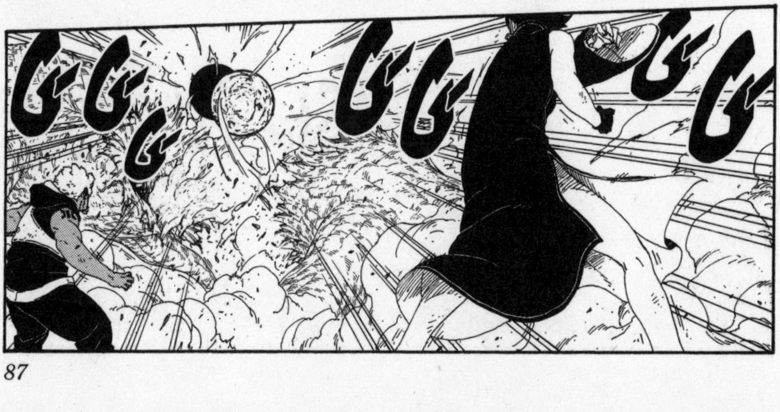
GGG
GGG
GGG

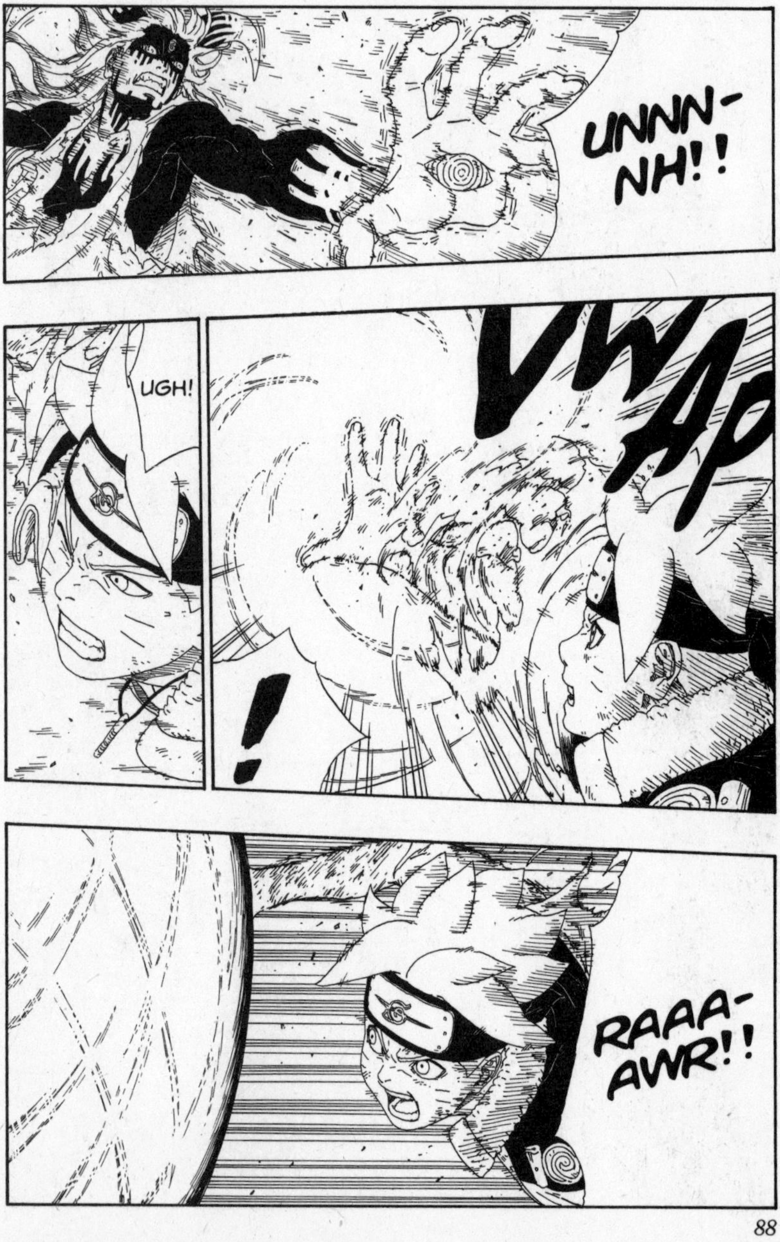
UNNN-NH!!
VWAP
!
UGH!
RAAA-AWR!!

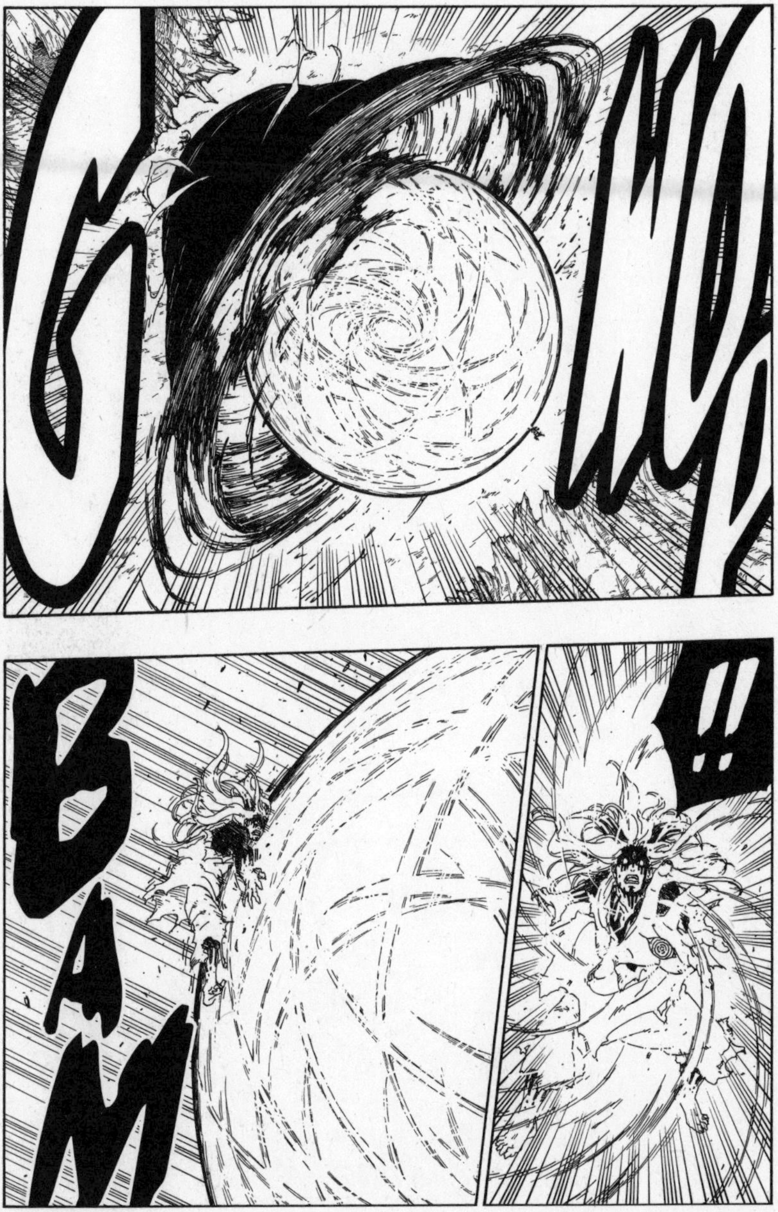
BAM!!

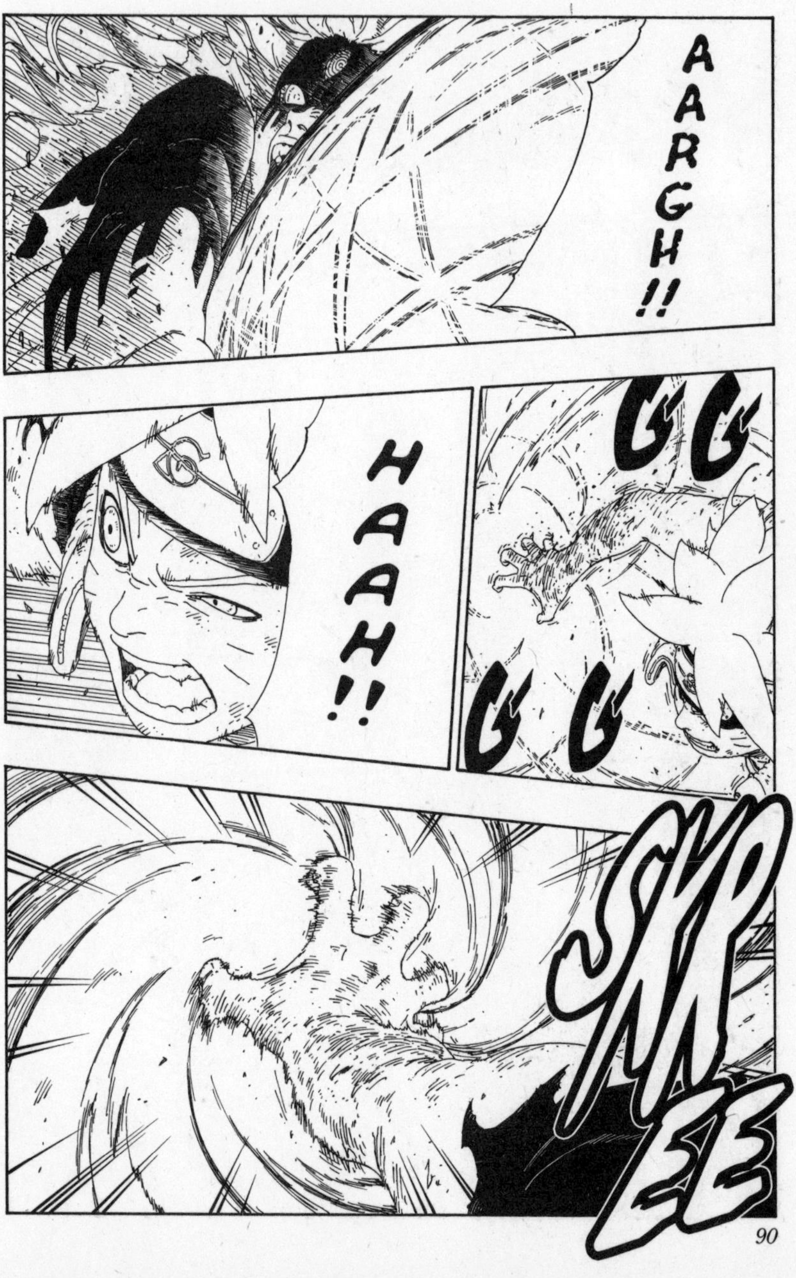
AARGH!!
GGGG
HAAAH!!

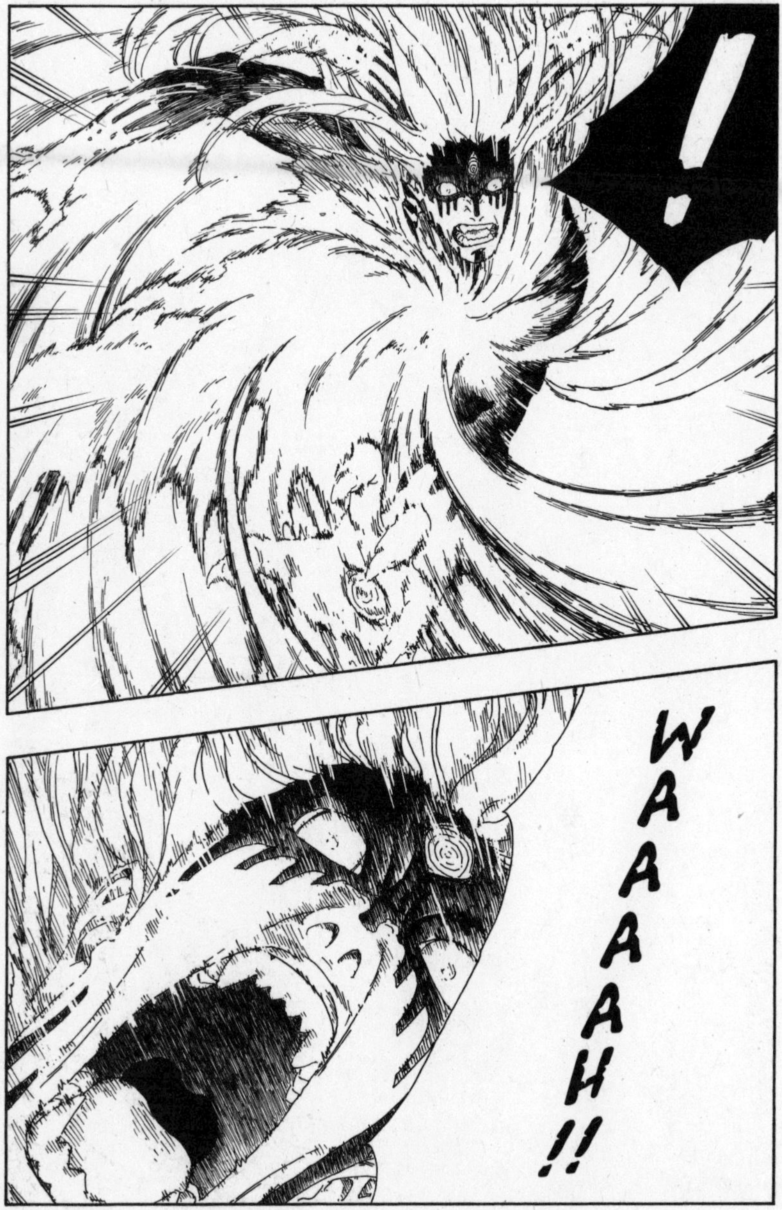
!
WAAAAAH!!

ZWP

92

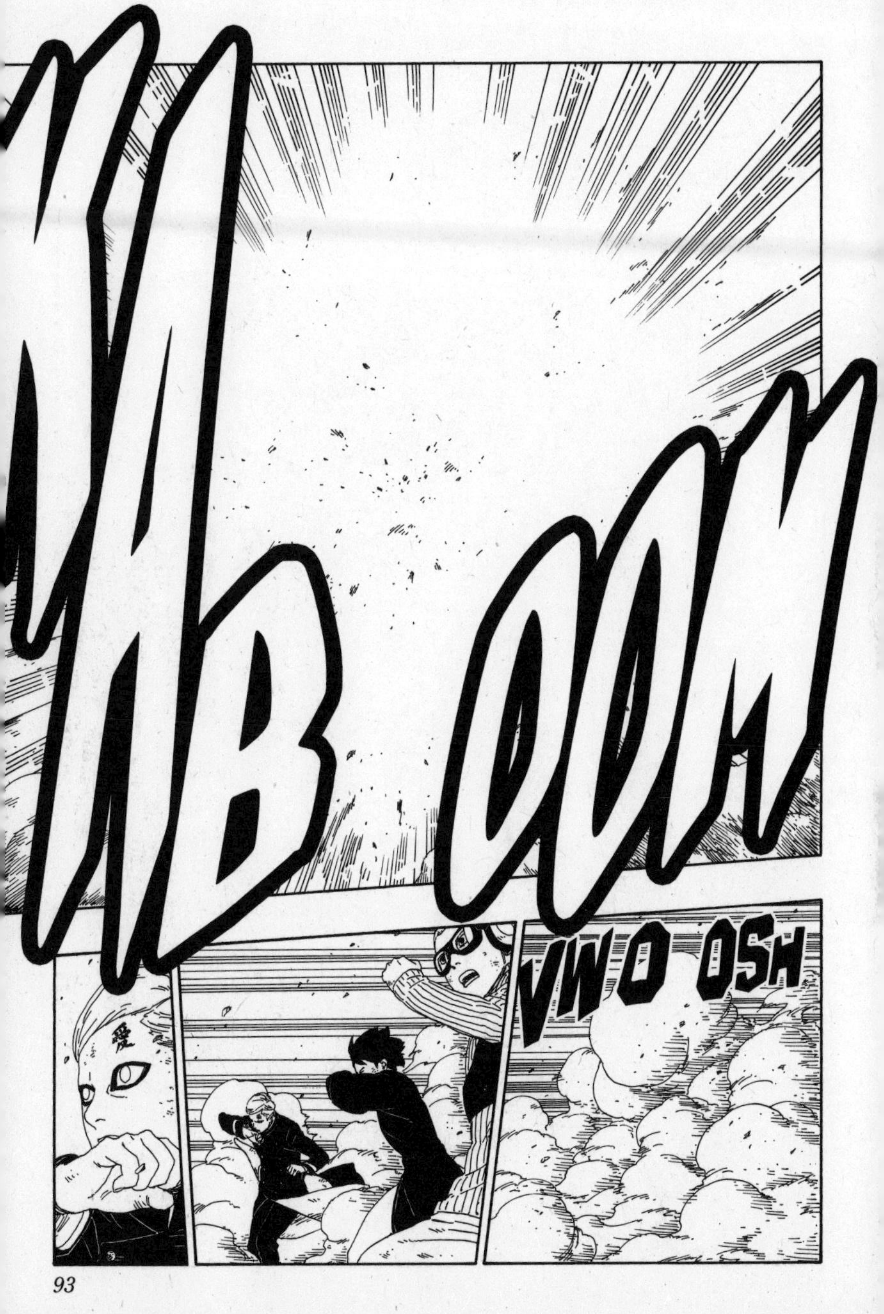
VWOOSH

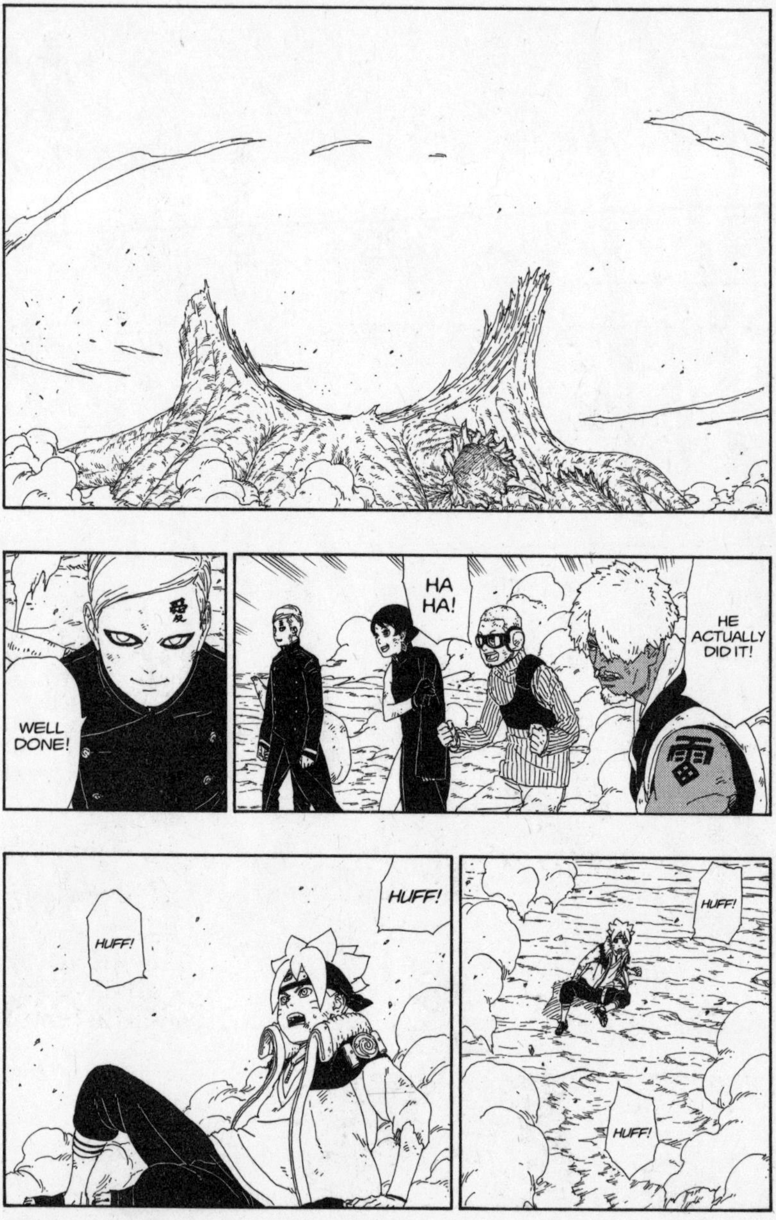
HE ACTUALLY DID IT!
HA HA!
WELL DONE!
HUFF!
HUFF!
HUFF!
HUFF!

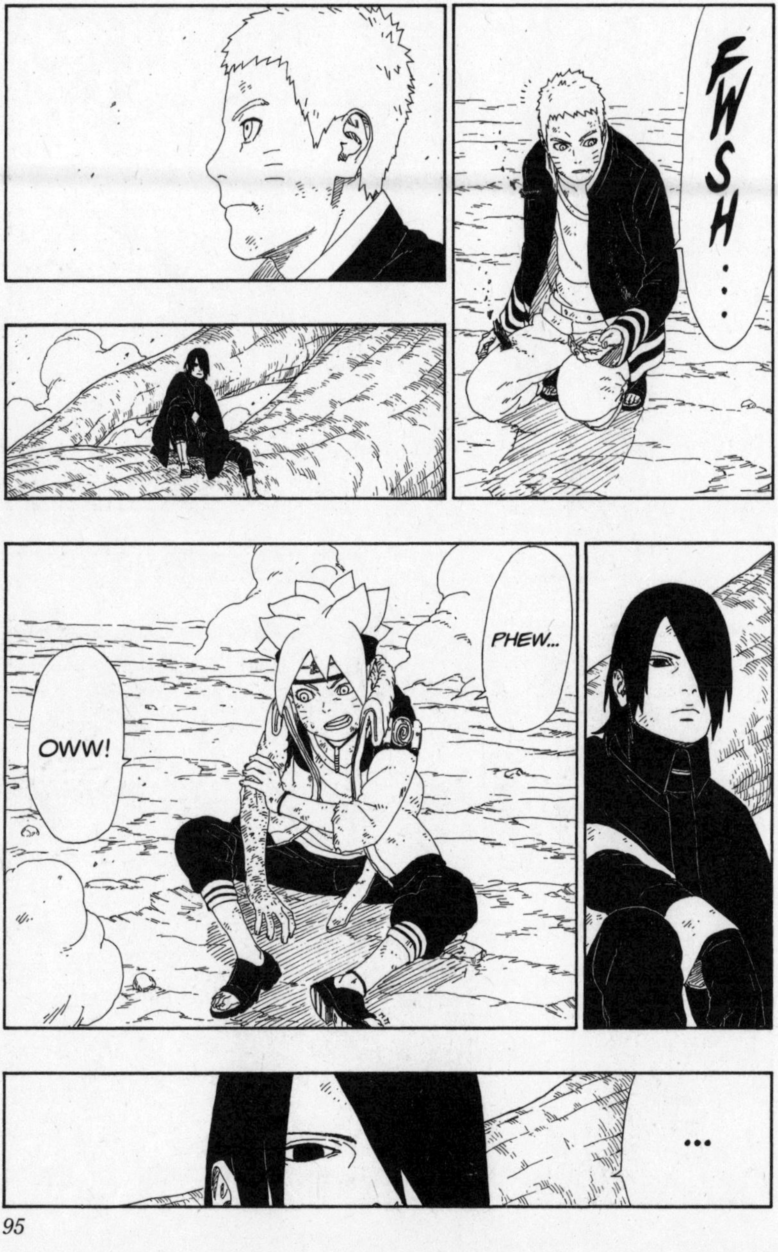
FWSH...
PHEW...
OWW!
...

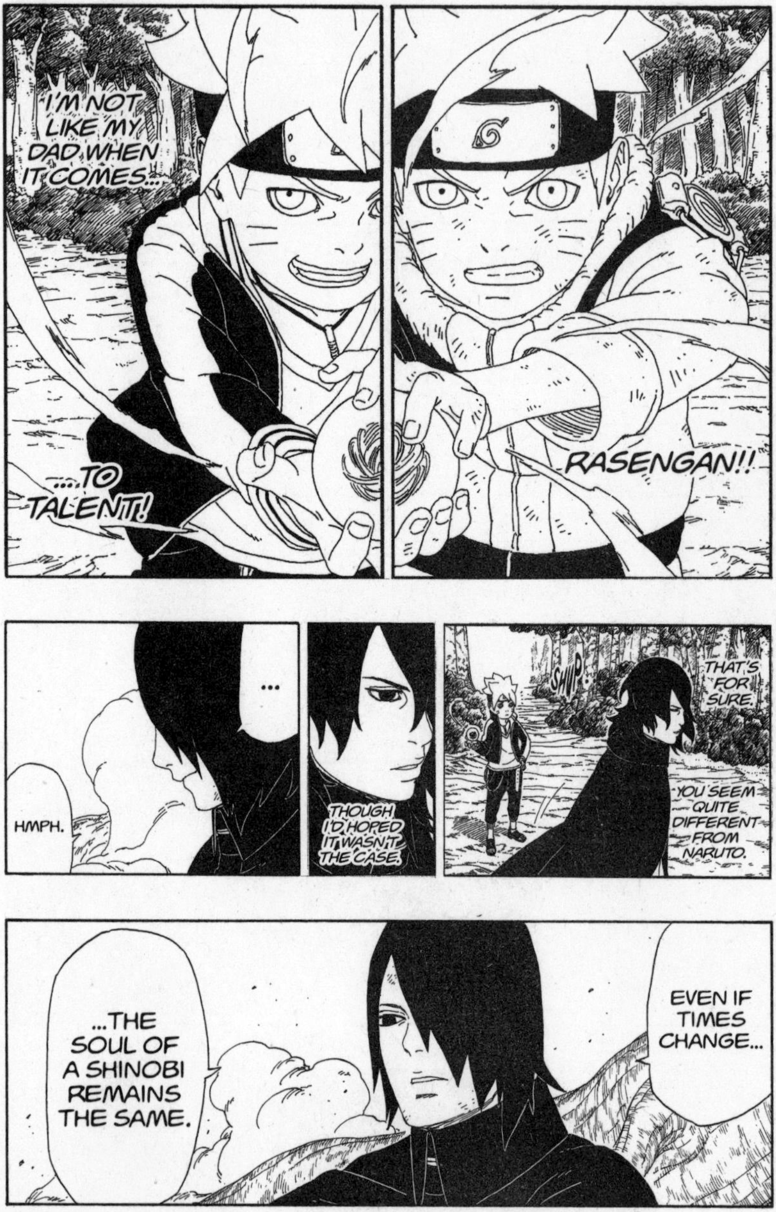
RASENGAN!!
I'M NOT LIKE MY DAD WHEN IT COMES...
...TO TALENT!
SHUP
THAT'S FOR SURE.
YOU SEEM QUITE DIFFERENT FROM NARUTO.
THOUGH I'D HOPED IT WASN'T THE CASE.
...
HMPH.
EVEN IF TIMES CHANGE...
...THE SOUL OF A SHINOBI REMAINS THE SAME.

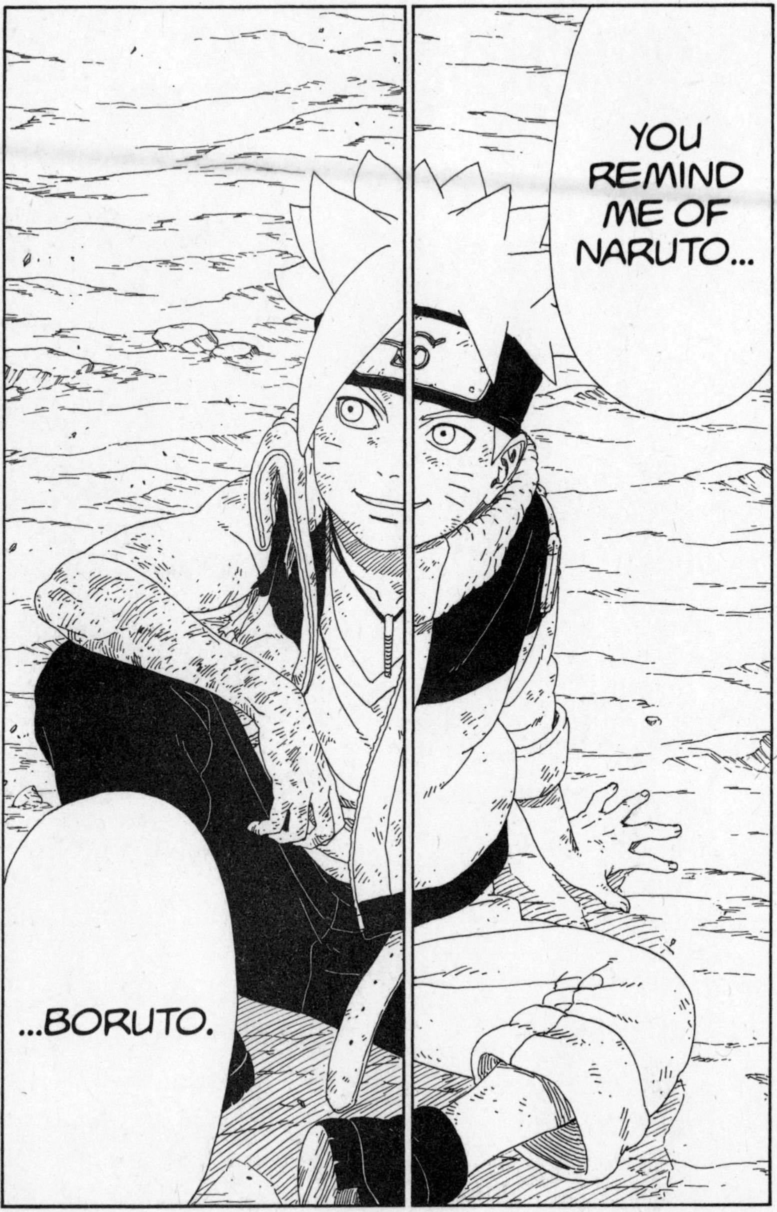
YOU REMIND ME OF NARUTO...
...BORUTO.

NINJA ENCYCLOPEDIA • ENTRY 8

UCHIHA SASUKE

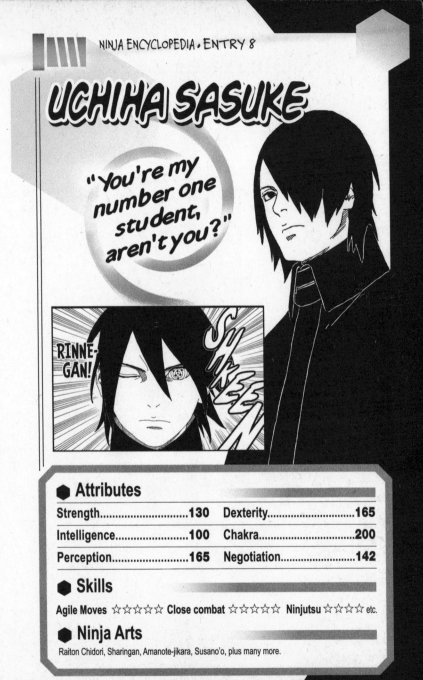

"You're my number one student, aren't you?"

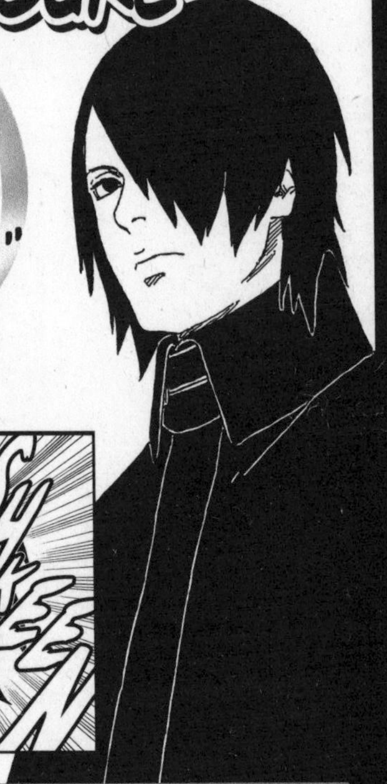

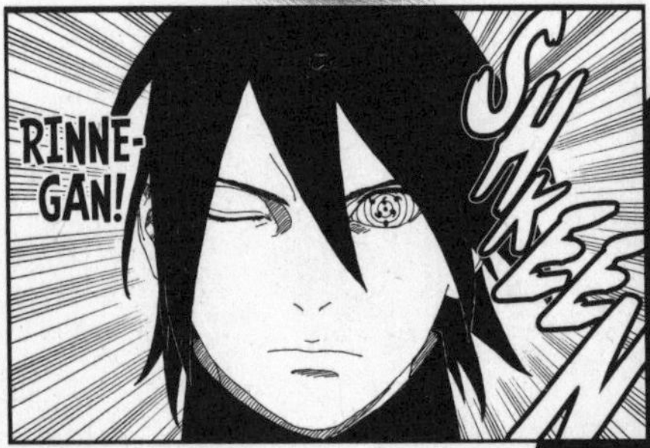
SHKEEN
RINNE-GAN!

Attributes

Strength	130	Dexterity	165
Intelligence	100	Chakra	200
Perception	165	Negotiation	142

Skills

Agile Moves ☆☆☆☆☆ **Close combat** ☆☆☆☆☆ **Ninjutsu** ☆☆☆☆ etc.

Ninja Arts

Raiton Chidori, Sharingan, Amanote-jikara, Susano'o, plus many more.

*Average attribute value is 60 for ordinary people and 90 for genin. Skill values range from 1 to 5☆with 5☆signifying super top-notch.

Number 10: My Story!!

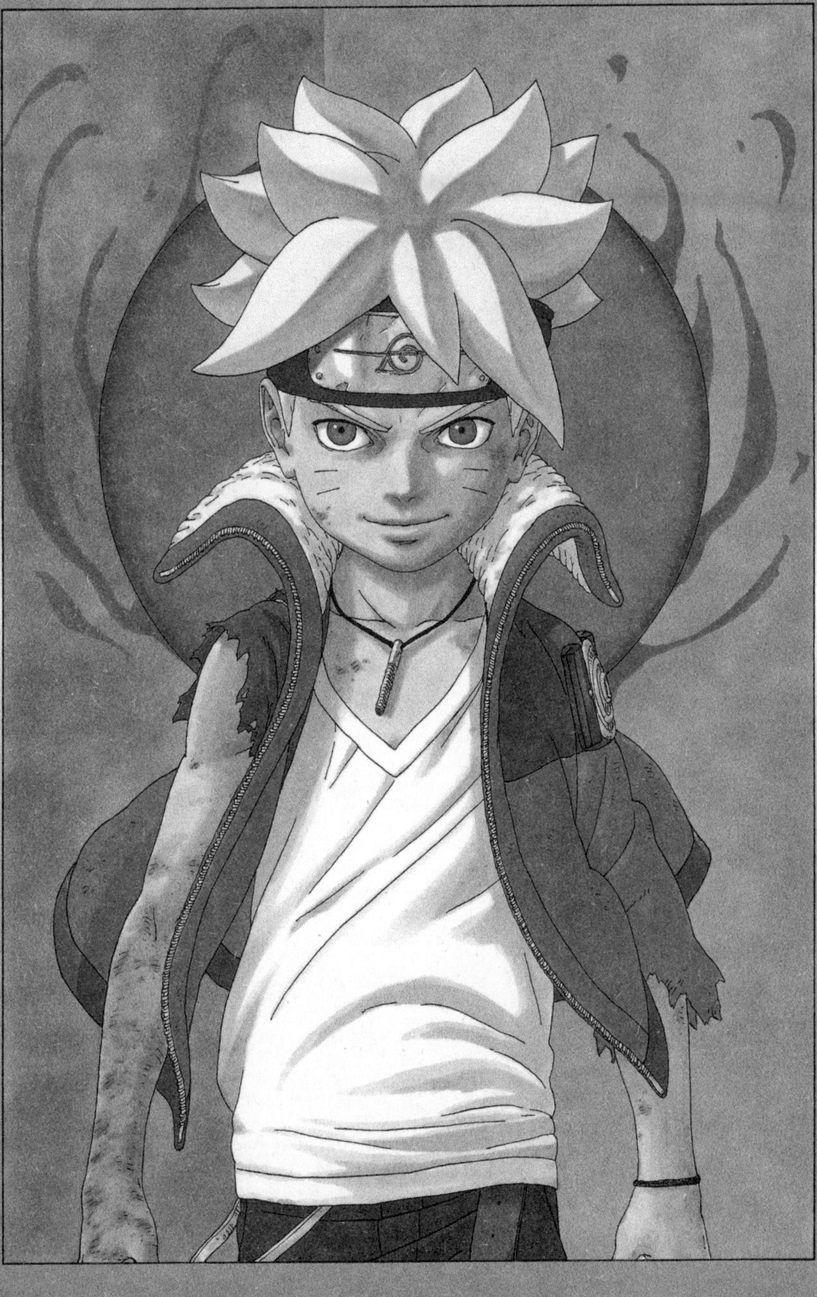

BORUTO

-NARUTO NEXT GENERATIONS-

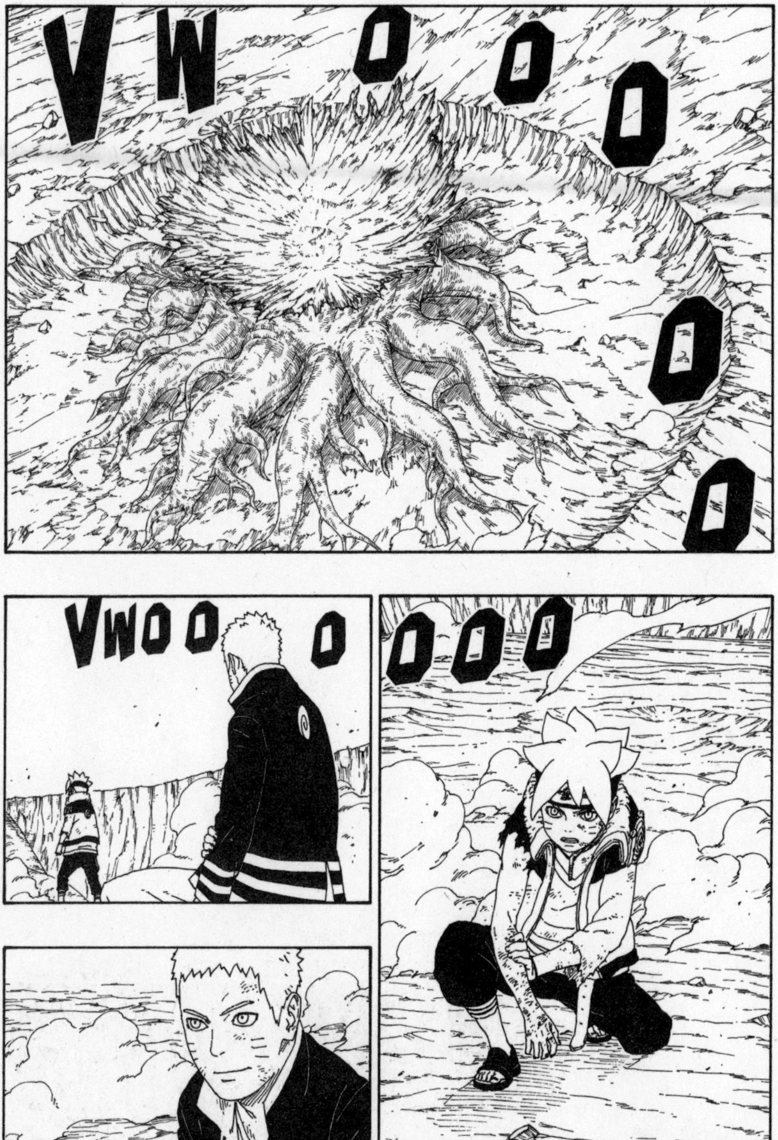
VWOOOOO
VWOOOOOO

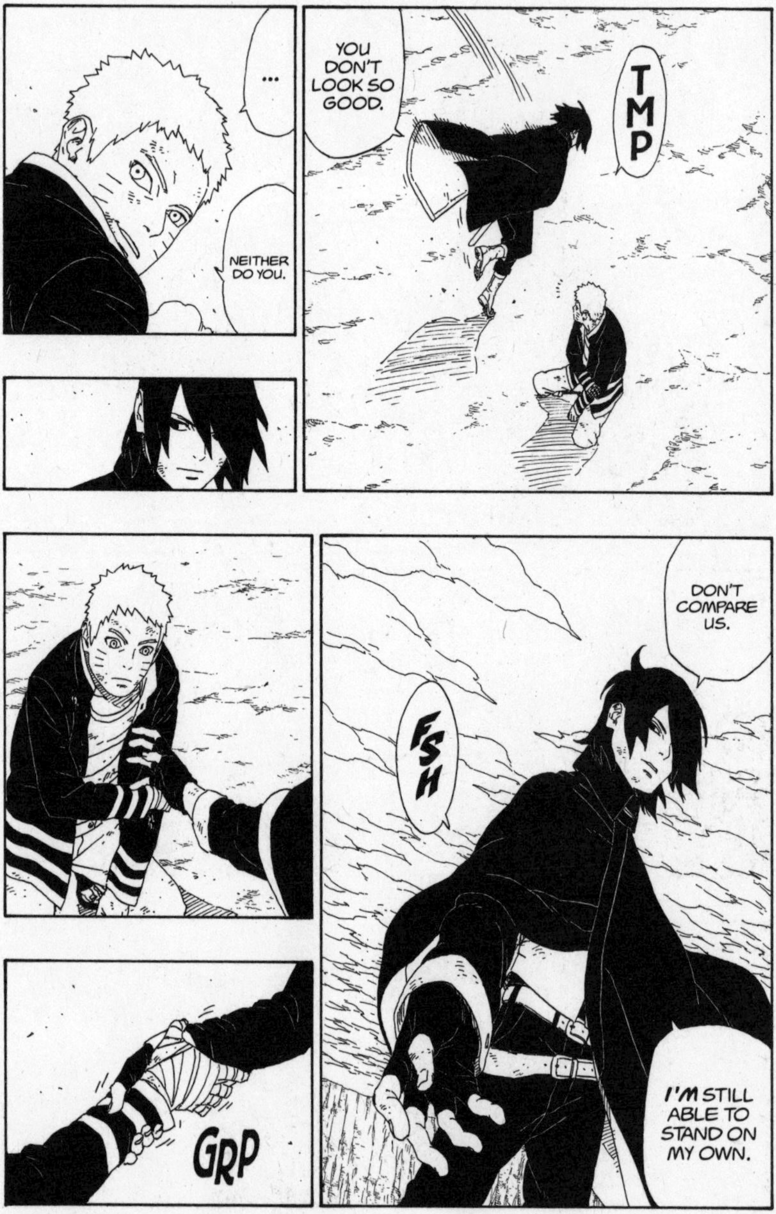
TMP
YOU DON'T LOOK SO GOOD.
...
NEITHER DO YOU.
DON'T COMPARE US.
FSH
I'M STILL ABLE TO STAND ON MY OWN.
GRP

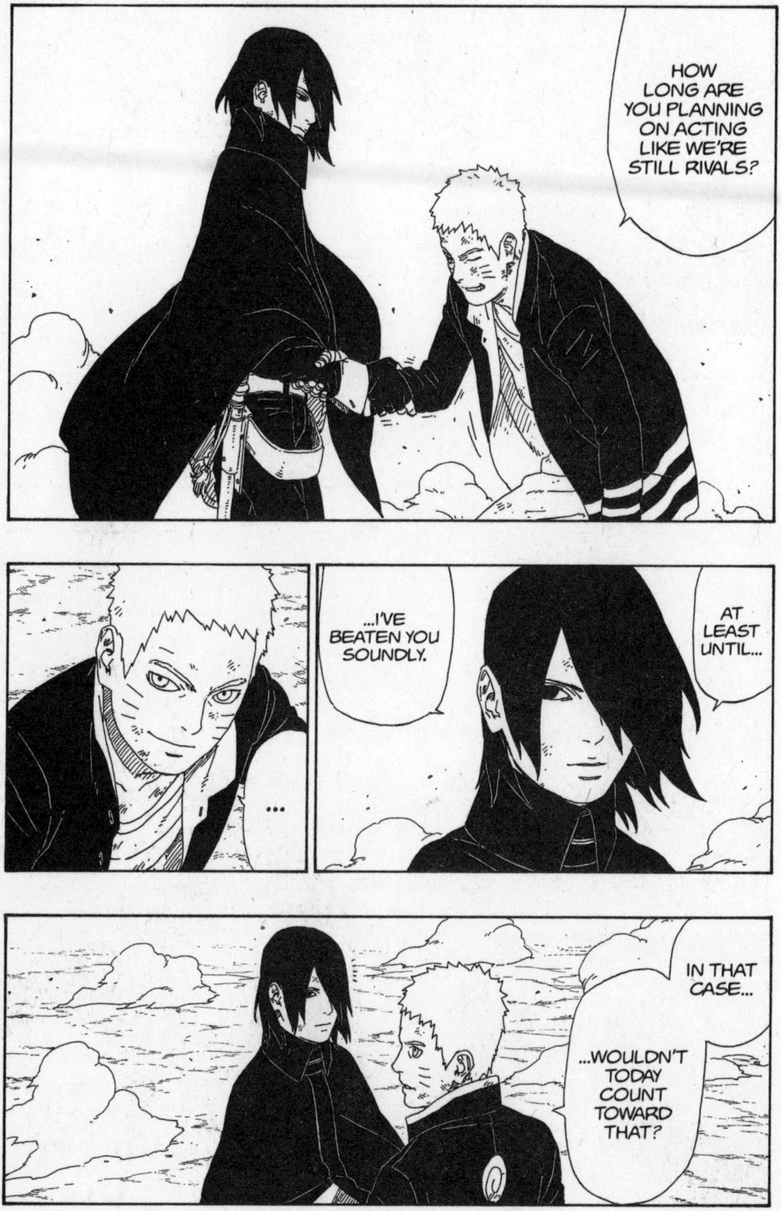
HOW LONG ARE YOU PLANNING ON ACTING LIKE WE'RE STILL RIVALS?
AT LEAST UNTIL...
...I'VE BEATEN YOU SOUNDLY.
...
IN THAT CASE...
...WOULDN'T TODAY COUNT TOWARD THAT?

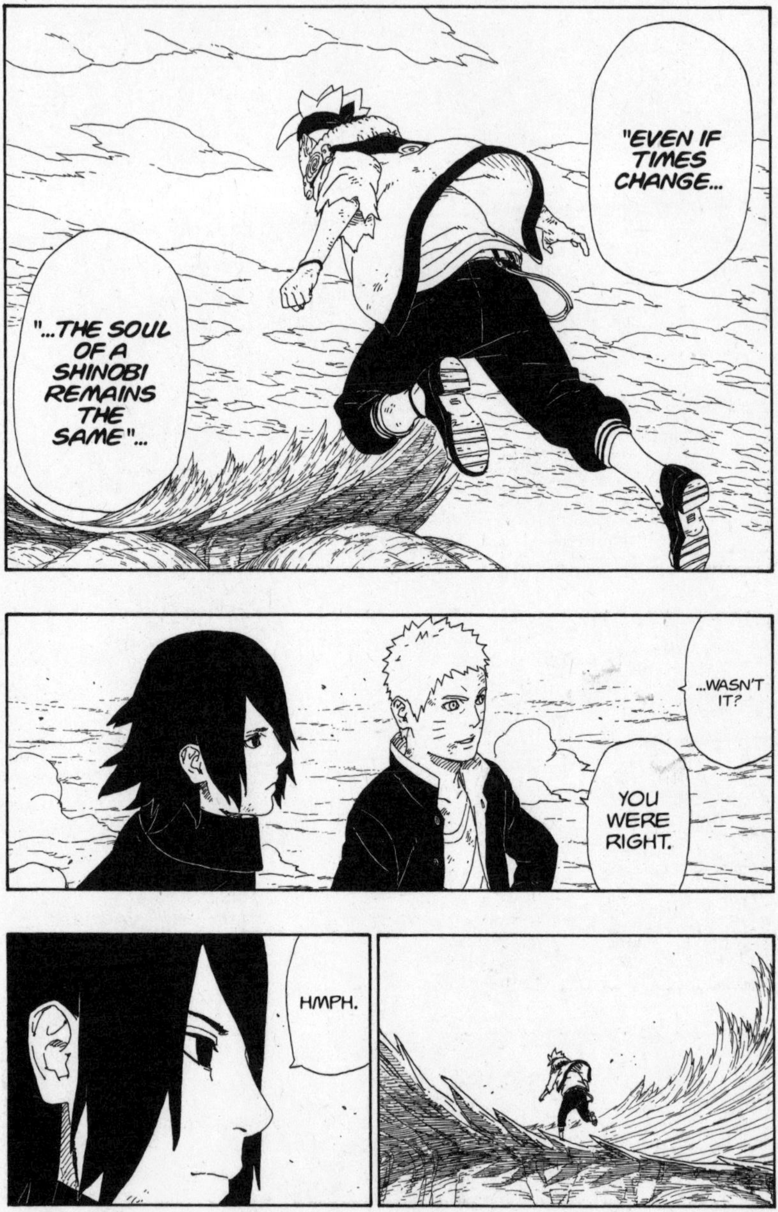
"EVEN IF TIMES CHANGE...
"...THE SOUL OF A SHINOBI REMAINS THE SAME"...
...WASN'T IT?
YOU WERE RIGHT.
HMPH.

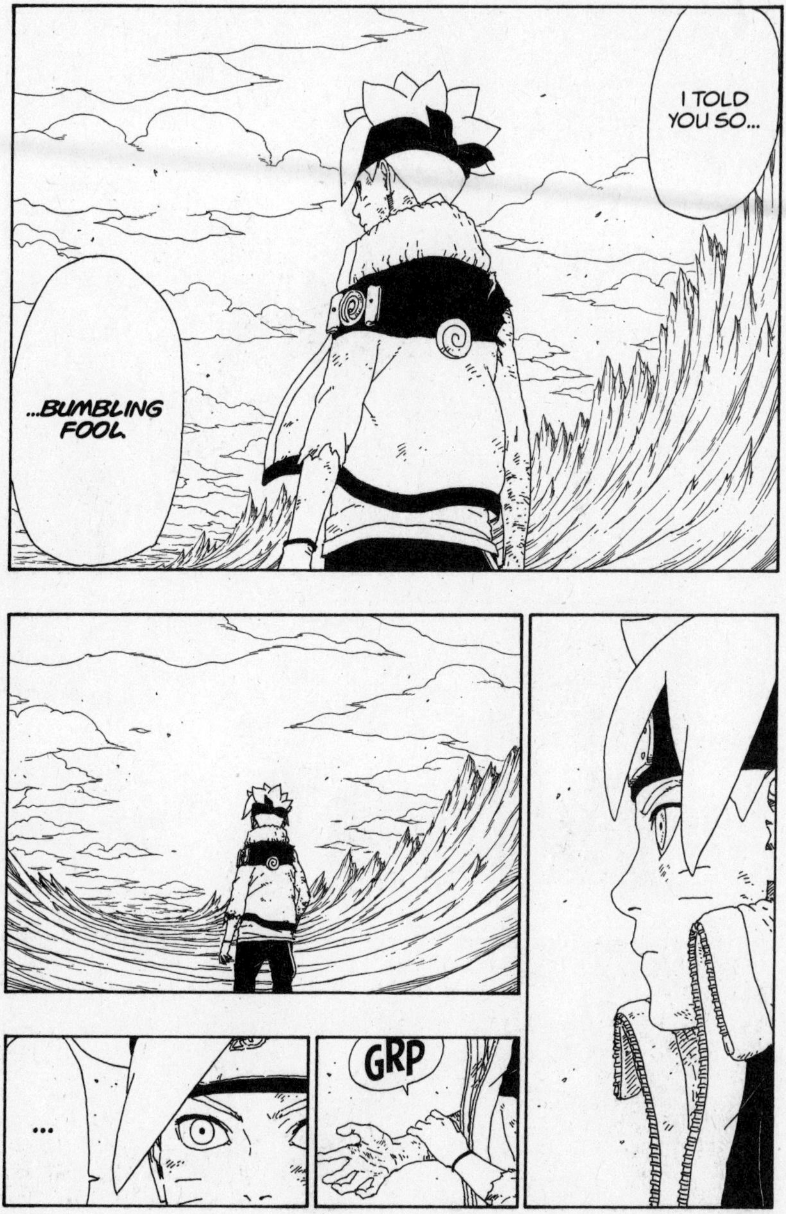
I TOLD YOU SO...
...BUMBLING FOOL.
GRP
...

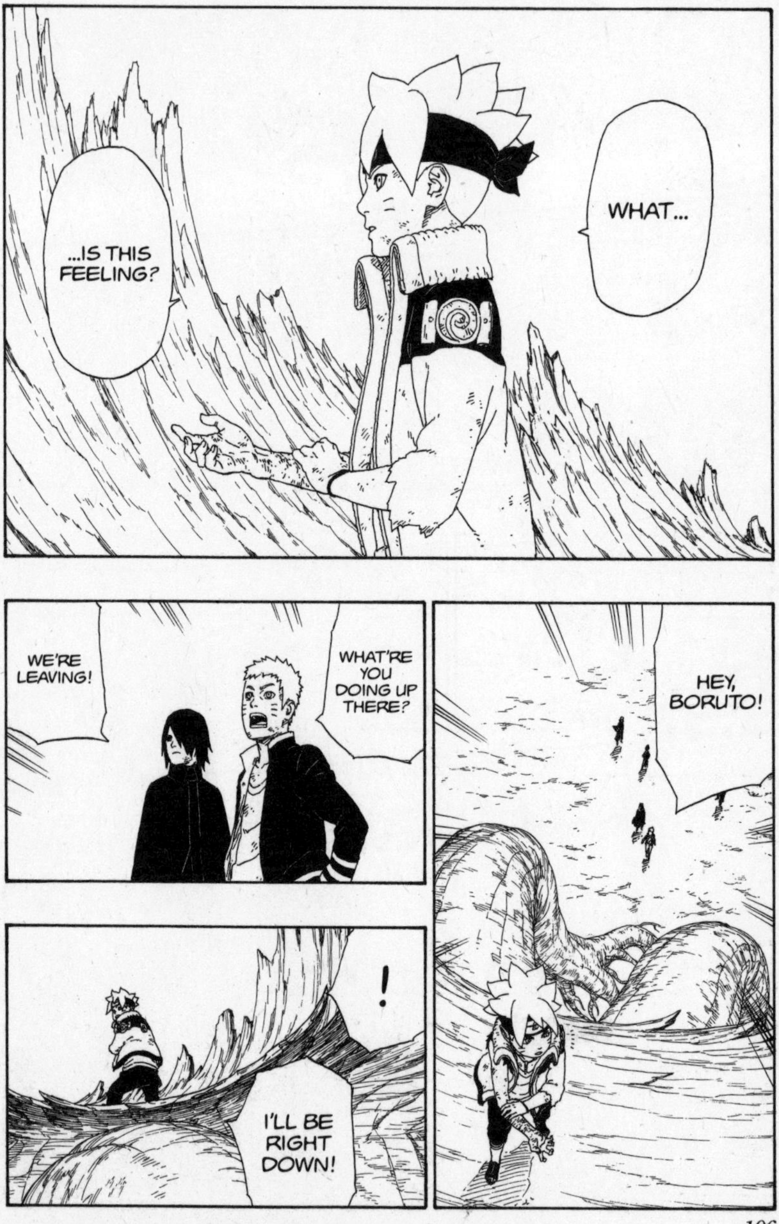
WHAT...
...IS THIS FEELING?
HEY, BORUTO!
WHAT'RE YOU DOING UP THERE?
WE'RE LEAVING!
!
I'LL BE RIGHT DOWN!

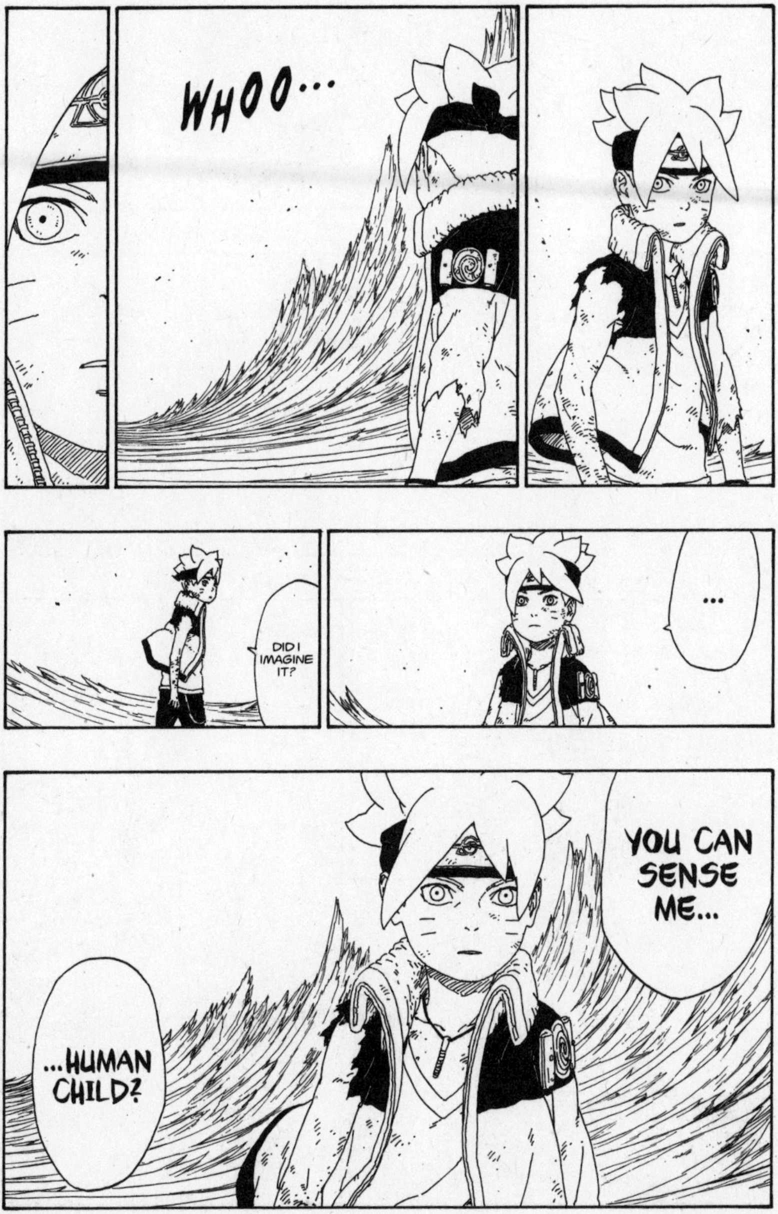
WHOO...
...
DID I IMAGINE IT?
YOU CAN SENSE ME...
...HUMAN CHILD?

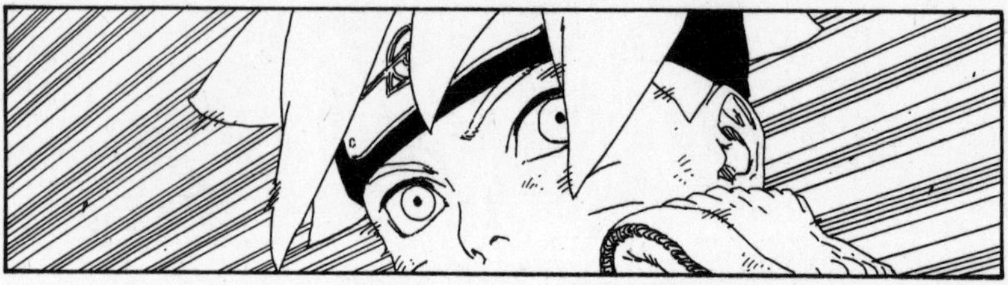

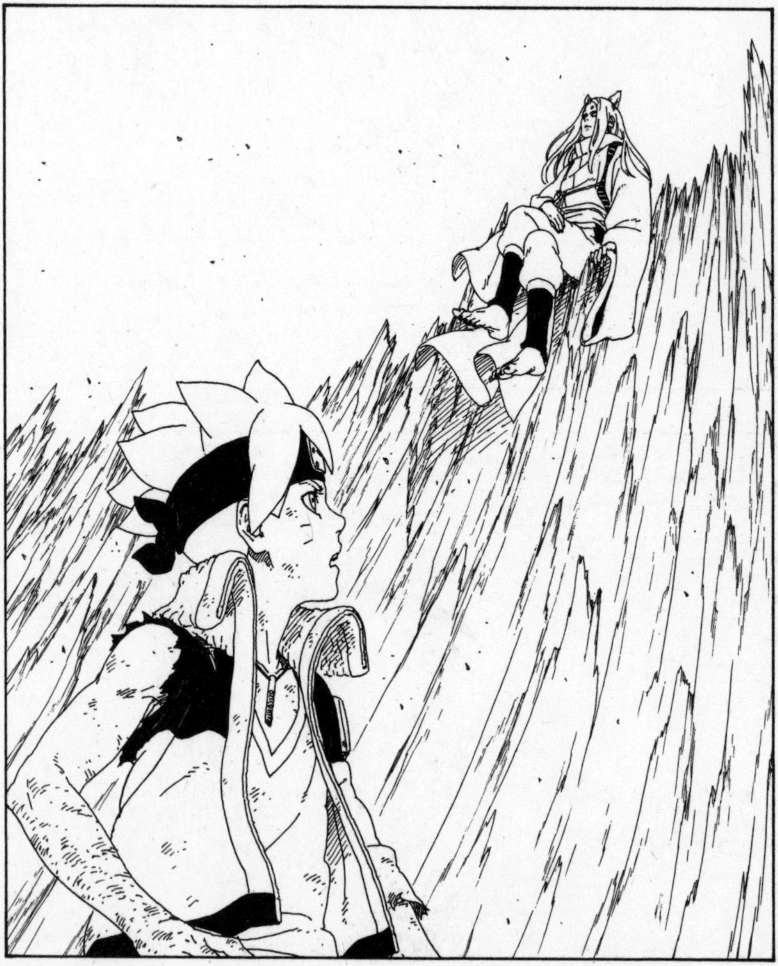

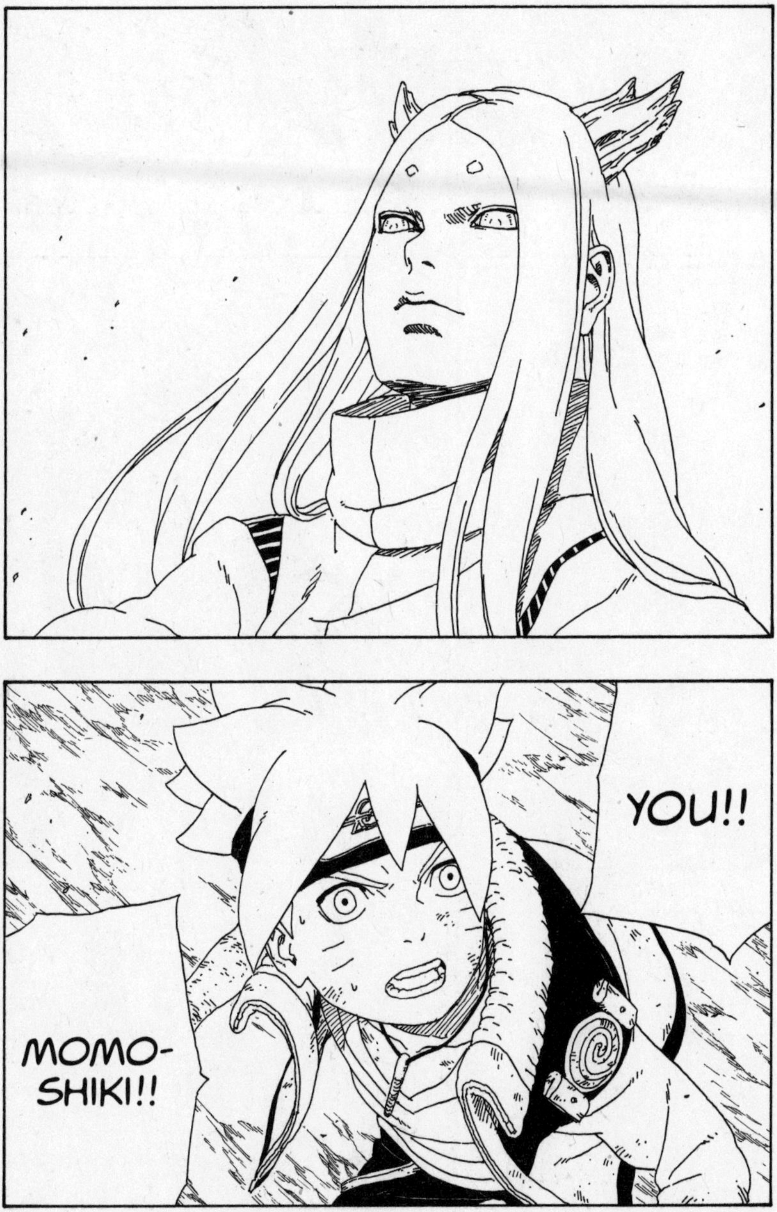
YOU!!
MOMO-
SHIKI!!

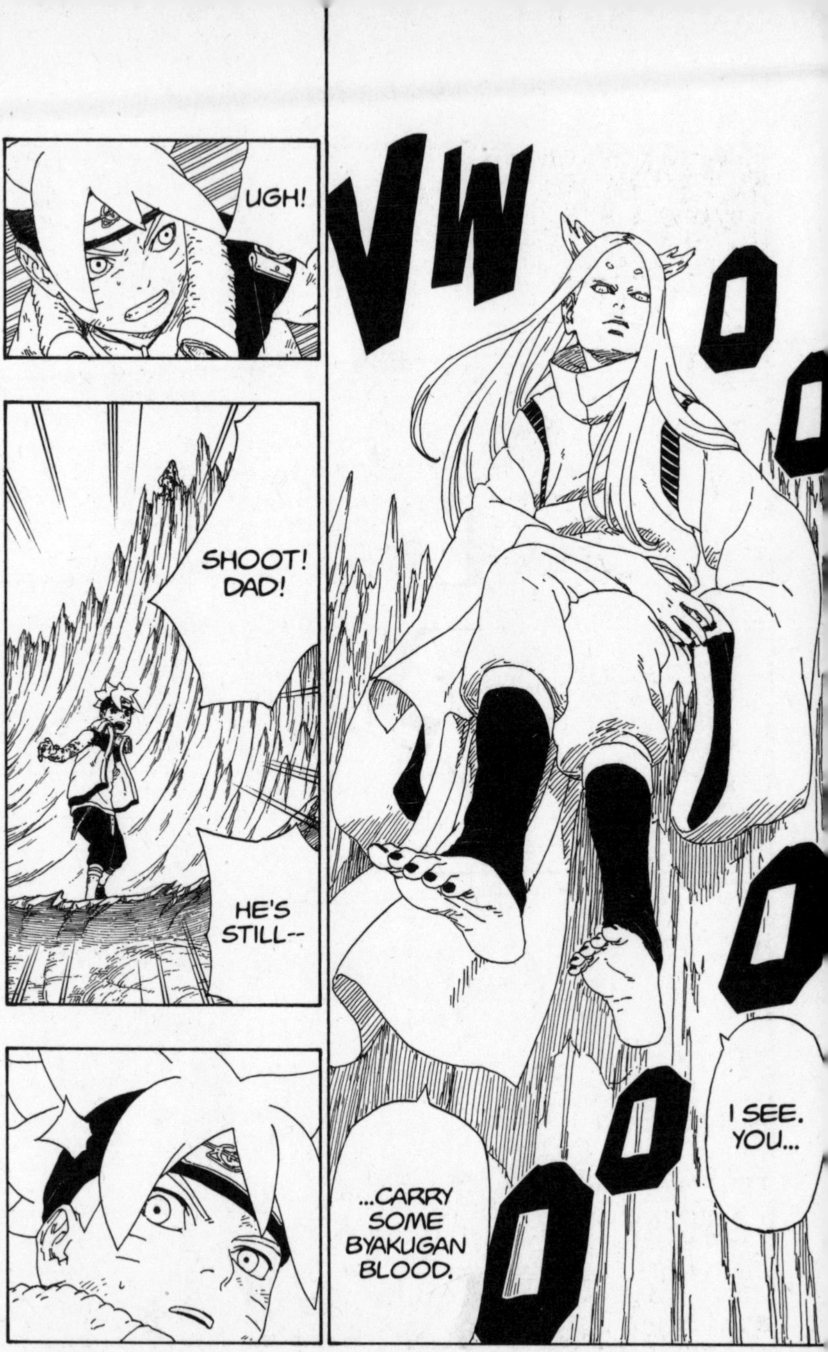
VWOOOOOOO
I SEE. YOU...
...CARRY SOME BYAKUGAN BLOOD.
UGH!
SHOOT! DAD!
HE'S STILL--

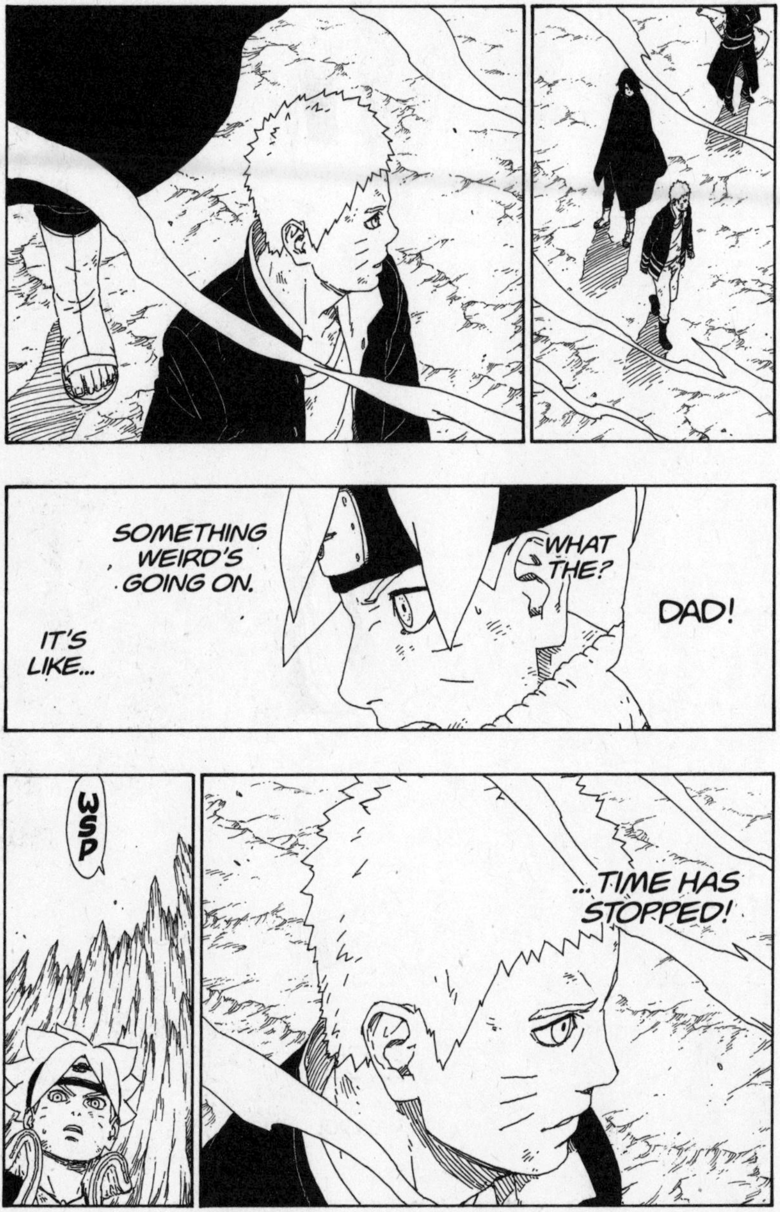
DAD!
WHAT THE?
SOMETHING WEIRD'S GOING ON.
IT'S LIKE...
...TIME HAS STOPPED!
WSP

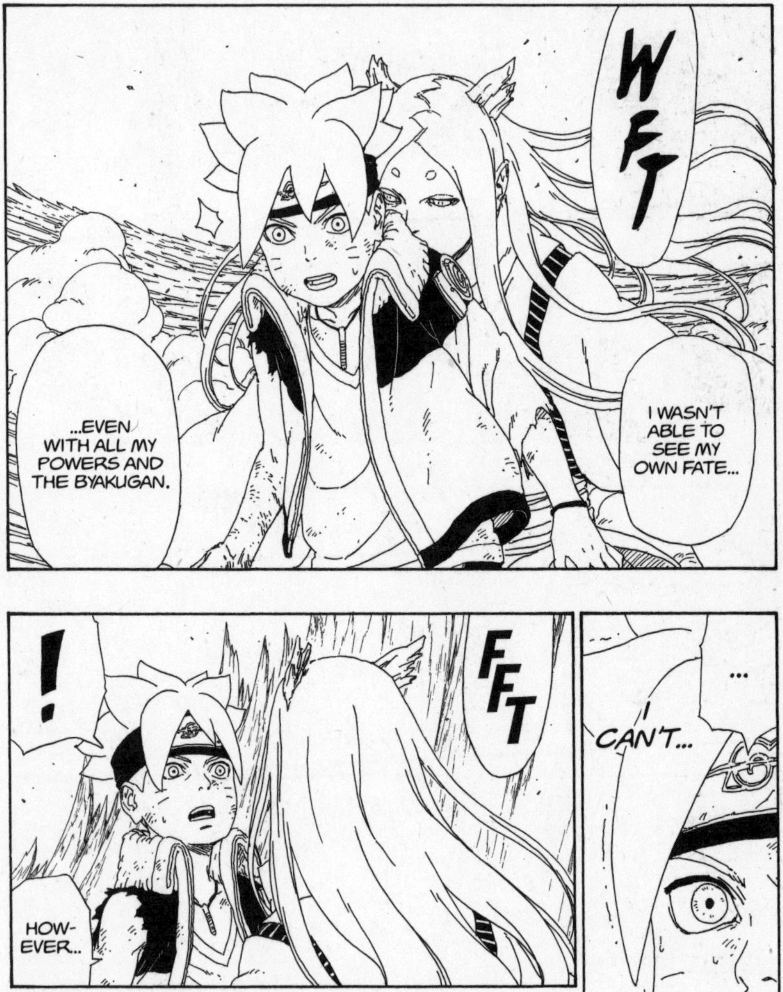
WFT
I WASN'T ABLE TO SEE MY OWN FATE...
...EVEN WITH ALL MY POWERS AND THE BYAKUGAN.
...
I CAN'T...
...MOVE...!!
FFT
!
HOW-EVER...
...I CAN SEE YOURS QUITE WELL!
SHKEEN

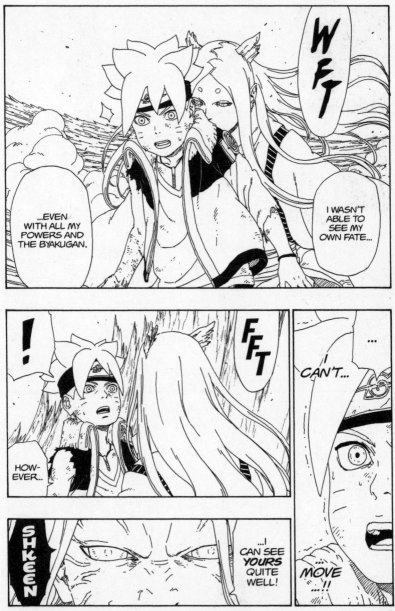

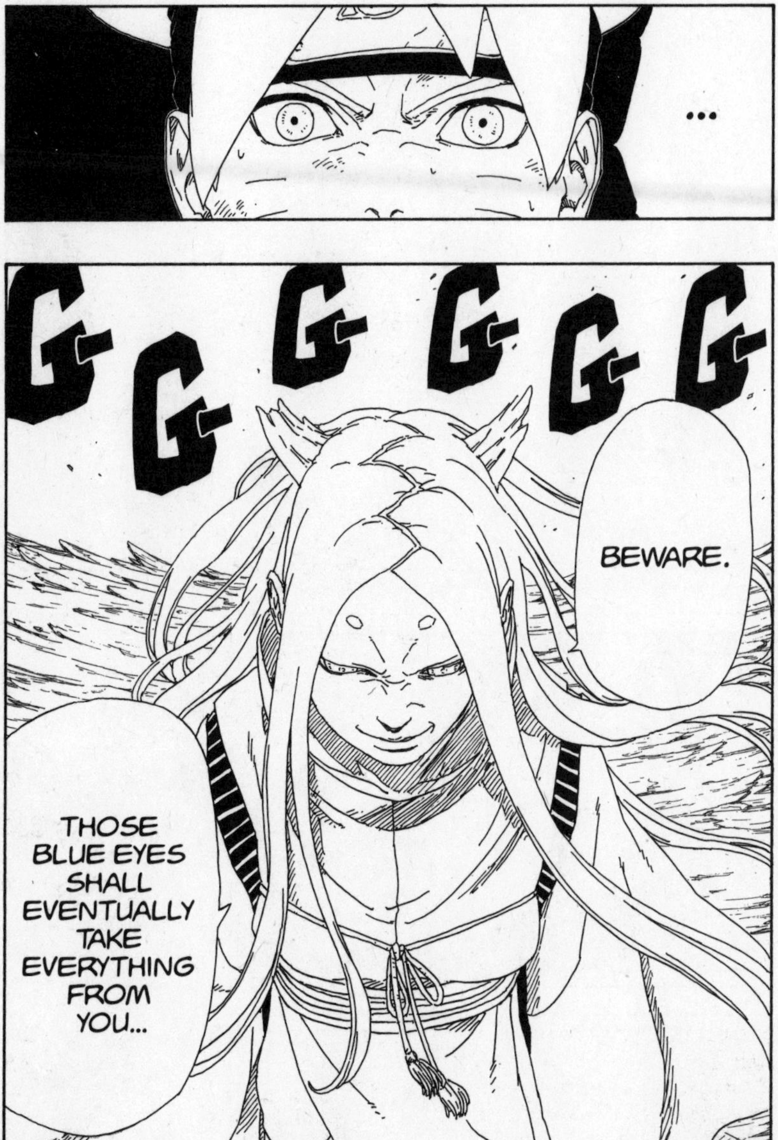
...
G-G-G-G-G-G-
BEWARE.
THOSE BLUE EYES SHALL EVENTUALLY TAKE EVERYTHING FROM YOU...

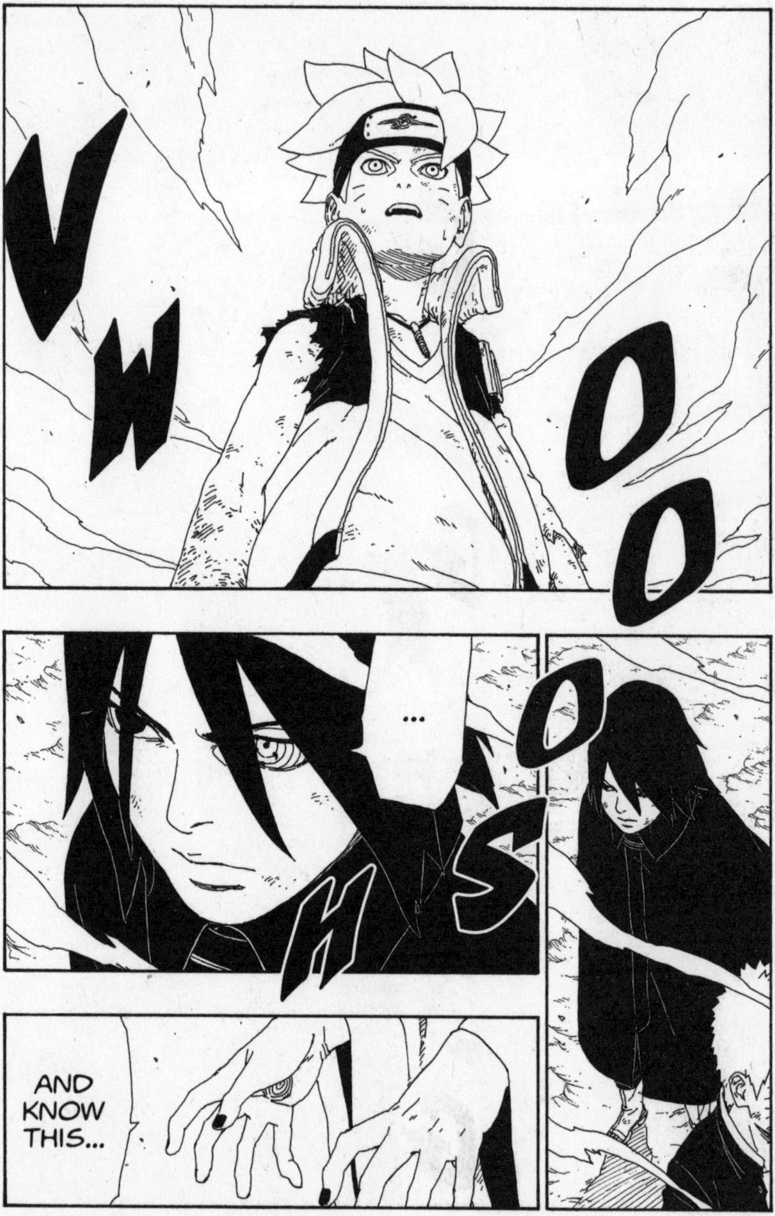
VWOOOSH
...
AND KNOW THIS...

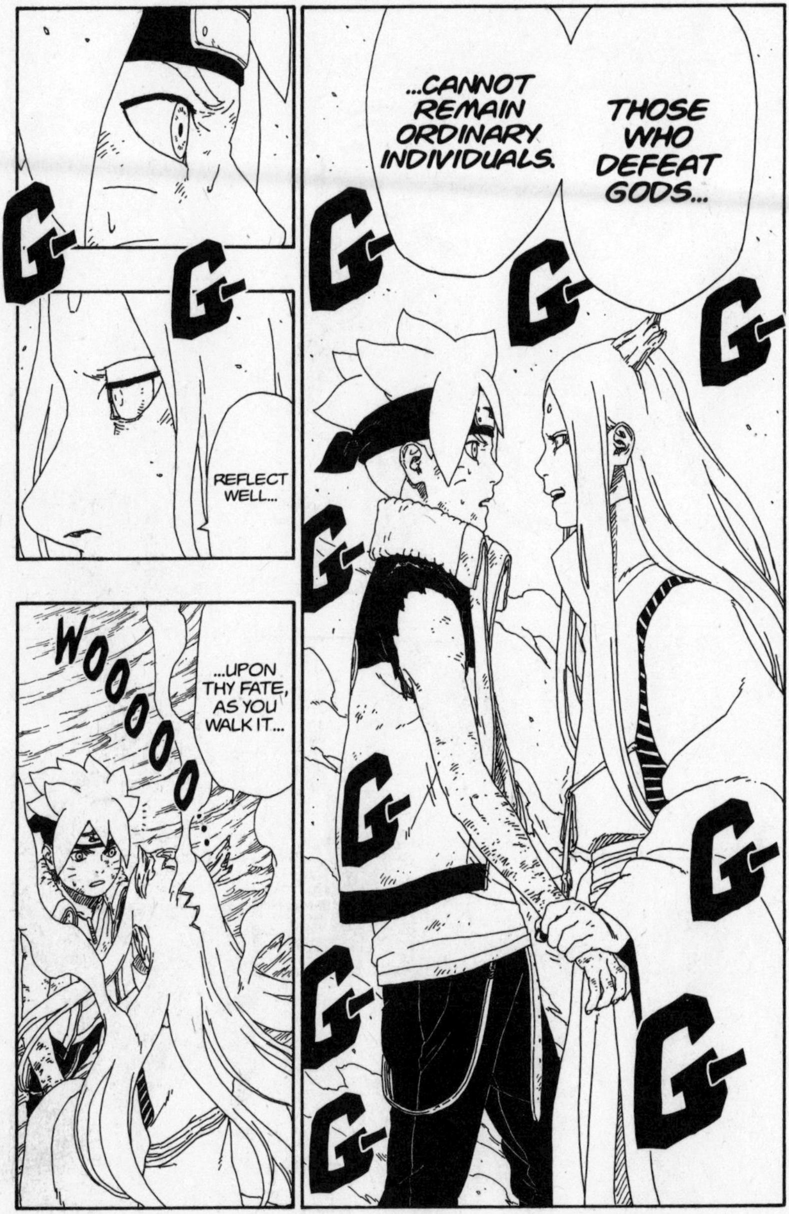
THOSE WHO DEFEAT GODS...
...CANNOT REMAIN ORDINARY INDIVIDUALS.
G- G- G- G- G- G- G- G-
G- G-
REFLECT WELL...
WOOOOOO
...UPON THY FATE, AS YOU WALK IT...

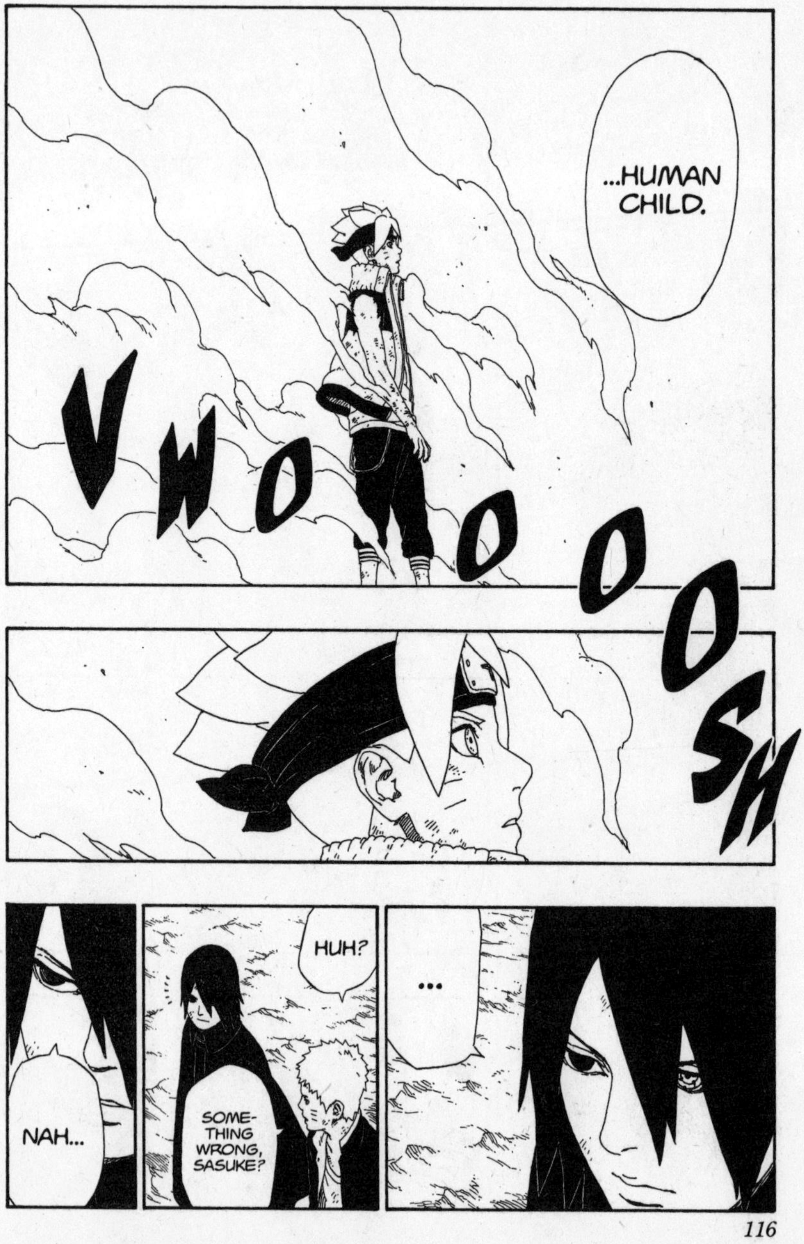
...HUMAN CHILD.
VWOOOOSH
...
HUH?
SOME-THING WRONG, SASUKE?
NAH...

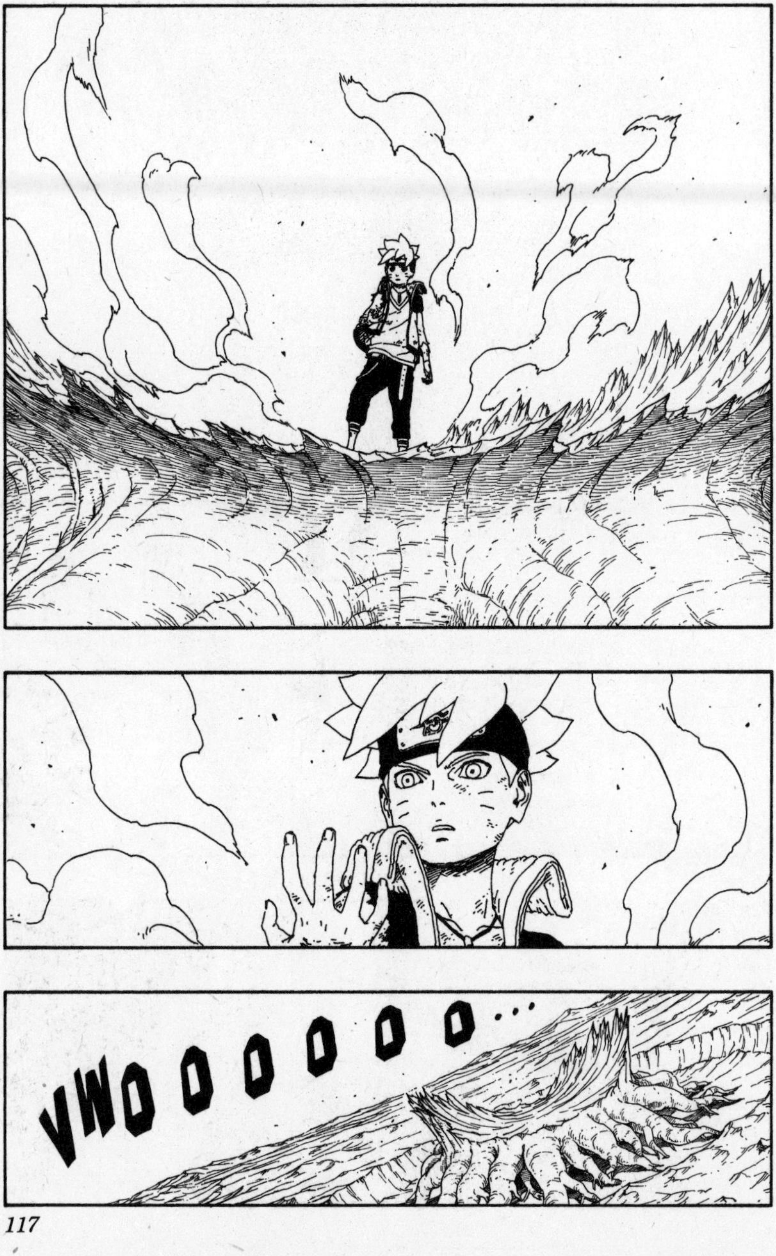
VWOOOOOO...

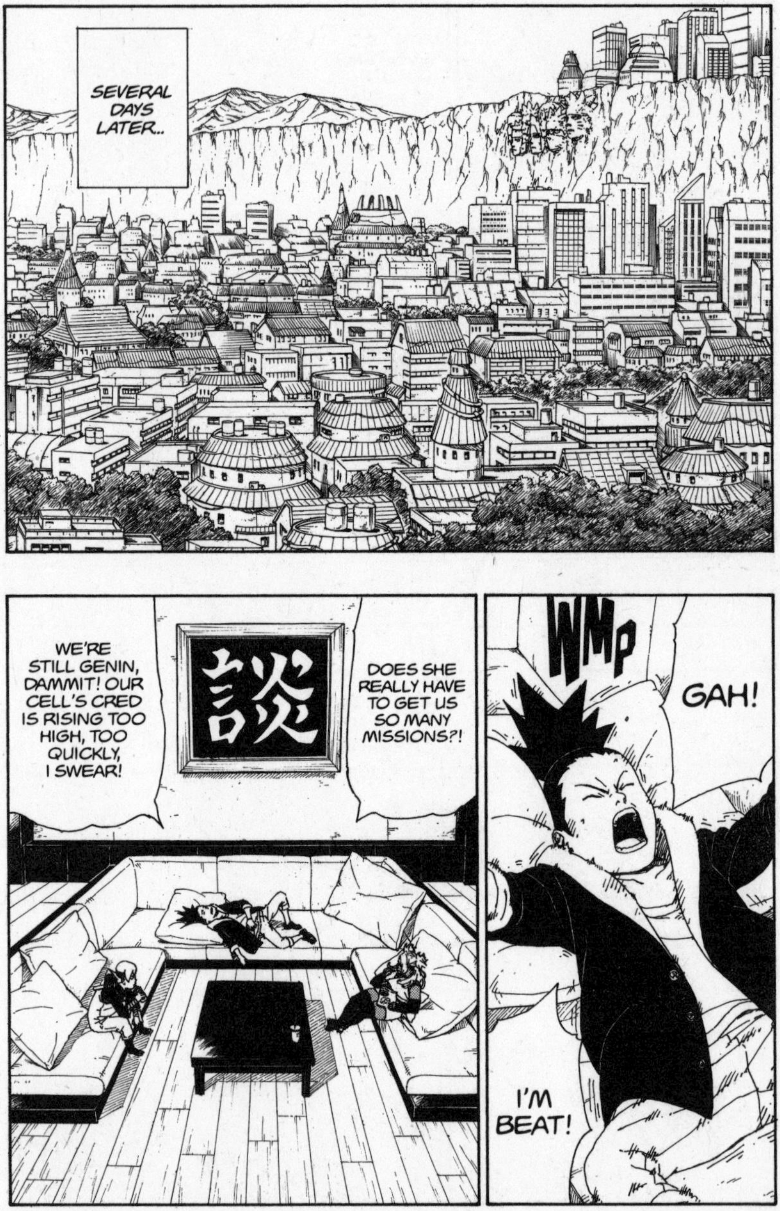
SEVERAL DAYS LATER...
WMP
GAH!
I'M BEAT!
DOES SHE REALLY HAVE TO GET US SO MANY MISSIONS?!
談
WE'RE STILL GENIN, DAMMIT! OUR CELL'S CRED IS RISING TOO HIGH, TOO QUICKLY, I SWEAR!

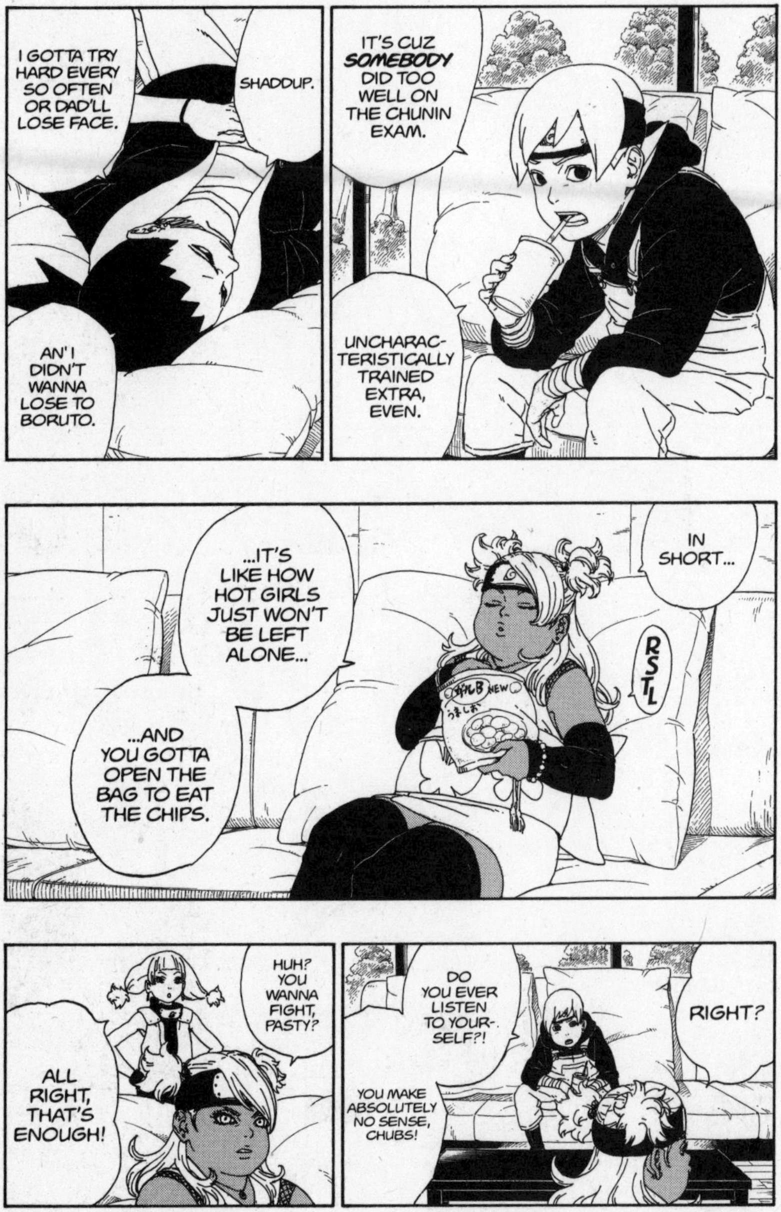
IT'S CUZ *SOMEBODY* DID TOO WELL ON THE CHUNIN EXAM.
UNCHARACTERISTICALLY TRAINED EXTRA, EVEN.
SHADDUP.
I GOTTA TRY HARD EVERY SO OFTEN OR DAD'LL LOSE FACE.
AN' I DIDN'T WANNA LOSE TO BORUTO.
IN SHORT...
RSTL
...IT'S LIKE HOW HOT GIRLS JUST WON'T BE LEFT ALONE...
...AND YOU GOTTA OPEN THE BAG TO EAT THE CHIPS.
RIGHT?
DO YOU EVER LISTEN TO YOURSELF?!
YOU MAKE ABSOLUTELY NO SENSE, CHUBS!
HUH? YOU WANNA FIGHT, PASTY?
ALL RIGHT, THAT'S ENOUGH!

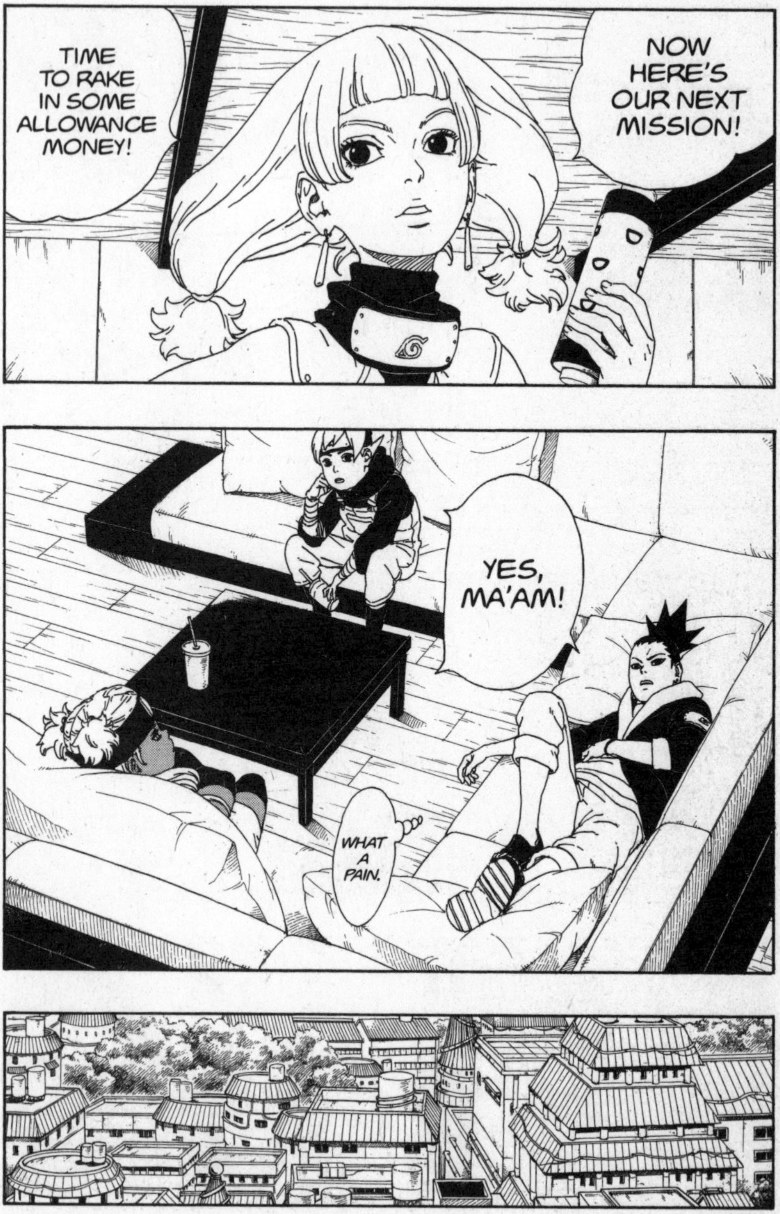
NOW HERE'S OUR NEXT MISSION!
TIME TO RAKE IN SOME ALLOWANCE MONEY!
YES, MA'AM!
WHAT A PAIN.

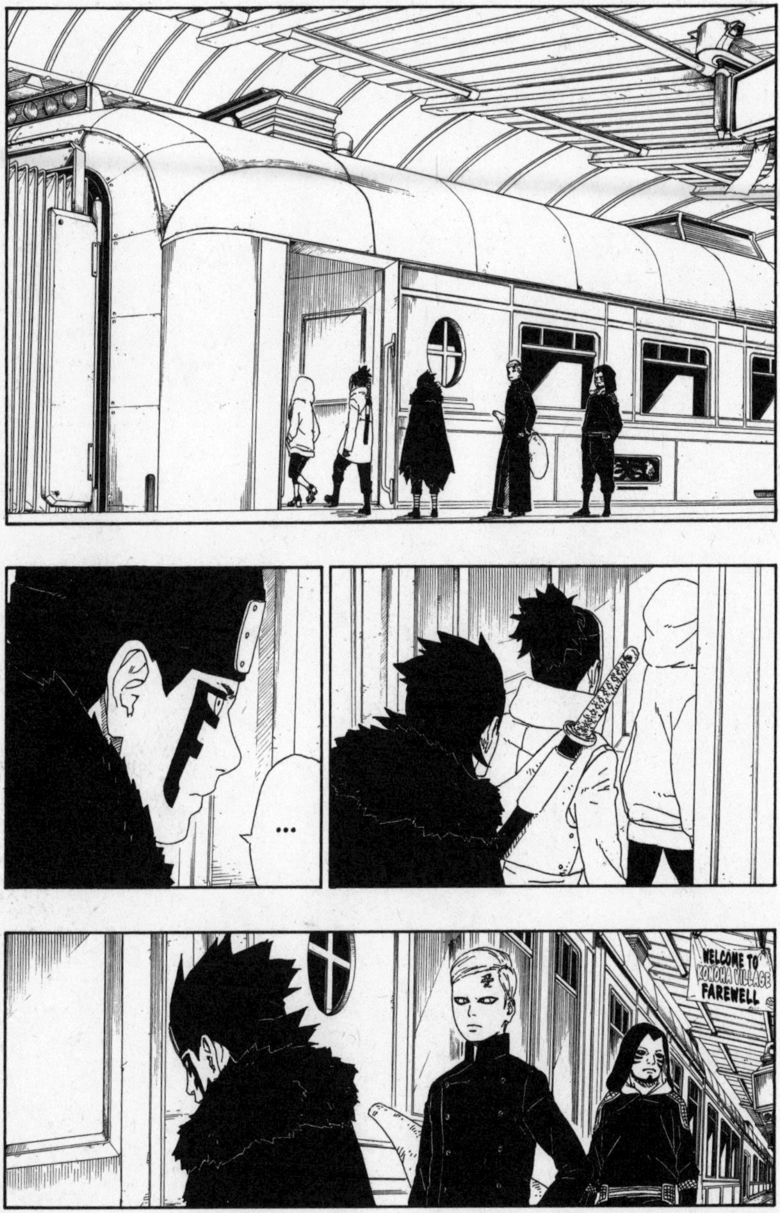
...
WELCOME TO KONOHA VILLAGE
FAREWELL

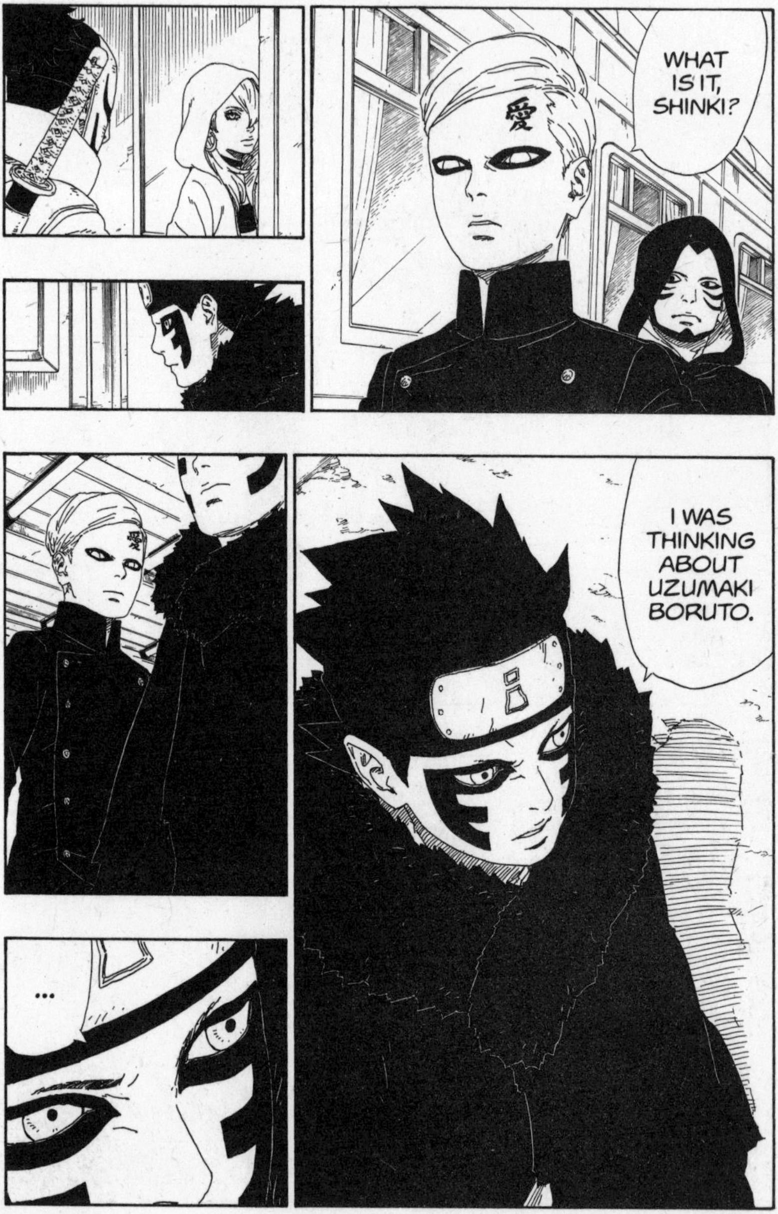
WHAT IS IT, SHINKI?
I WAS THINKING ABOUT UZUMAKI BORUTO.
...

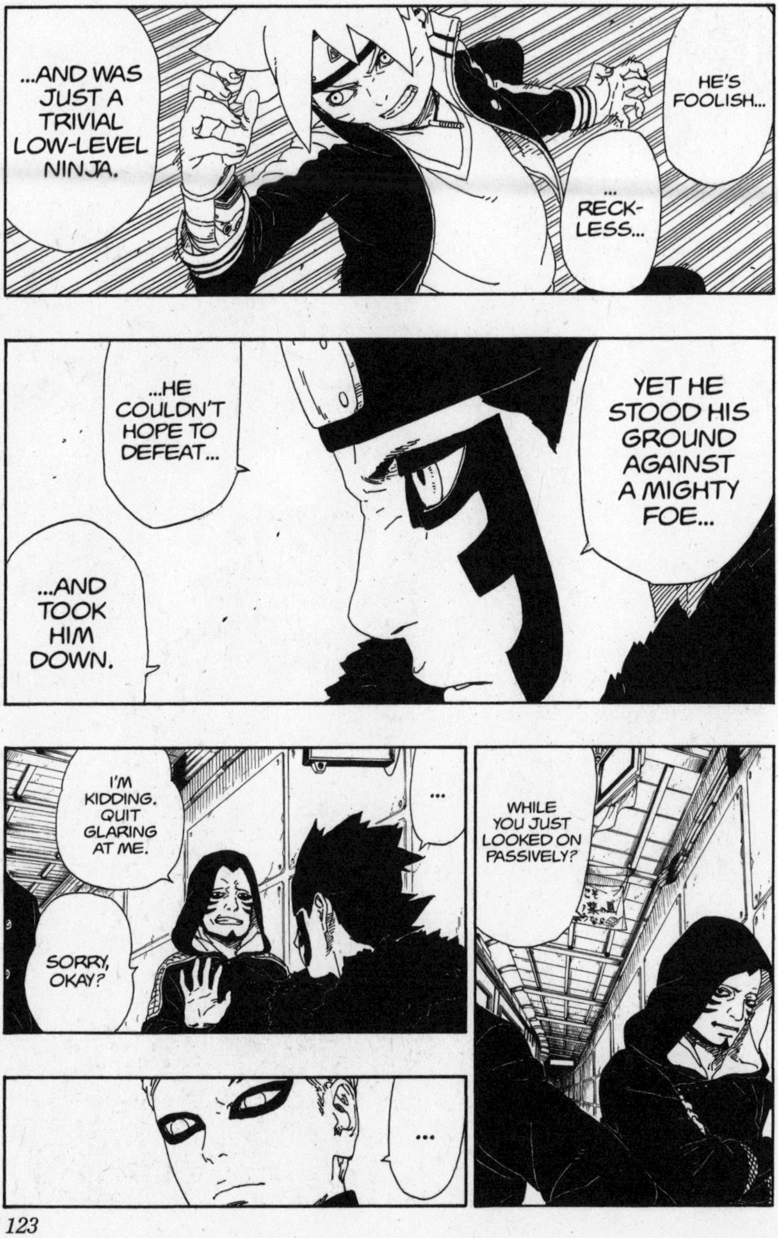
HE'S FOOLISH...
...RECKLESS...
...AND WAS JUST A TRIVIAL LOW-LEVEL NINJA.
YET HE STOOD HIS GROUND AGAINST A MIGHTY FOE...
...HE COULDN'T HOPE TO DEFEAT...
...AND TOOK HIM DOWN.
WHILE YOU JUST LOOKED ON PASSIVELY?
...
I'M KIDDING. QUIT GLARING AT ME.
SORRY, OKAY?
...

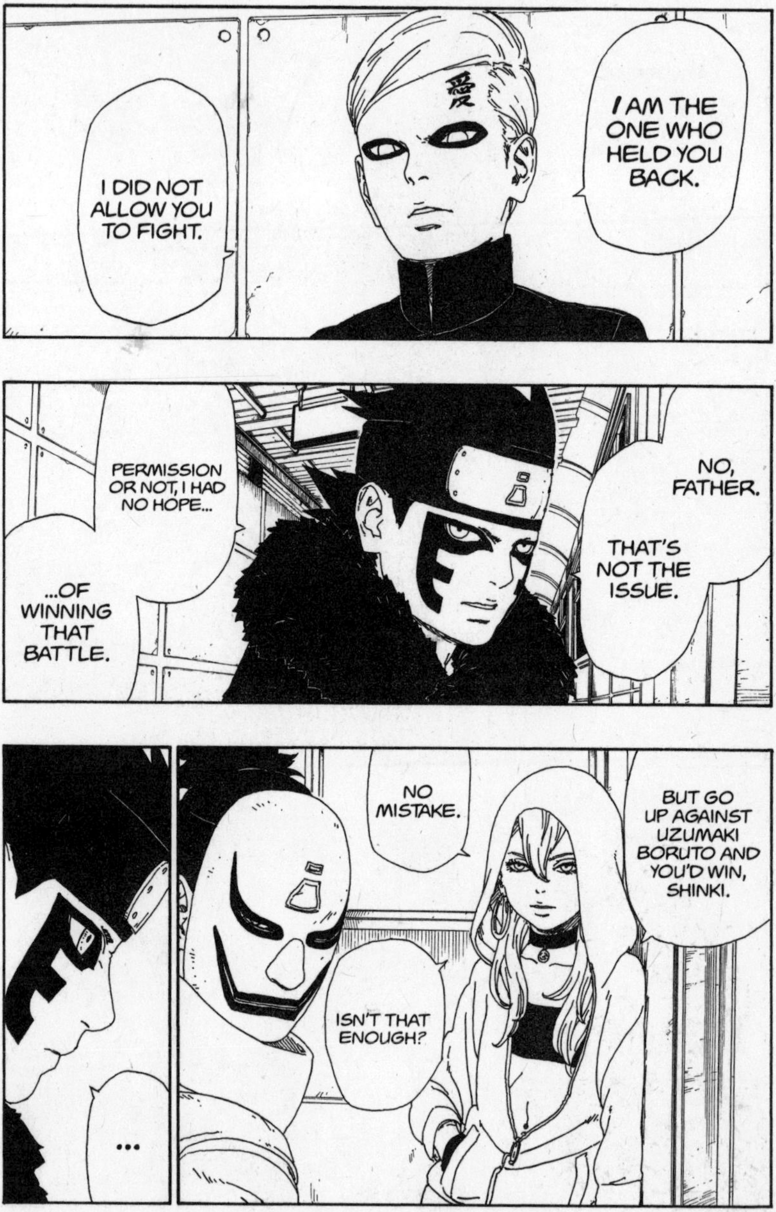
I AM THE ONE WHO HELD YOU BACK.
I DID NOT ALLOW YOU TO FIGHT.
NO, FATHER.
THAT'S NOT THE ISSUE.
PERMISSION OR NOT, I HAD NO HOPE...
...OF WINNING THAT BATTLE.
BUT GO UP AGAINST UZUMAKI BORUTO AND YOU'D WIN, SHINKI.
NO MISTAKE.
ISN'T THAT ENOUGH?
...

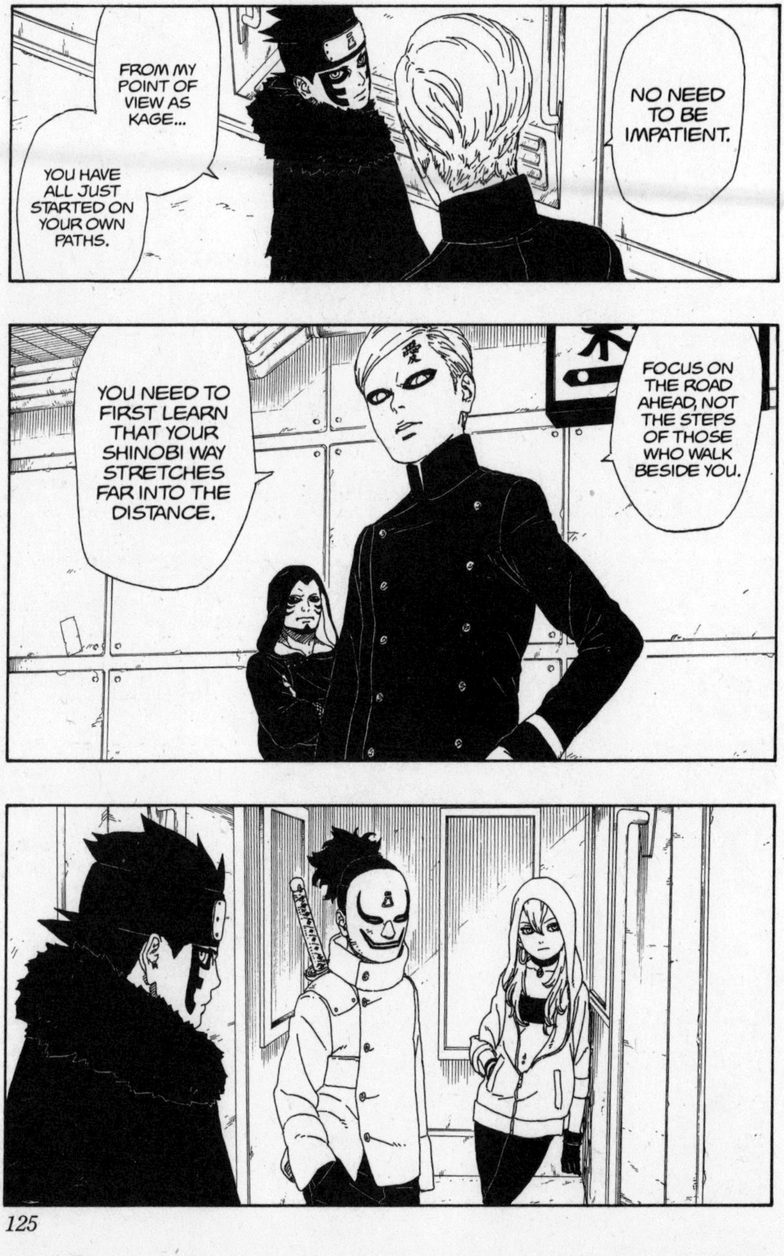
NO NEED TO BE IMPATIENT.
FROM MY POINT OF VIEW AS KAGE...
YOU HAVE ALL JUST STARTED ON YOUR OWN PATHS.
FOCUS ON THE ROAD AHEAD, NOT THE STEPS OF THOSE WHO WALK BESIDE YOU.
YOU NEED TO FIRST LEARN THAT YOUR SHINOBI WAY STRETCHES FAR INTO THE DISTANCE.

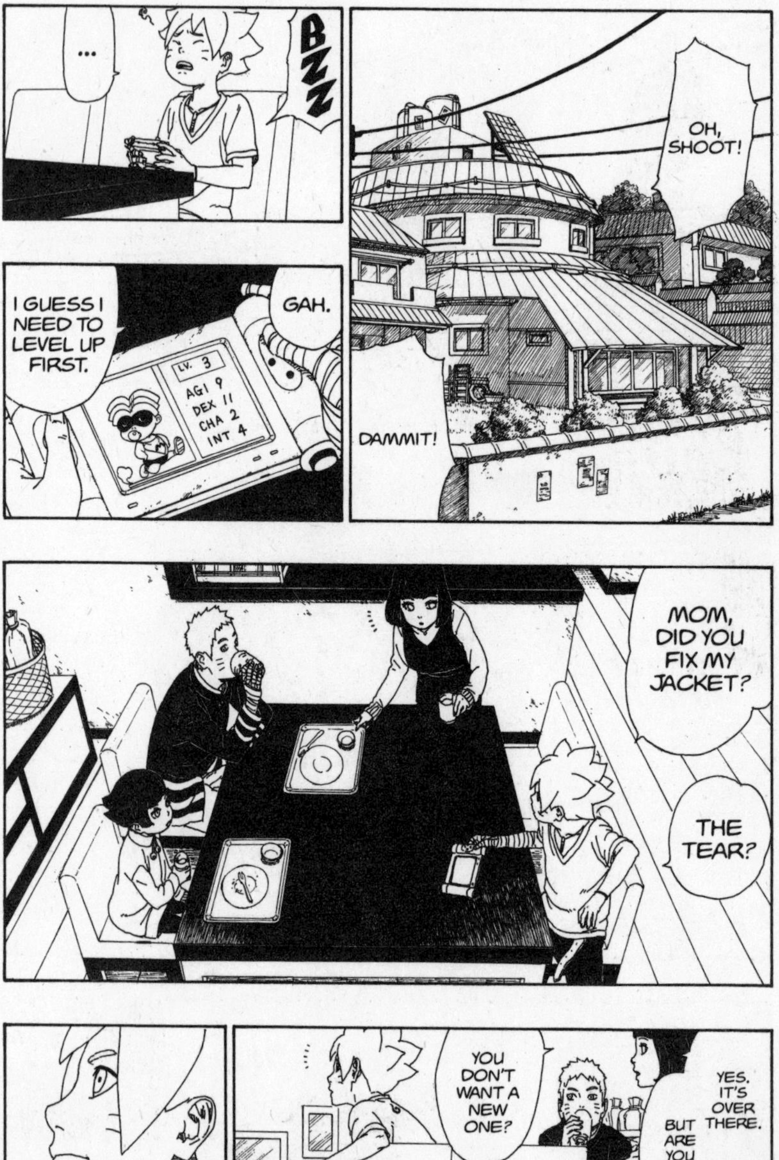
OH, SHOOT!
DAMMIT!
BZZ
...
GAH.
I GUESS I NEED TO LEVEL UP FIRST.
LV. 3
AGI 9
DEX 11
CHA 2
INT 4
MOM, DID YOU FIX MY JACKET?
THE TEAR?
YES. IT'S OVER THERE.
BUT ARE YOU SURE?
YOU DON'T WANT A NEW ONE?

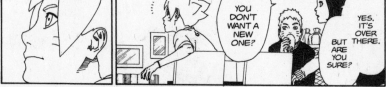

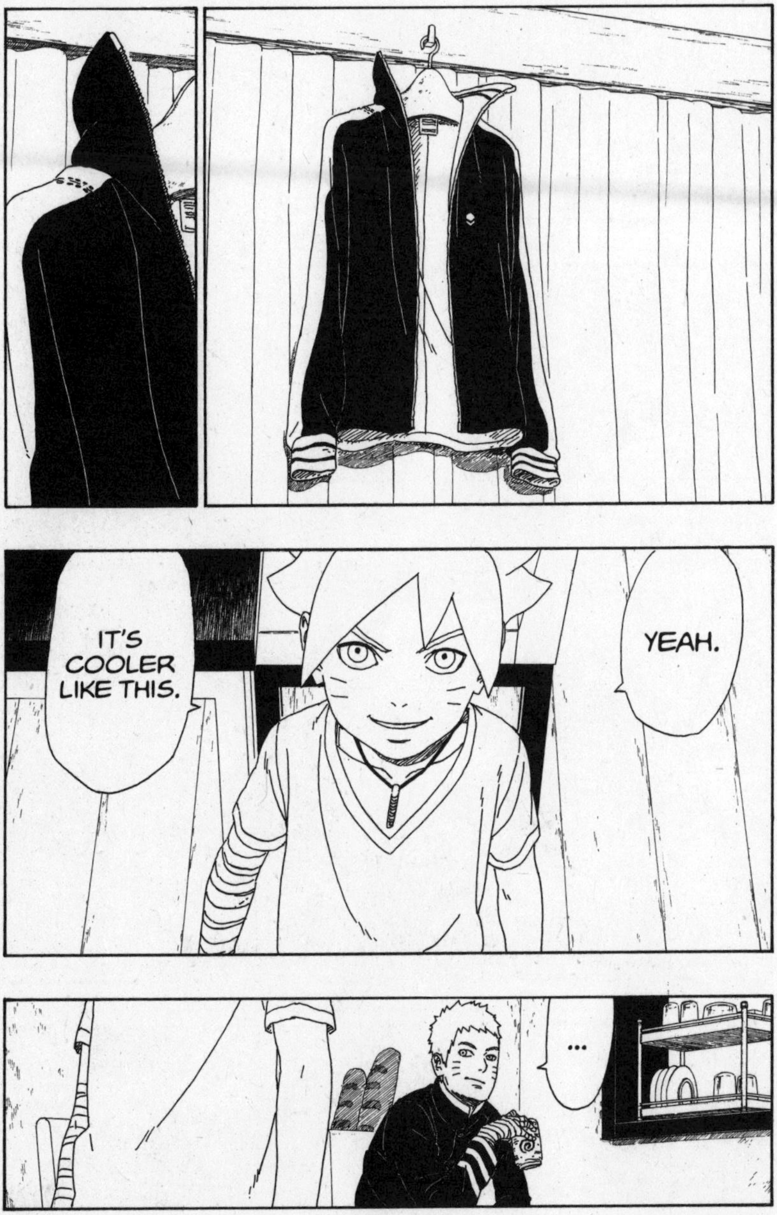
YEAH.
IT'S COOLER LIKE THIS.
...

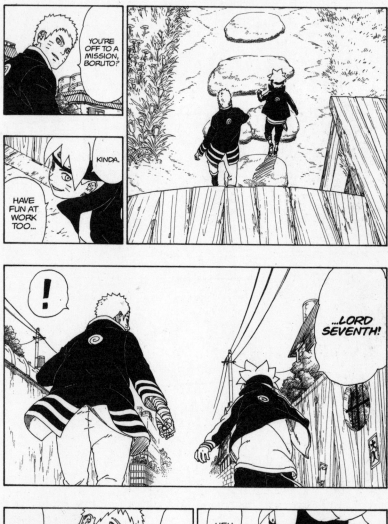

YOU'RE OFF TO A MISSION, BORUTO?

KINDA.

HAVE FUN AT WORK TOO...

!

...LORD SEVENTH!

CHEEKY LITTLE...

...

HEH HEH.

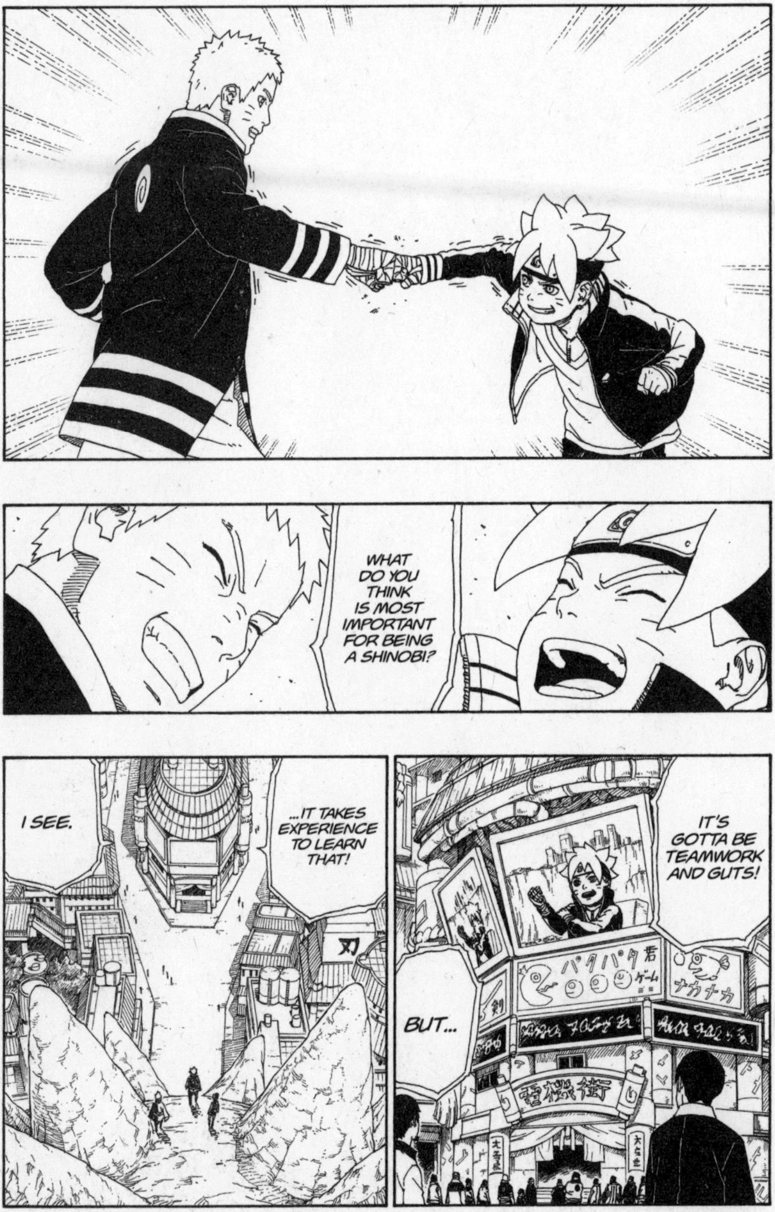
WHAT DO YOU THINK IS MOST IMPORTANT FOR BEING A SHINOBI?
IT'S GOTTA BE TEAMWORK AND GUTS!
BUT...
...IT TAKES EXPERIENCE TO LEARN THAT!
I SEE.

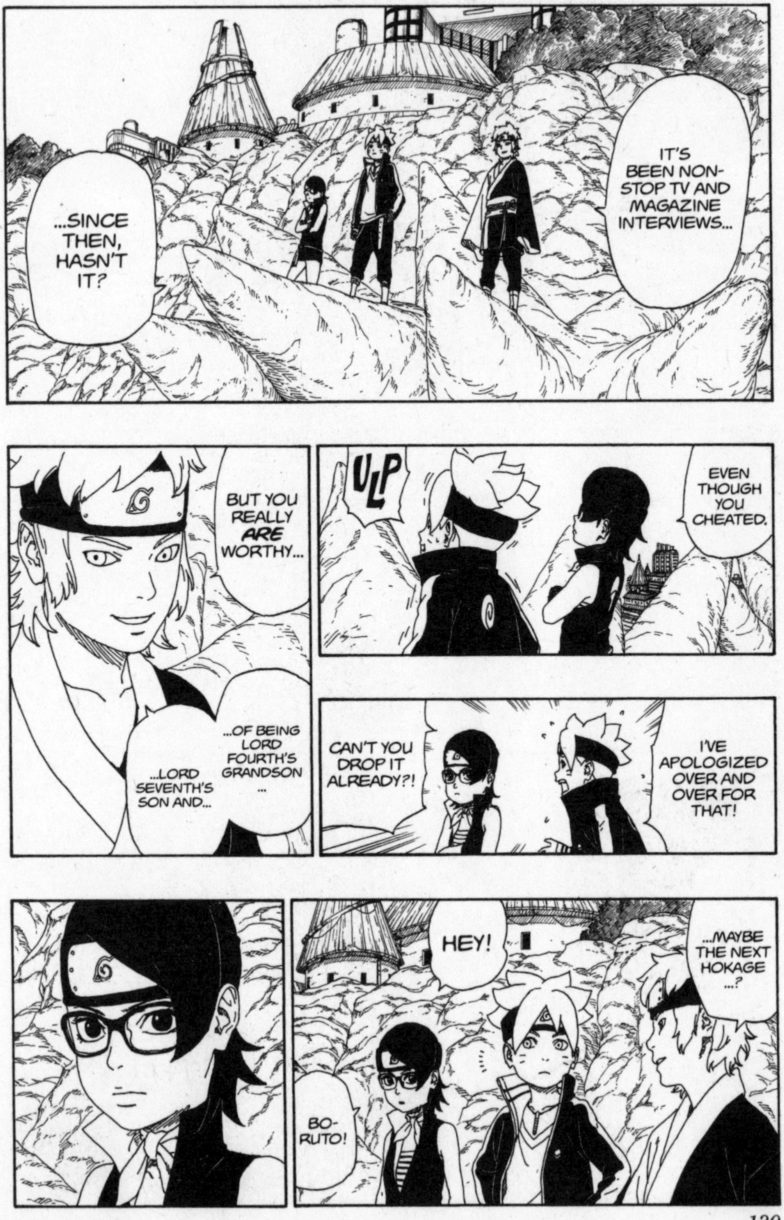
IT'S BEEN NON-STOP TV AND MAGAZINE INTERVIEWS...
...SINCE THEN, HASN'T IT?
EVEN THOUGH YOU CHEATED.
ULP
I'VE APOLOGIZED OVER AND OVER FOR THAT!
CAN'T YOU DROP IT ALREADY?!
BUT YOU REALLY ARE WORTHY...
...OF BEING LORD FOURTH'S GRANDSON ...
...LORD SEVENTH'S SON AND...
...MAYBE THE NEXT HOKAGE ...?
HEY!
BO-RUTO!
...

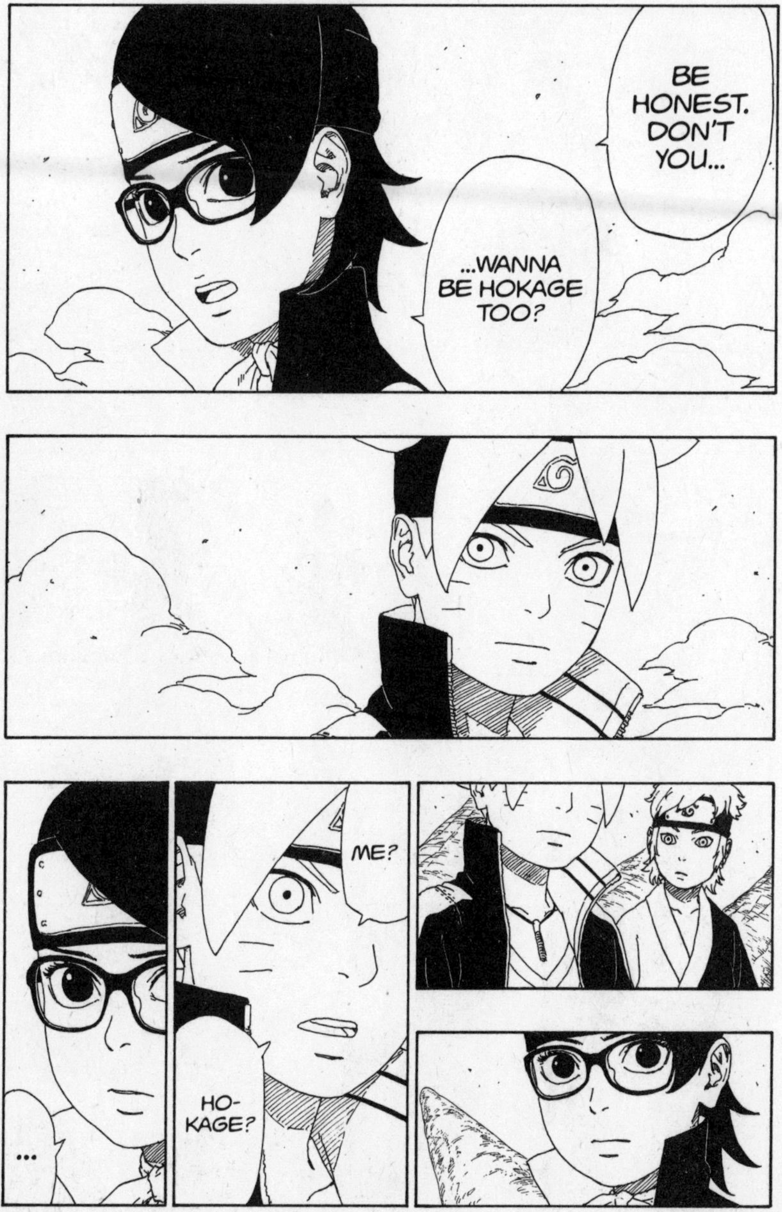
BE HONEST. DON'T YOU...
...WANNA BE HOKAGE TOO?
ME?
HO-KAGE?
...

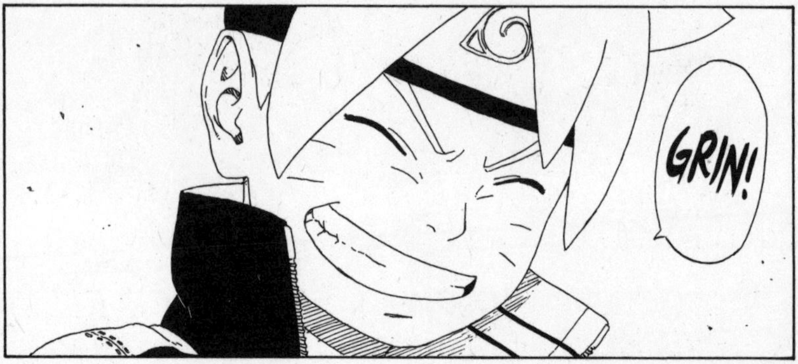
GRIN!

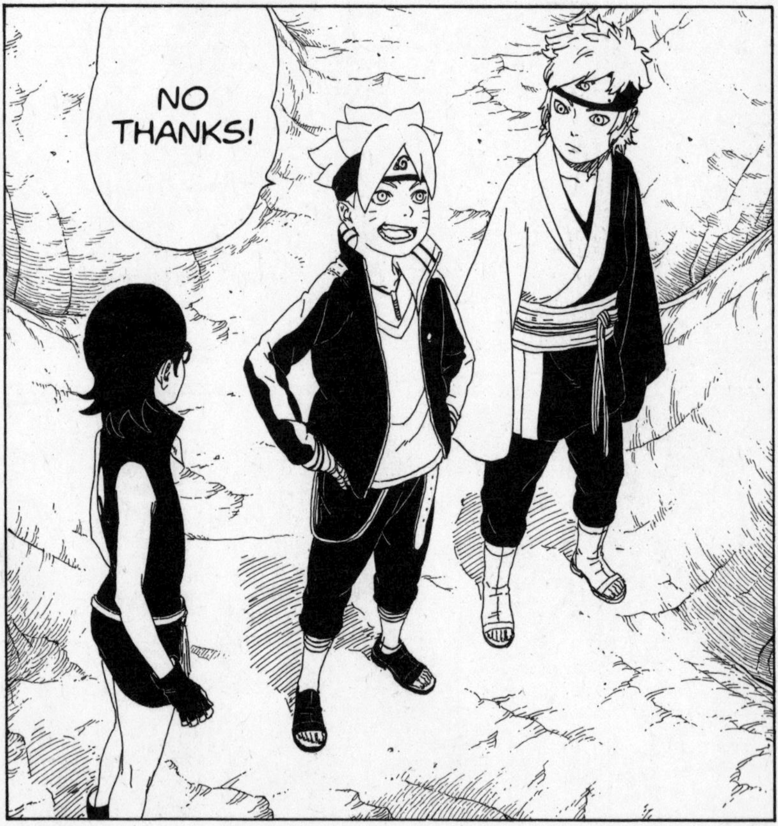
NO THANKS!

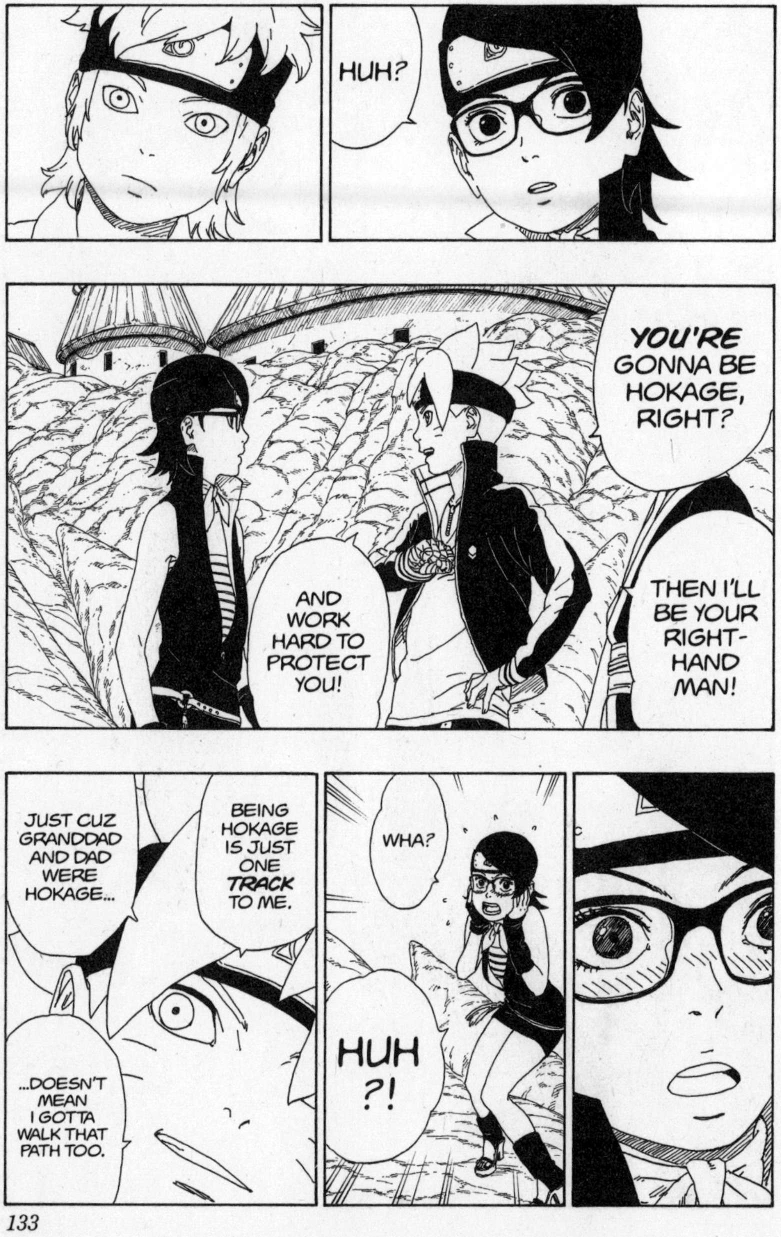
HUH?
YOU'RE GONNA BE HOKAGE, RIGHT?
THEN I'LL BE YOUR RIGHT-HAND MAN!
AND WORK HARD TO PROTECT YOU!
WHA?
HUH ?!
BEING HOKAGE IS JUST ONE TRACK TO ME.
JUST CUZ GRANDDAD AND DAD WERE HOKAGE...
...DOESN'T MEAN I GOTTA WALK THAT PATH TOO.

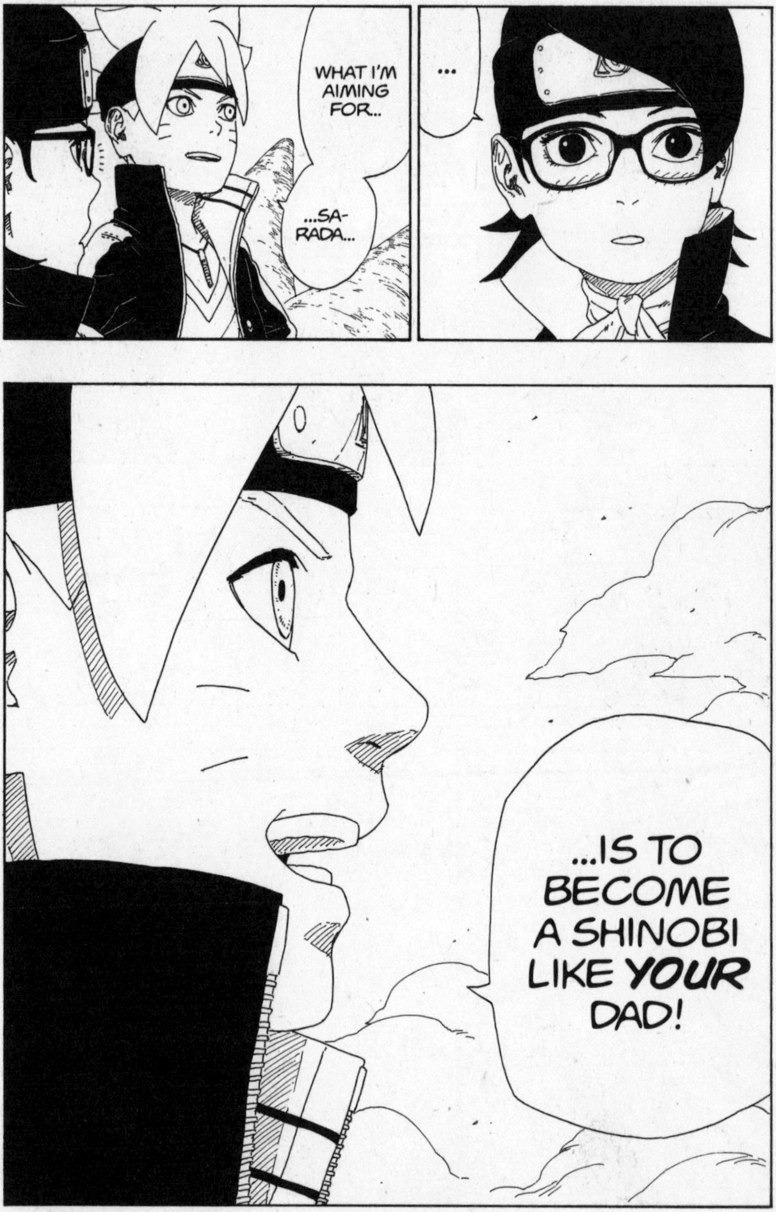
...
WHAT I'M AIMING FOR...
...SA-RADA...
...IS TO BECOME A SHINOBI LIKE *YOUR* DAD!

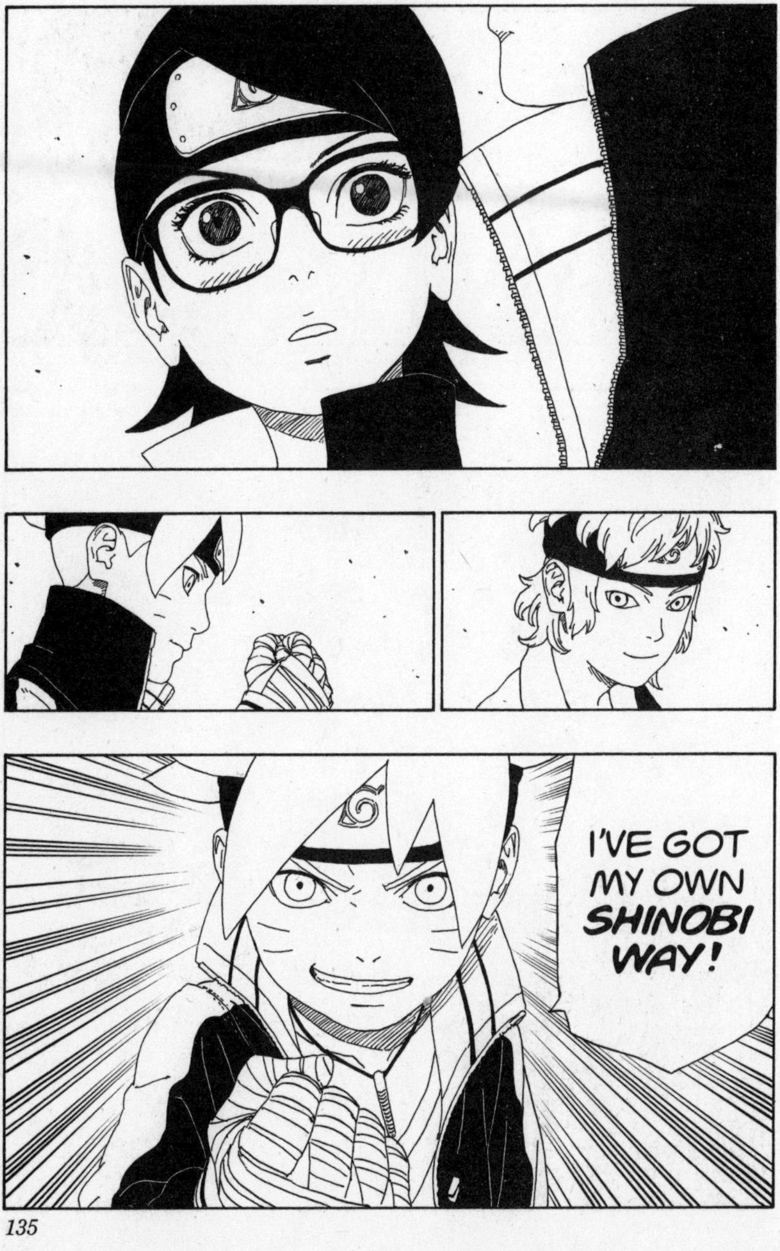
I'VE GOT MY OWN SHINOBI WAY!

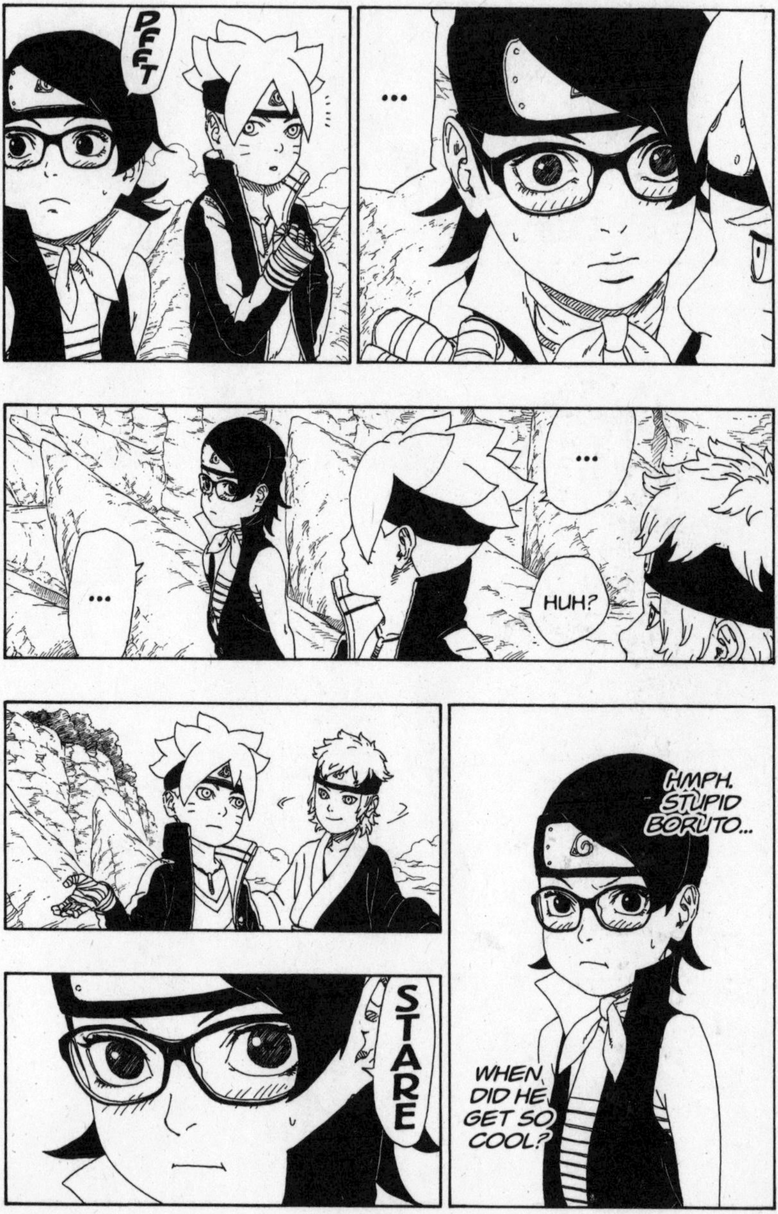
...
PFFT
...
HUH?
...
HMPH. STUPID BORUTO...
WHEN DID HE GET SO COOL?
STARE

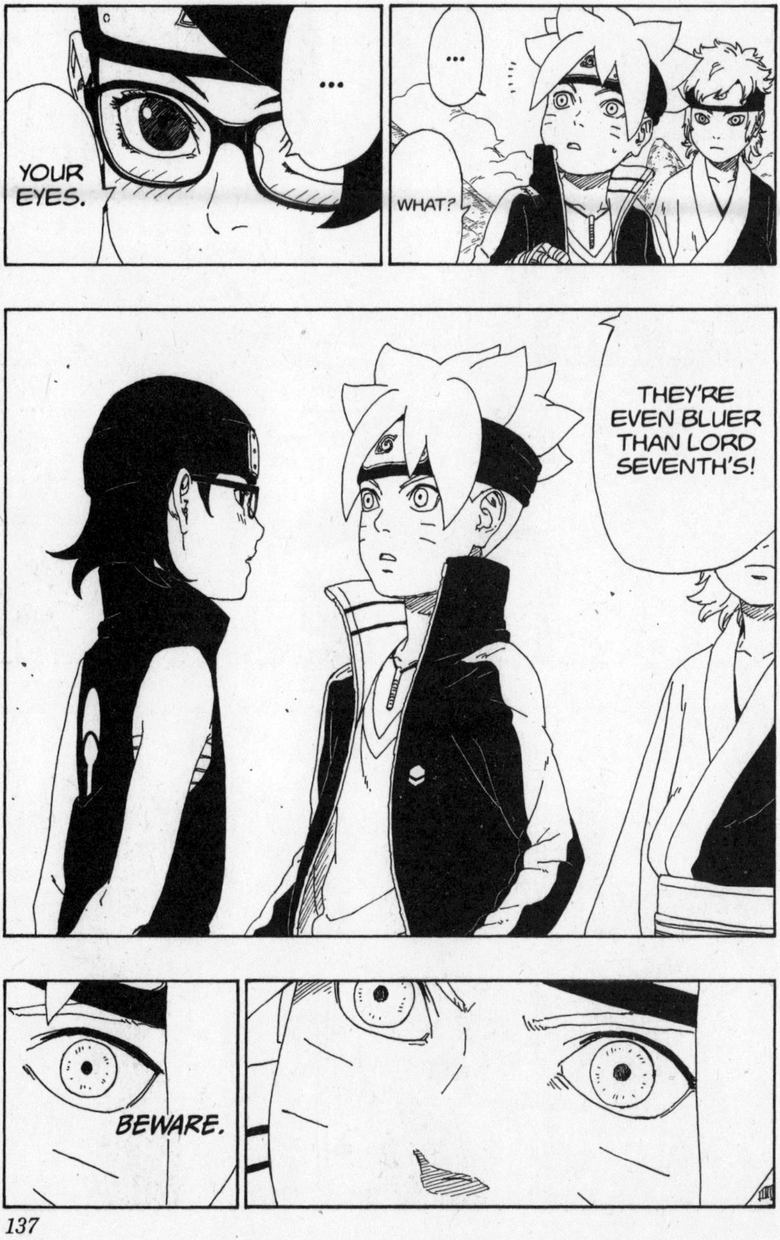
...
WHAT?
...
YOUR EYES.
THEY'RE EVEN BLUER THAN LORD SEVENTH'S!
BEWARE.

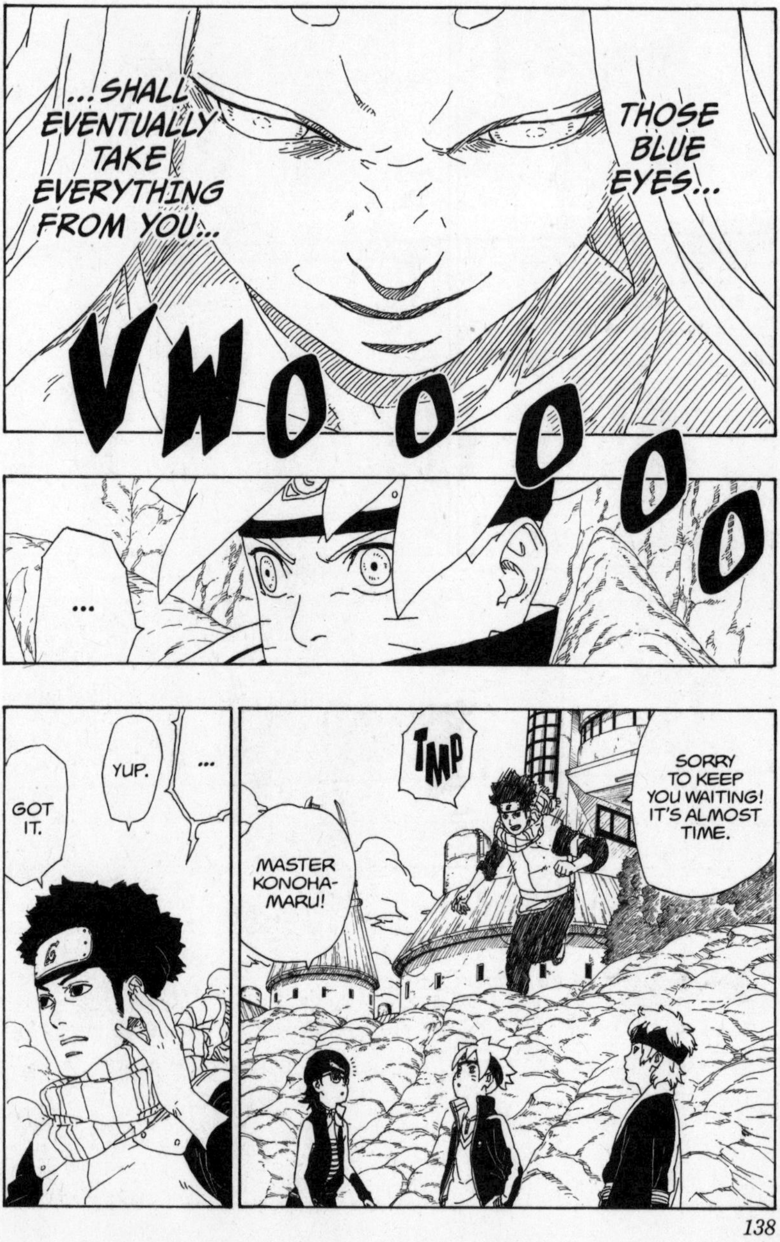
THOSE BLUE EYES...
...SHALL EVENTUALLY TAKE EVERYTHING FROM YOU...
VWOOOOOO
...
SORRY TO KEEP YOU WAITING! IT'S ALMOST TIME.
TMP
MASTER KONOHAMARU!
...
YUP.
GOT IT.

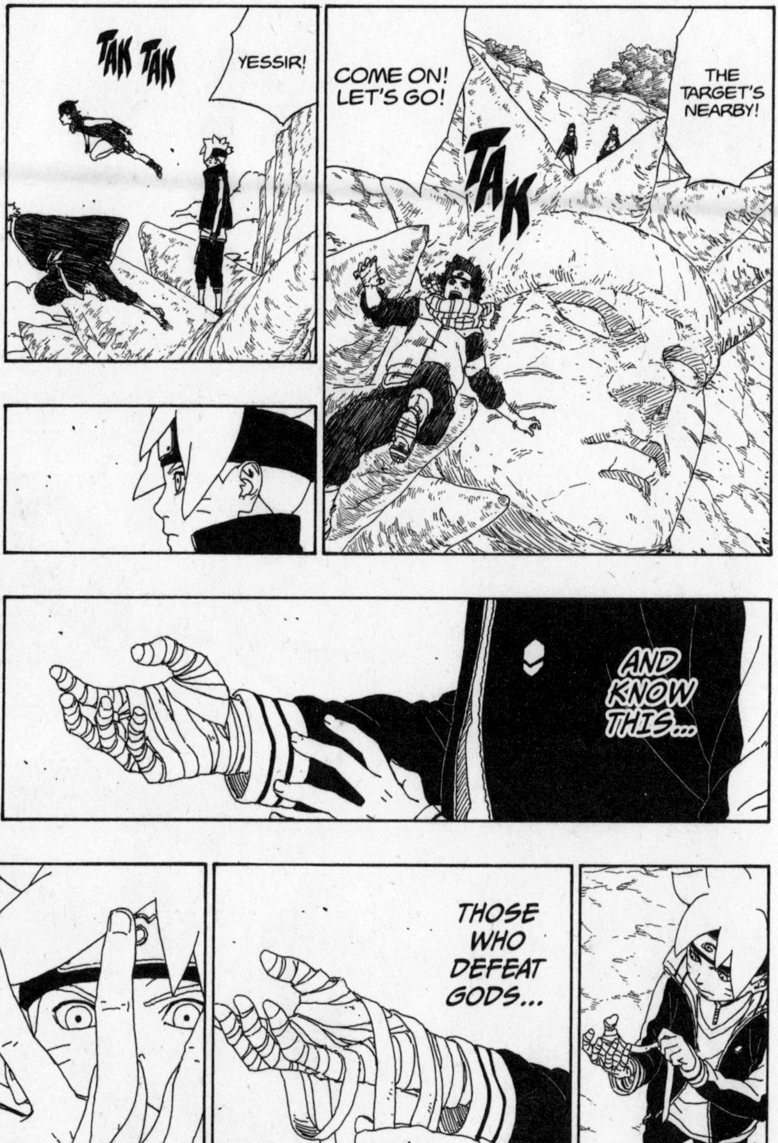
THE TARGET'S NEARBY!
COME ON! LET'S GO!
TAK
YESSIR!
TAK TAK
AND KNOW THIS...
THOSE WHO DEFEAT GODS...

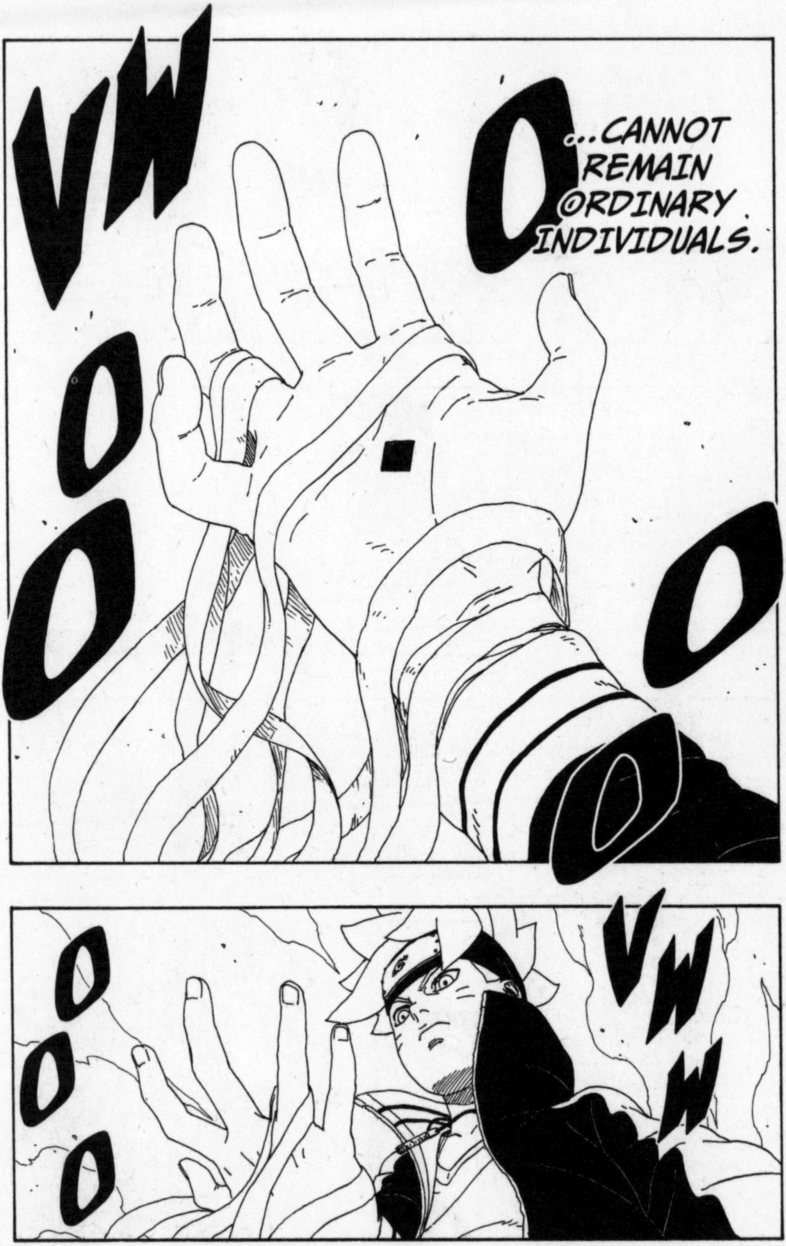

...CANNOT REMAIN ORDINARY INDIVIDUALS.
VWOOOO
VWWOOO

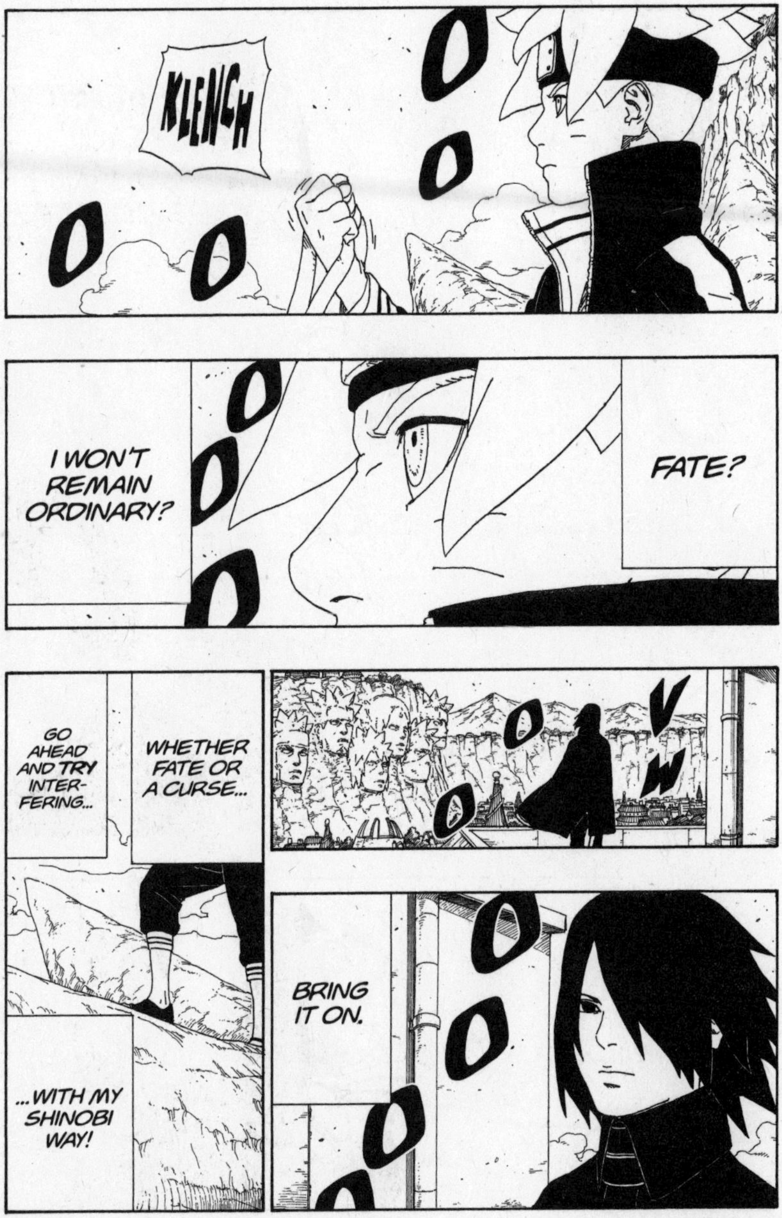

KLENCH
FATE?
I WON'T REMAIN ORDINARY?
VW
BRING IT ON.
WHETHER FATE OR A CURSE...
GO AHEAD AND TRY INTER-FERING...
...WITH MY SHINOBI WAY!

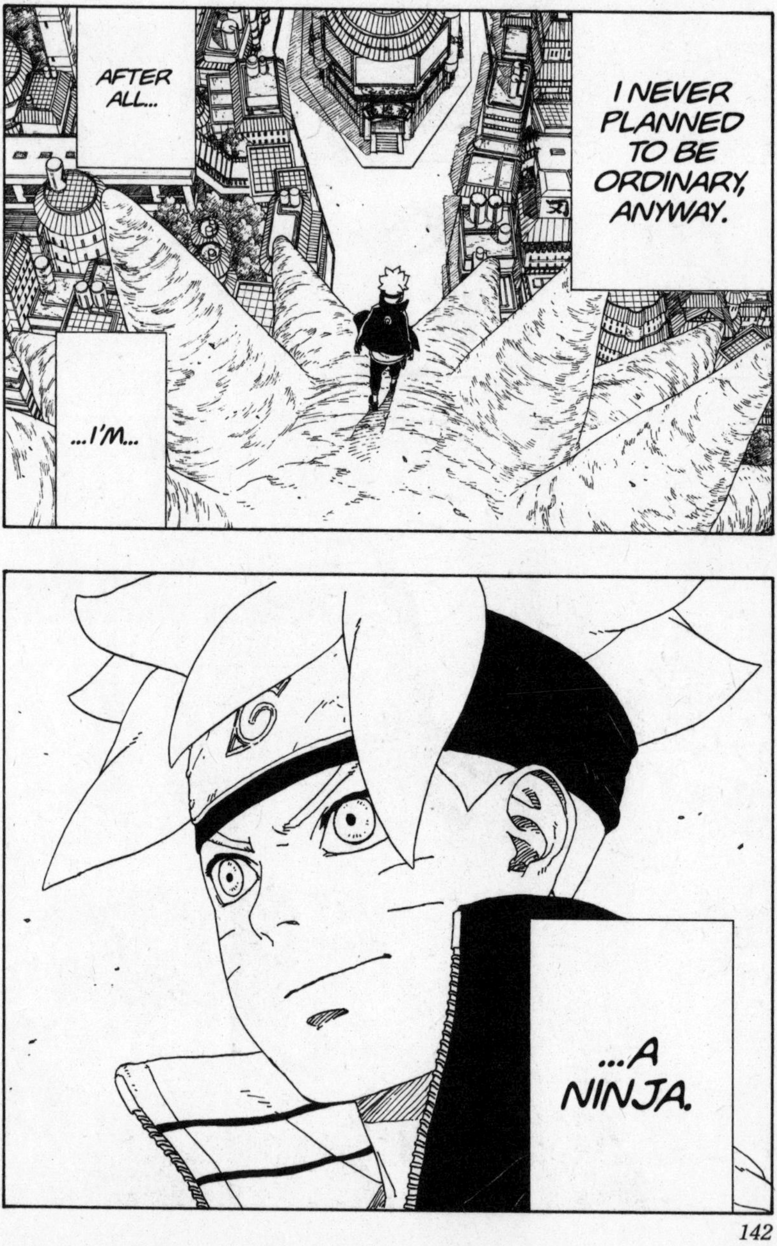
I NEVER PLANNED TO BE ORDINARY, ANYWAY.
AFTER ALL...
...I'M...
...A NINJA.

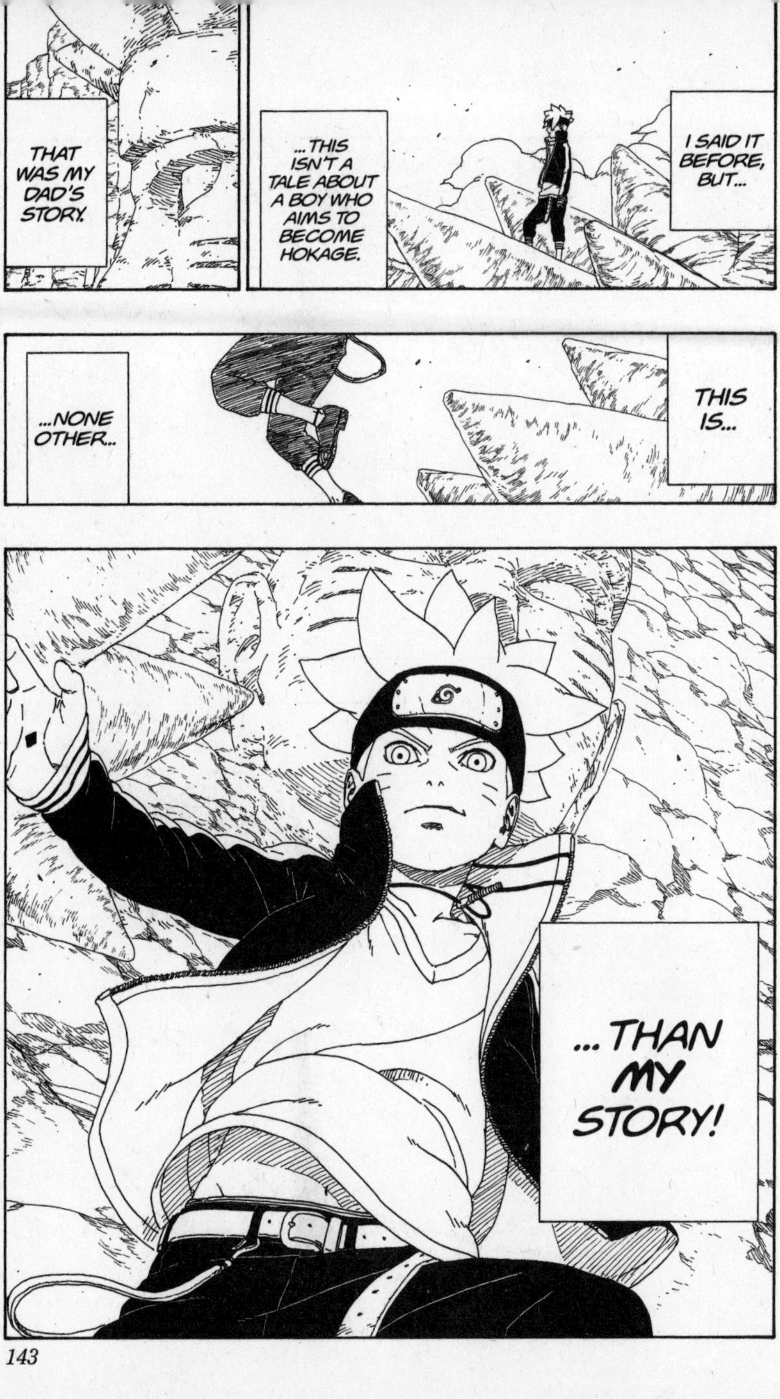
I SAID IT BEFORE, BUT...
...THIS ISN'T A TALE ABOUT A BOY WHO AIMS TO BECOME HOKAGE.
THAT WAS MY DAD'S STORY.
THIS IS...
...NONE OTHER...
...THAN MY STORY!

NINJA ENCYCLOPEDIA • ENTRY 9

UCHIHA SAKURA

"Don't worry... she'll be okay."

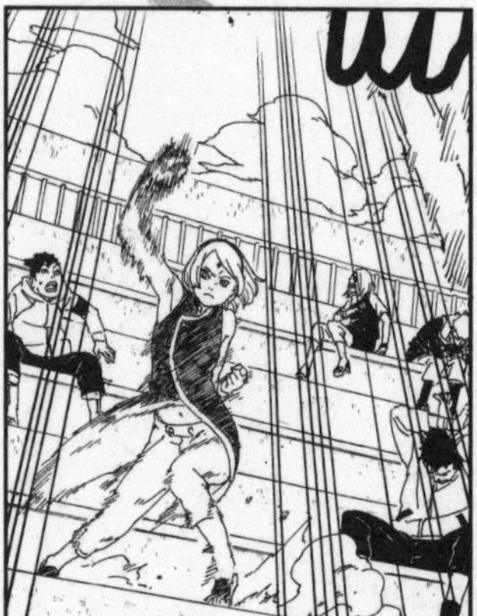

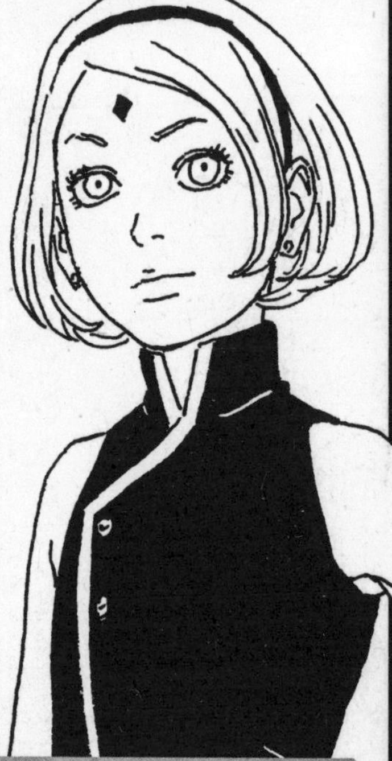

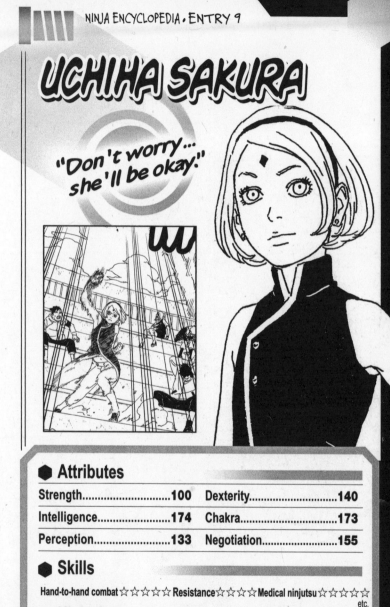

Attributes

Strength..............................100	Dexterity..............................140
Intelligence........................174	Chakra.................................173
Perception..........................133	Negotiation..........................155

Skills

Hand-to-hand combat ☆☆☆☆☆ Resistance ☆☆☆☆ Medical ninjutsu ☆☆☆☆☆ etc.

Ninja Arts

Taijutsu: Sakura Blossom Shock, Healing Power Transmutation Jutsu, Kuchiyose Summoning: Katsuyu, etc.

*Average attribute value is 60 for ordinary people and 90 for genin. Skill values range from 1 to 5☆with 5☆signifying super top-notch.

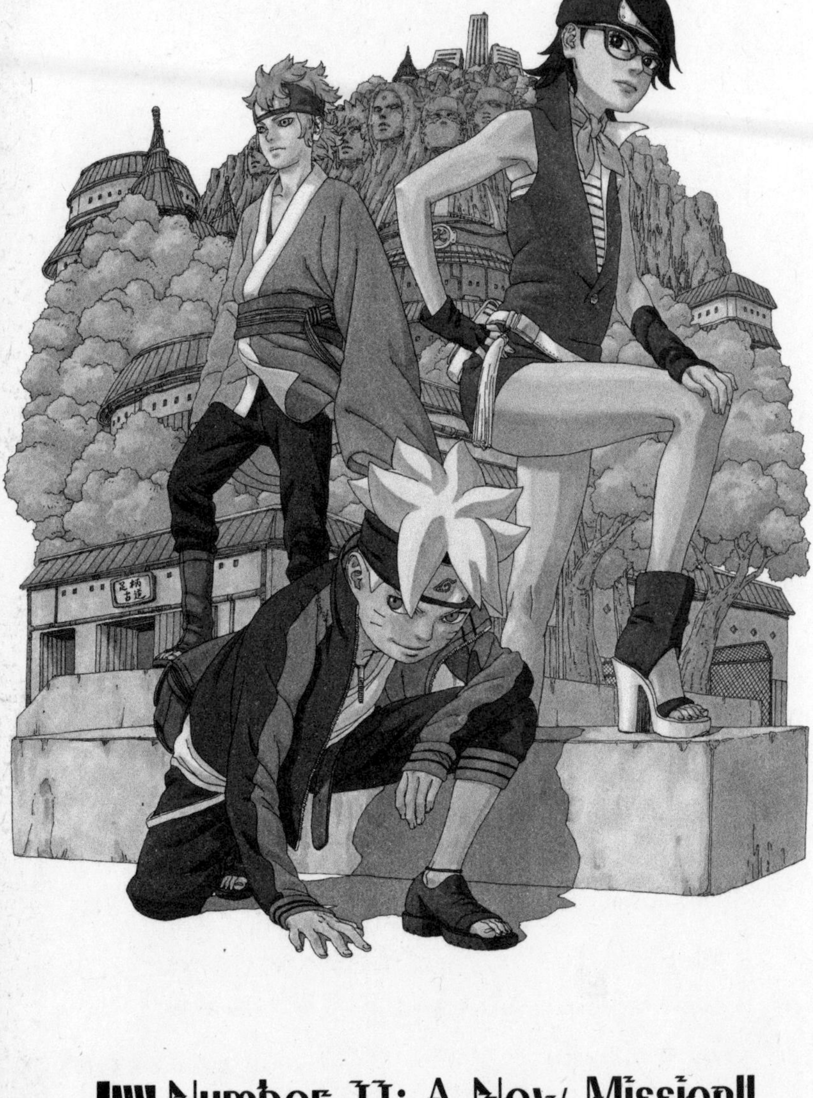

Number 11: A New Mission!!

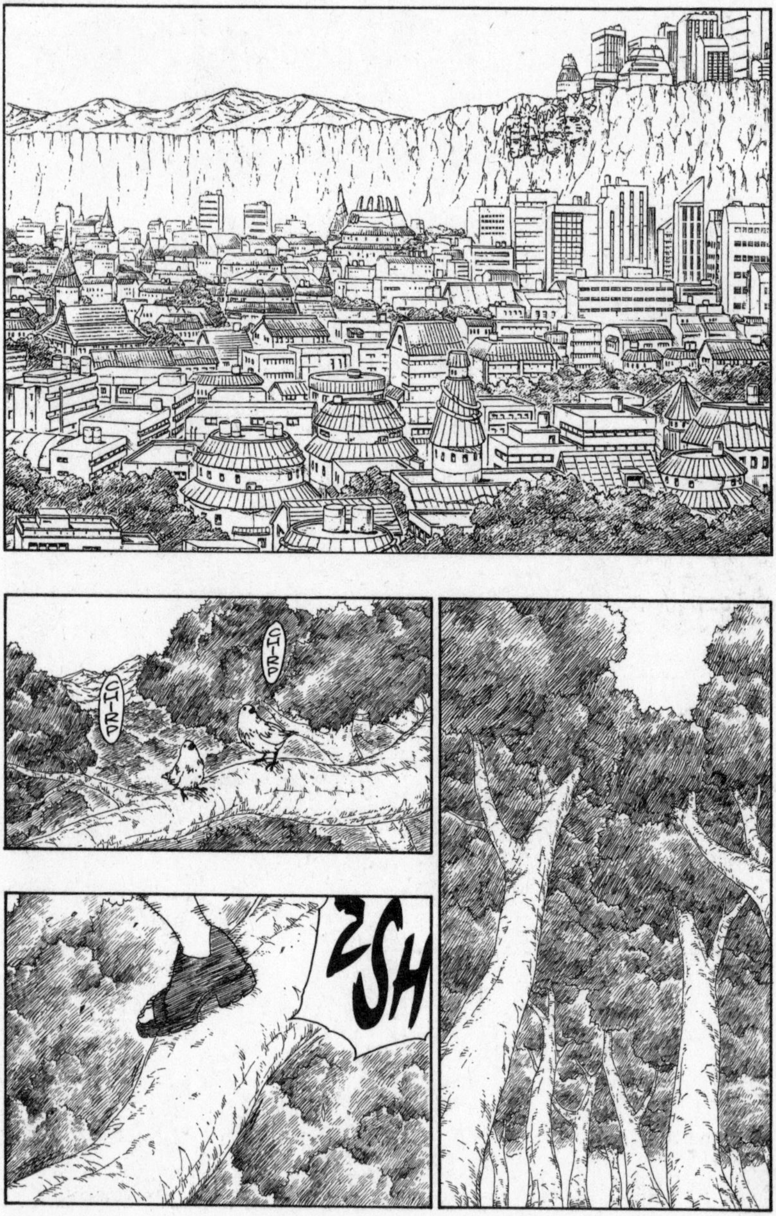
CHIRP
CHIRP
ZSH

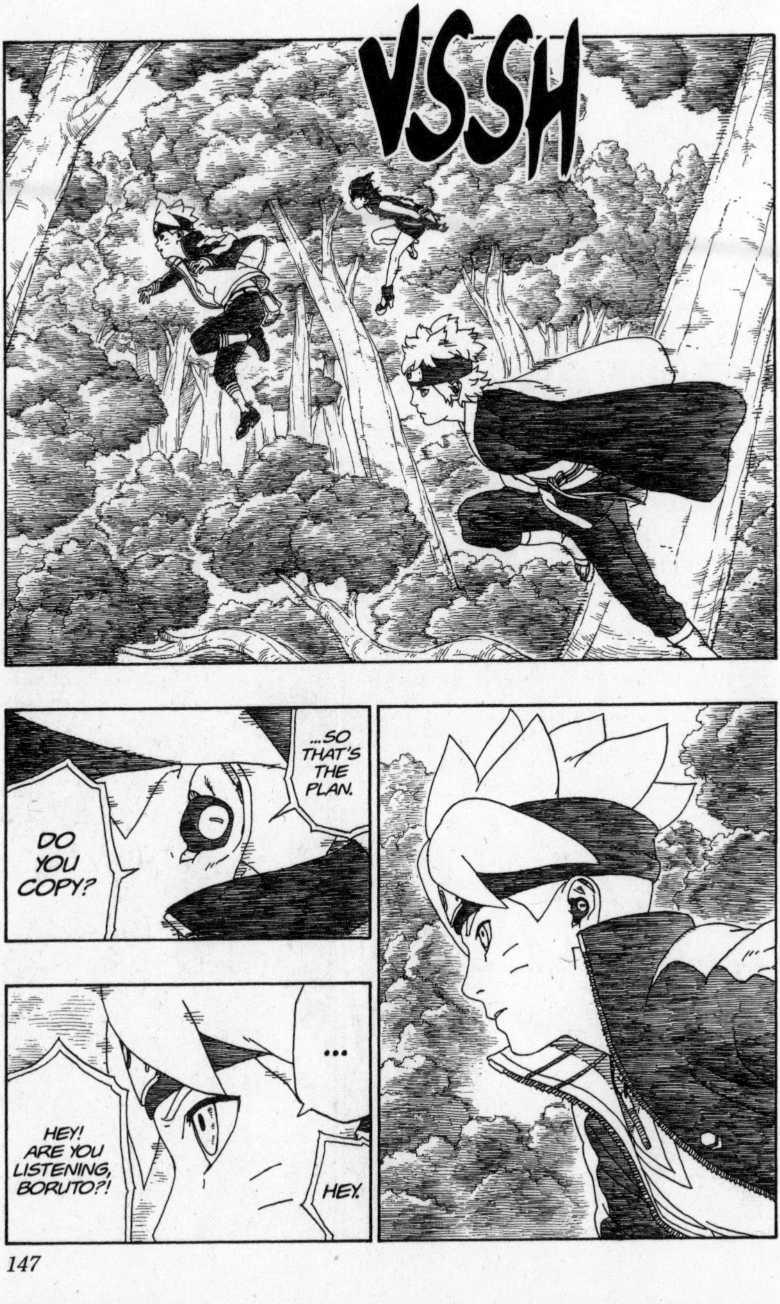
VSSH
...SO THAT'S THE PLAN.
DO YOU COPY?
...
HEY.
HEY! ARE YOU LISTENING, BORUTO?!

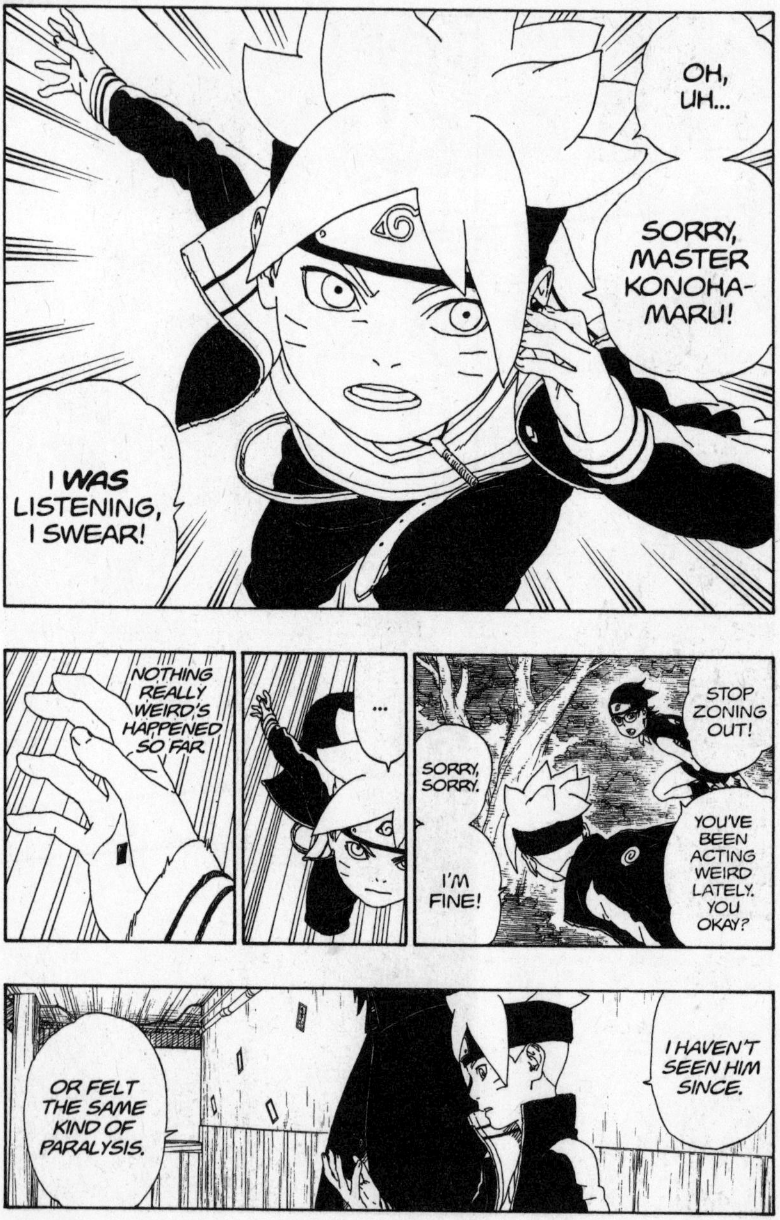
OH, UH...
SORRY, MASTER KONOHA-MARU!
I **WAS** LISTENING, I SWEAR!
STOP ZONING OUT!
YOU'VE BEEN ACTING WEIRD LATELY. YOU OKAY?
SORRY, SORRY.
I'M FINE!
...
NOTHING REALLY WEIRD'S HAPPENED SO FAR
I HAVEN'T SEEN HIM SINCE.
OR FELT THE SAME KIND OF PARALYSIS.

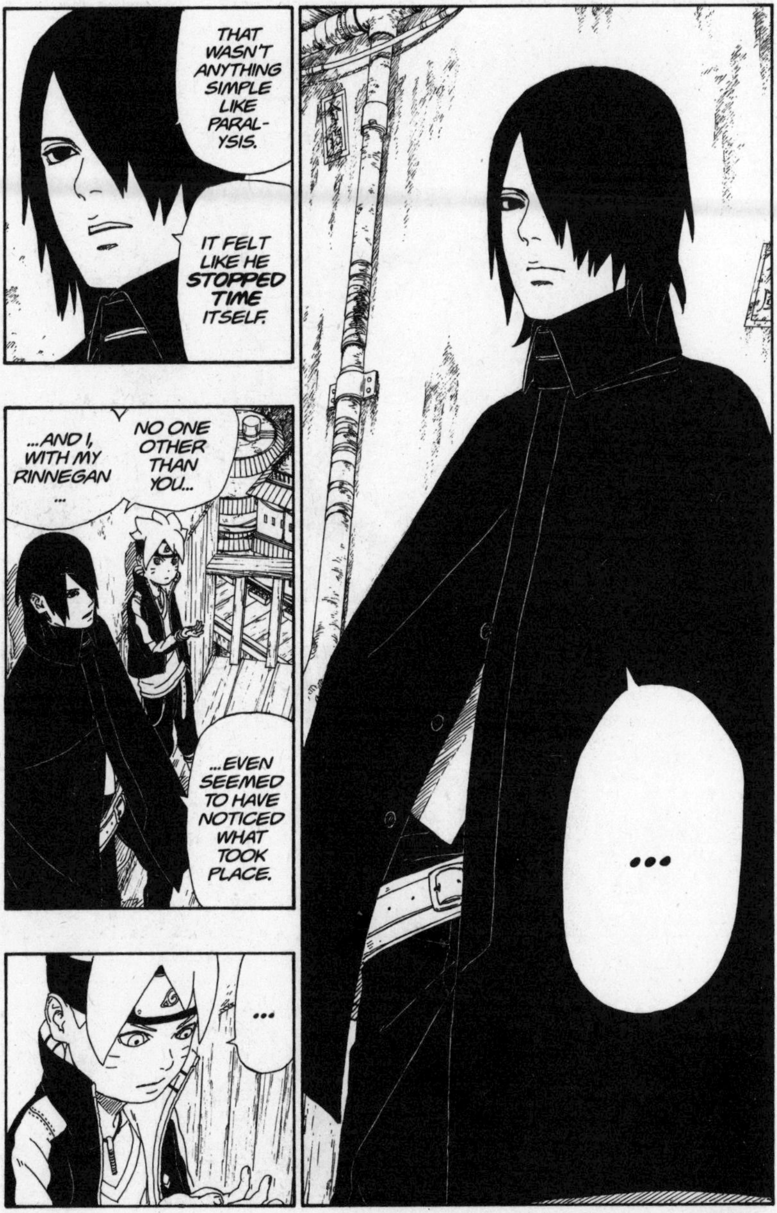
...
THAT WASN'T ANYTHING SIMPLE LIKE PARALYSIS.
IT FELT LIKE HE STOPPED TIME ITSELF.
NO ONE OTHER THAN YOU...
...AND I, WITH MY RINNEGAN...
...EVEN SEEMED TO HAVE NOTICED WHAT TOOK PLACE.
...

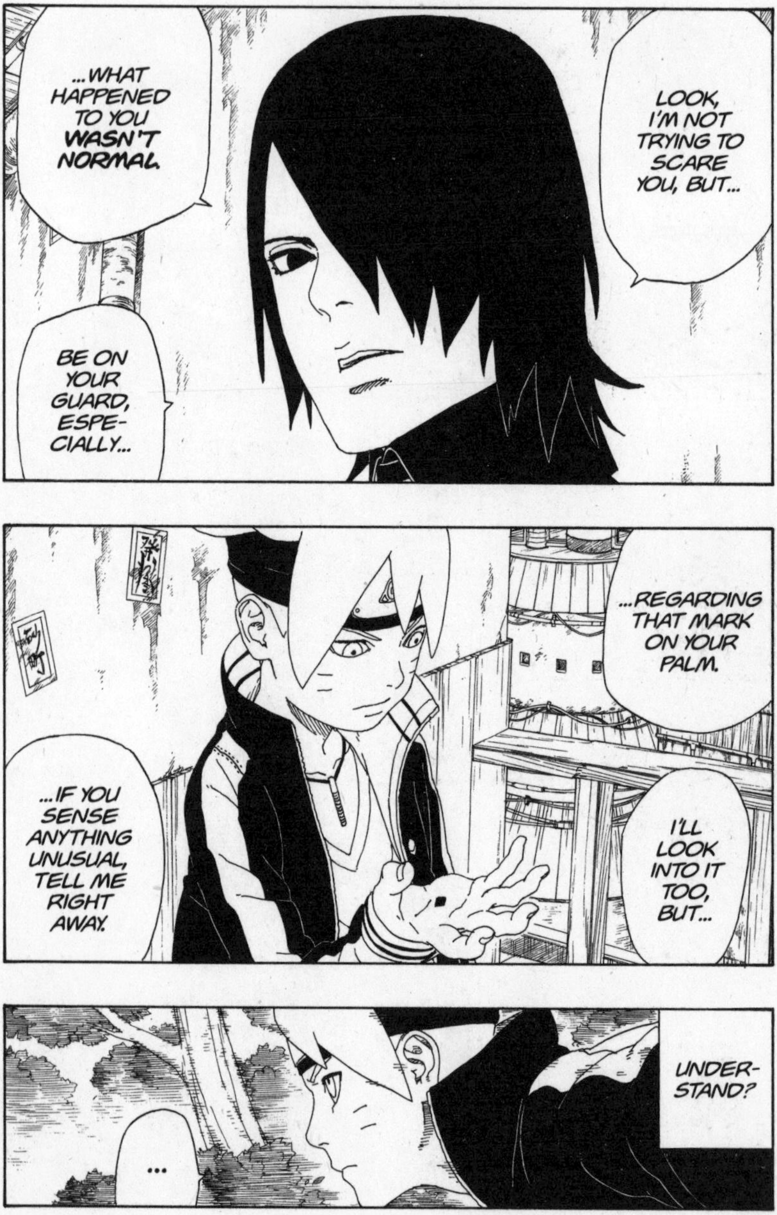
LOOK, I'M NOT TRYING TO SCARE YOU, BUT...
...WHAT HAPPENED TO YOU WASN'T NORMAL.
BE ON YOUR GUARD, ESPE-CIALLY...
...REGARDING THAT MARK ON YOUR PALM.
I'LL LOOK INTO IT TOO, BUT...
...IF YOU SENSE ANYTHING UNUSUAL, TELL ME RIGHT AWAY.
UNDER-STAND?
...

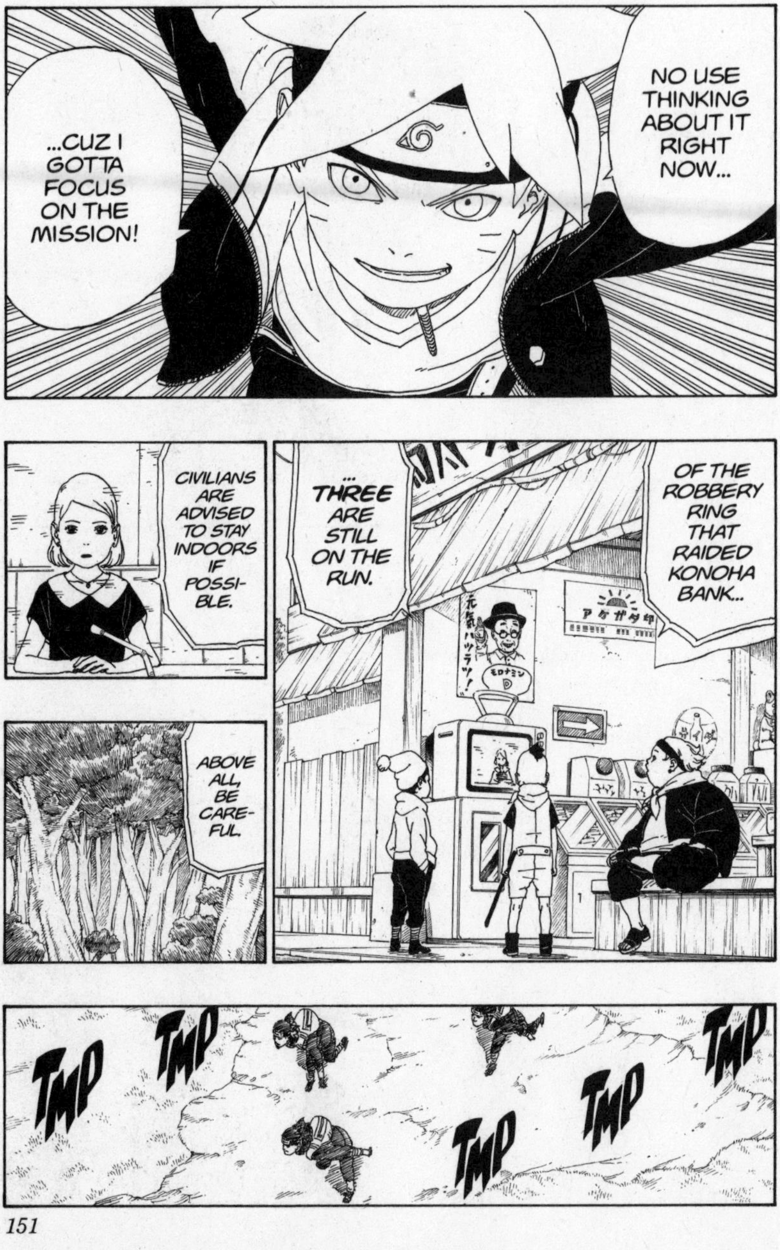
NO USE THINKING ABOUT IT RIGHT NOW...
...CUZ I GOTTA FOCUS ON THE MISSION!
OF THE ROBBERY RING THAT RAIDED KONOHA BANK...
...THREE ARE STILL ON THE RUN.
CIVILIANS ARE ADVISED TO STAY INDOORS IF POSSIBLE.
ABOVE ALL, BE CAREFUL.
TMP
TMP
TMP
TMP
TMP
TMP

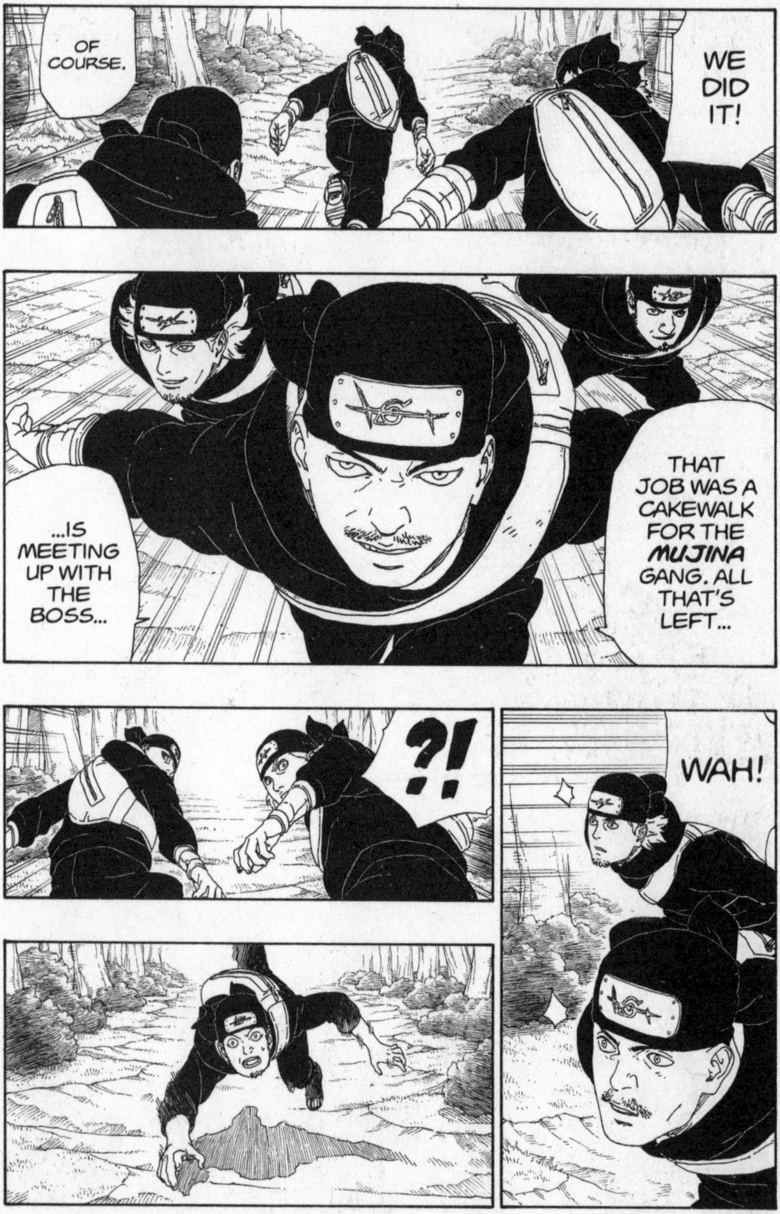
WE DID IT!
OF COURSE.
THAT JOB WAS A CAKEWALK FOR THE MUJINA GANG. ALL THAT'S LEFT...
...IS MEETING UP WITH THE BOSS...
WAH!
?!

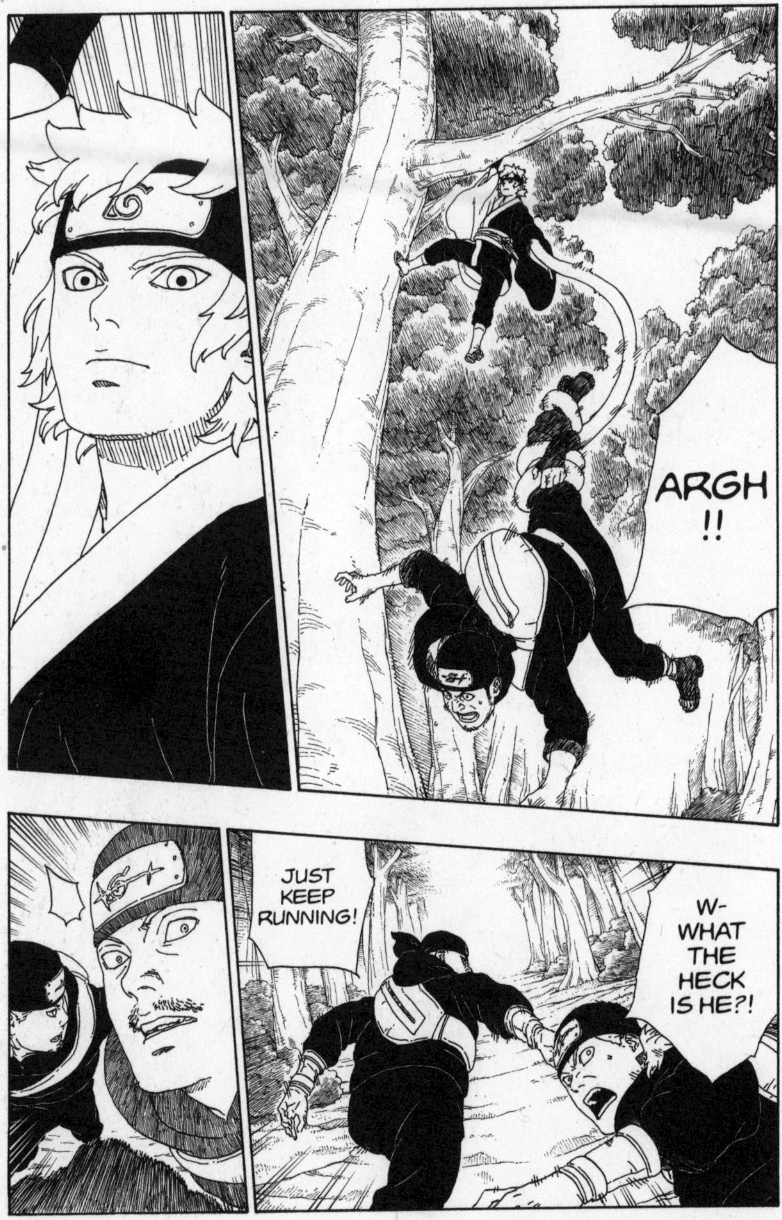
ARGH !!
W- WHAT THE HECK IS HE?!
JUST KEEP RUNNING!

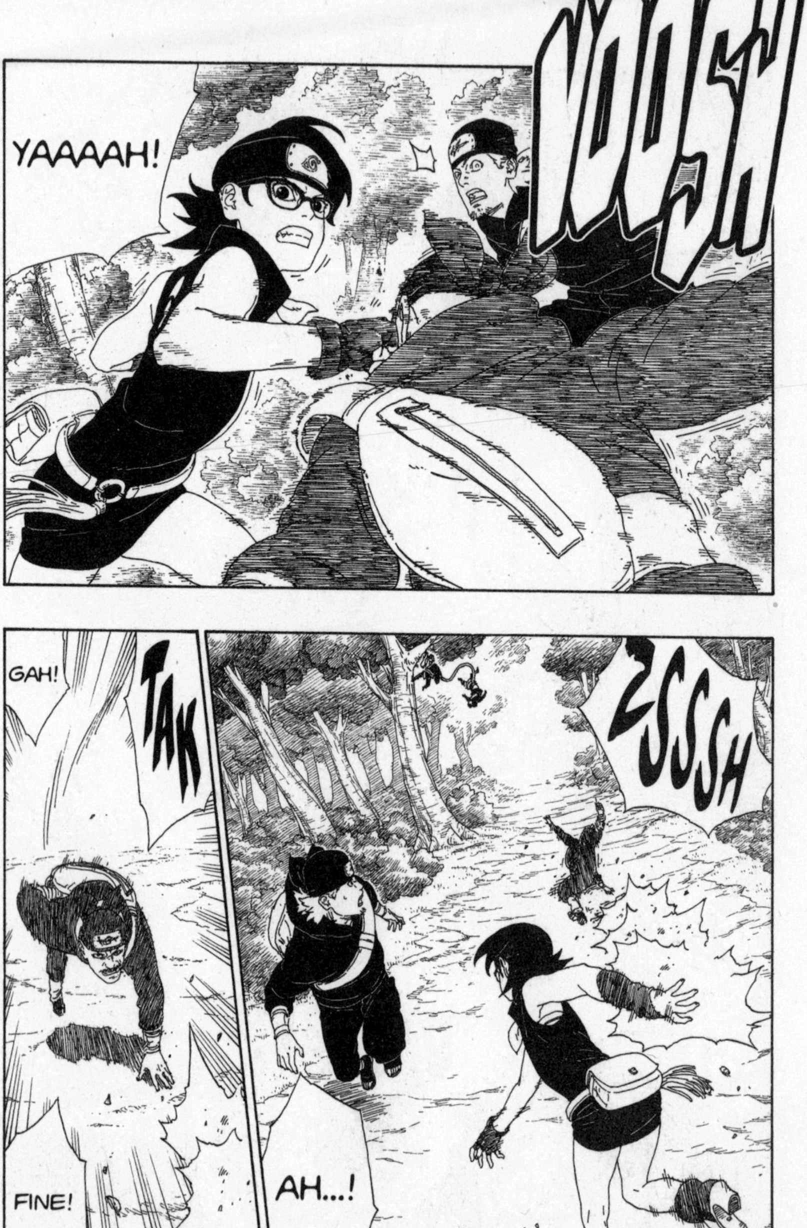
WOOSH
YAAAAH!
ZSSSH
AH...!
GAH!
TAK
FINE!

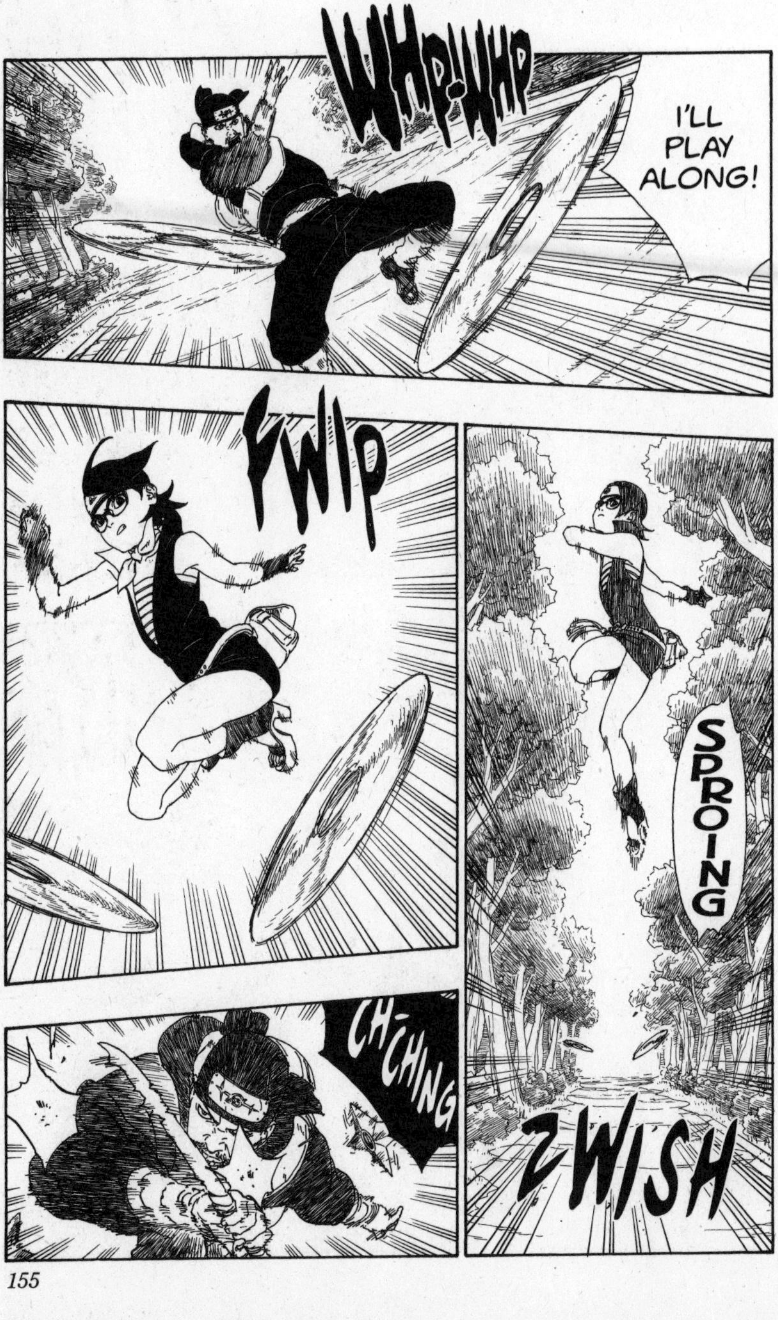
I'LL PLAY ALONG!
WHP-WHP
SPROING
ZWISH
FWIP
CH-CHING

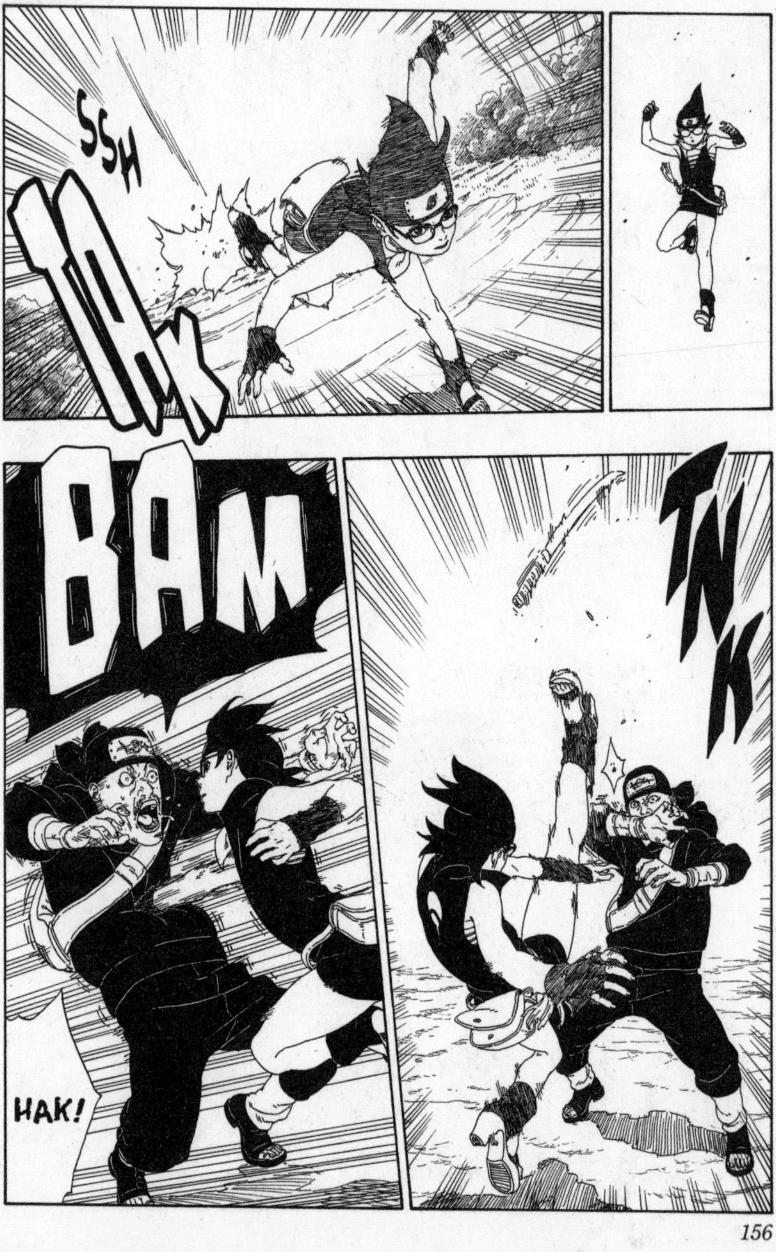
SSH
TAK
TNK
BAM
HAK!

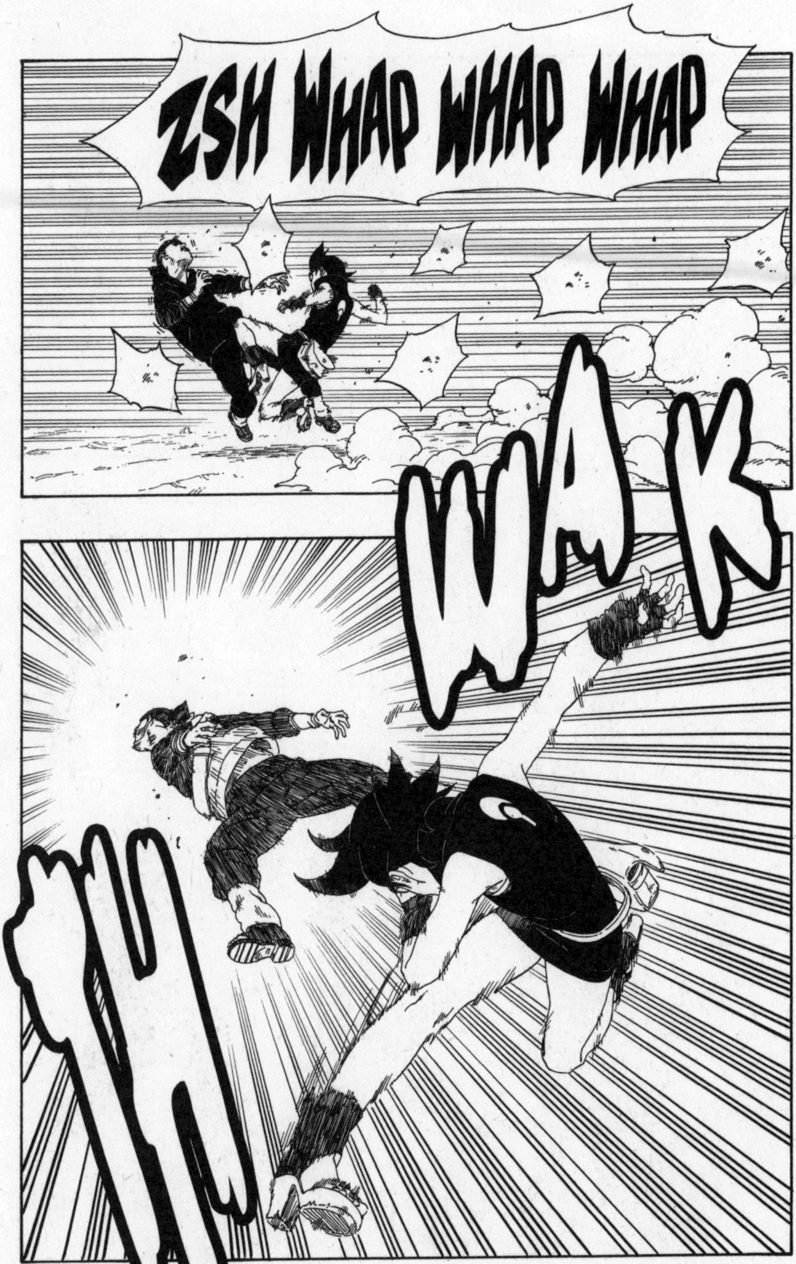
ZSH WHAP WHAP WHAP
WAK

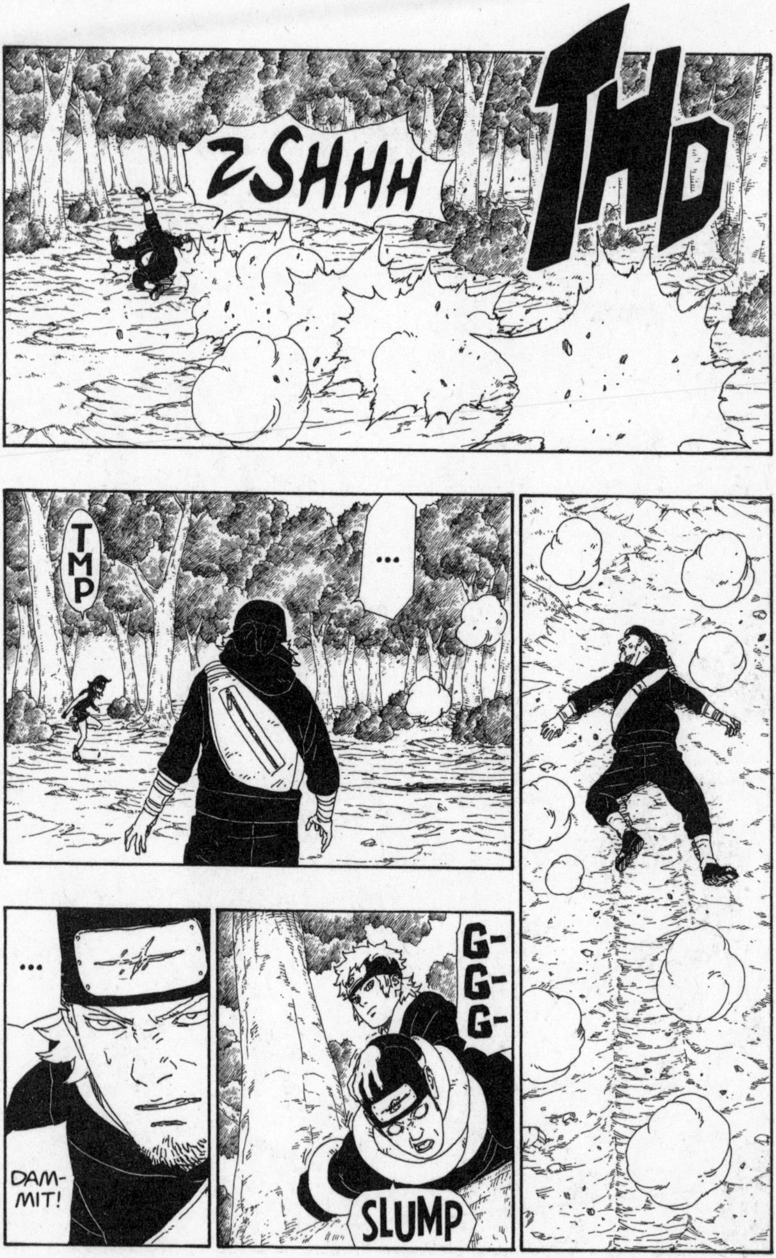
THD
ZSHHH
...
TMP
G-G-G-
SLUMP
...
DAM-MIT!

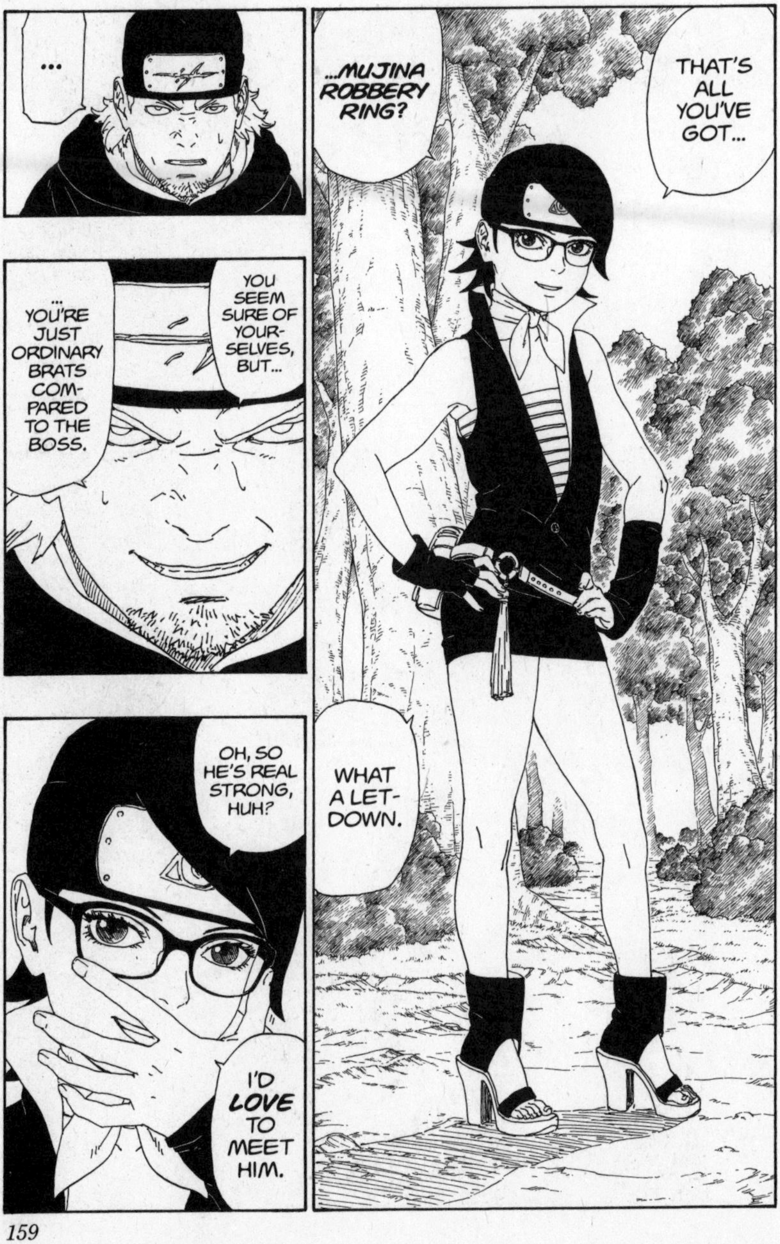
THAT'S ALL YOU'VE GOT...
...MUJINA ROBBERY RING?
WHAT A LET-DOWN.
...
YOU SEEM SURE OF YOUR-SELVES, BUT...
... YOU'RE JUST ORDINARY BRATS COM-PARED TO THE BOSS.
OH, SO HE'S REAL STRONG, HUH?
I'D *LOVE* TO MEET HIM.

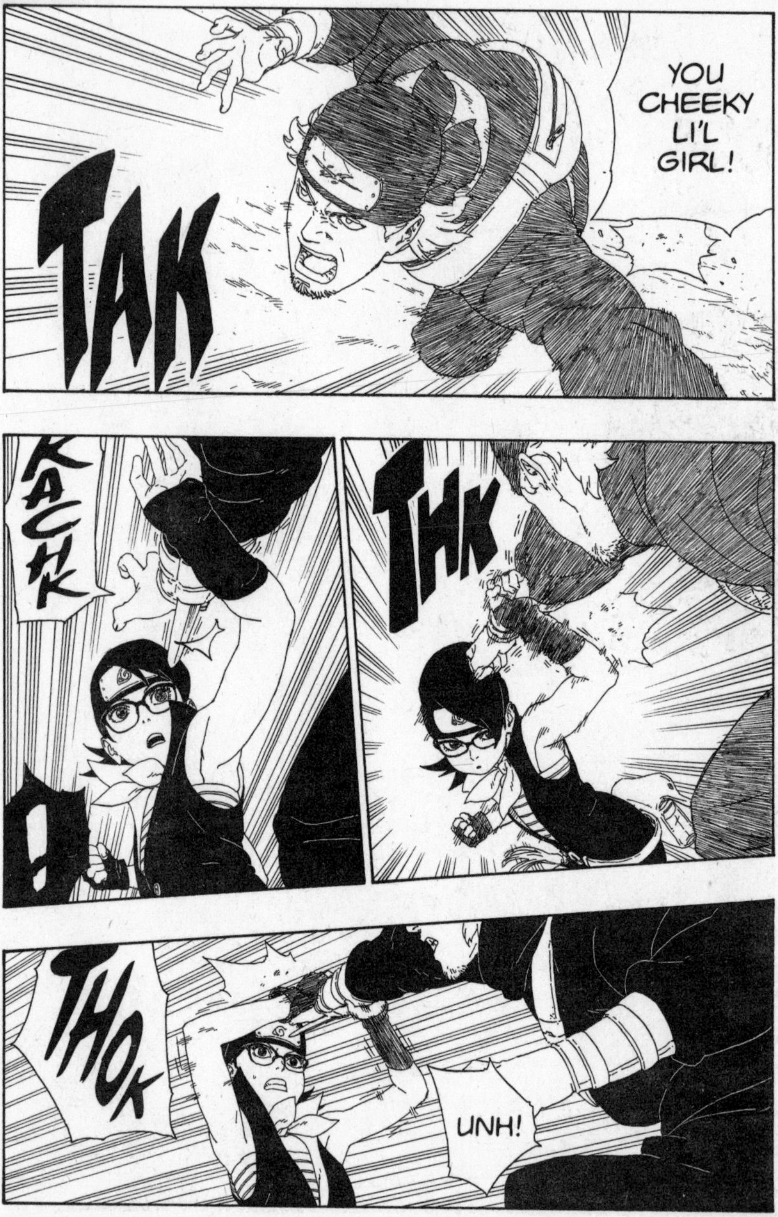
YOU CHEEKY LI'L GIRL!
TAK
THK
KACHK
THOK
UNH!

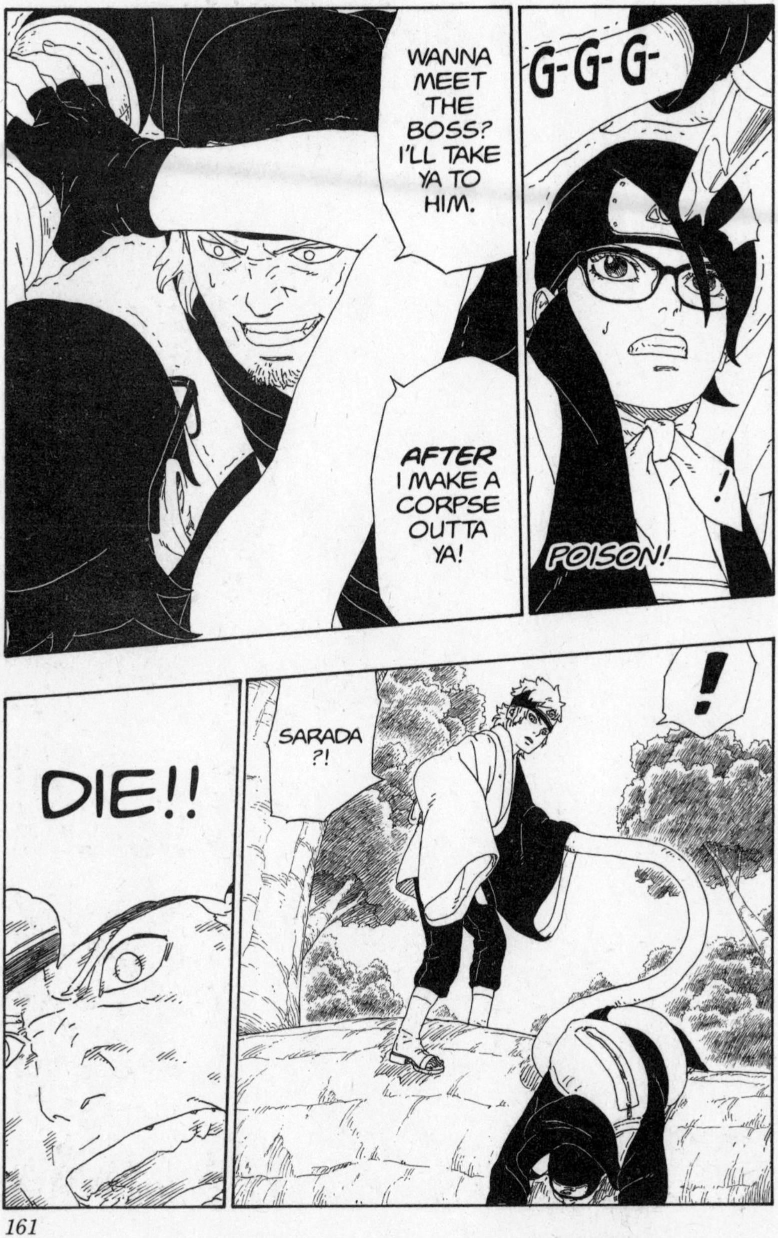
G-G-G-
!
POISON!
WANNA MEET THE BOSS? I'LL TAKE YA TO HIM.
AFTER I MAKE A CORPSE OUTTA YA!
!
SARADA?!
DIE!!

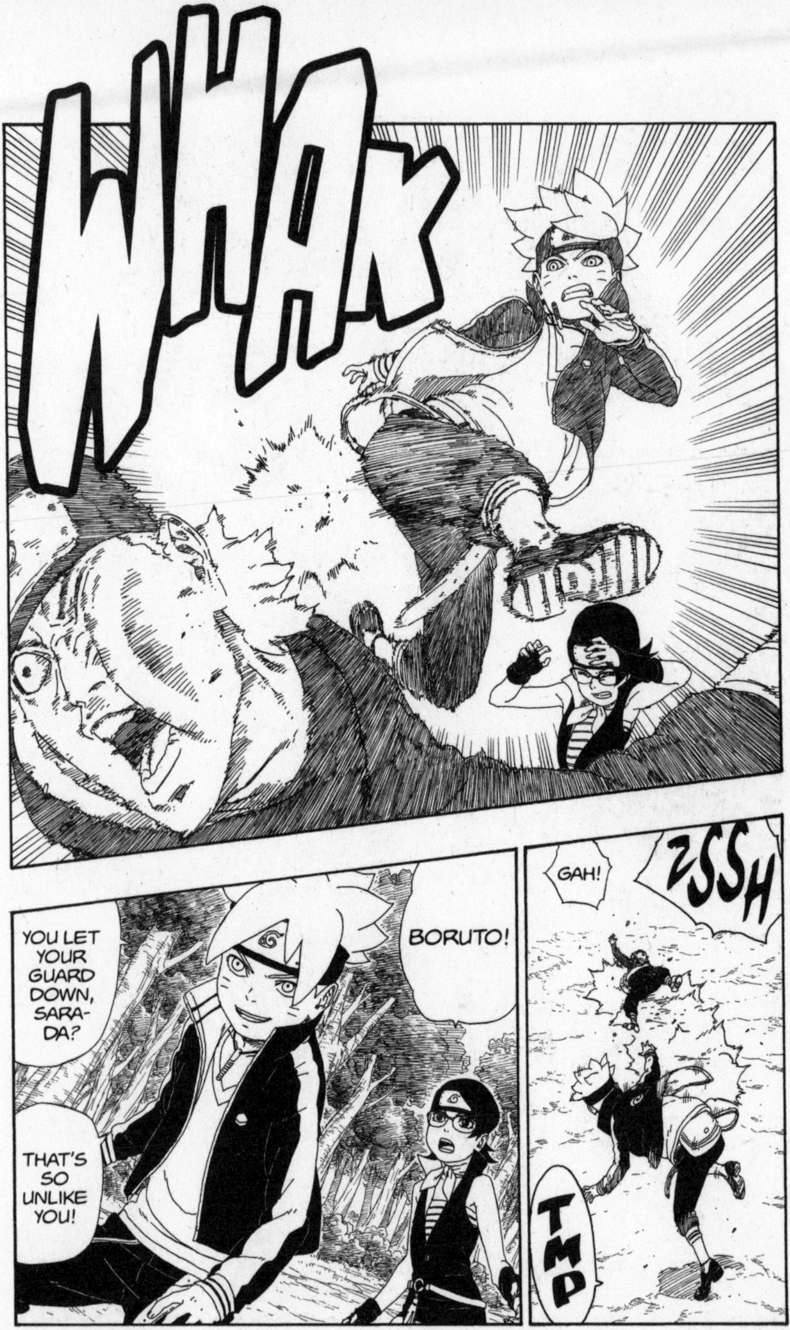
WHAK
ZSSH
GAH!
TMP
BORUTO!
YOU LET YOUR GUARD DOWN, SARADA?
THAT'S SO UNLIKE YOU!

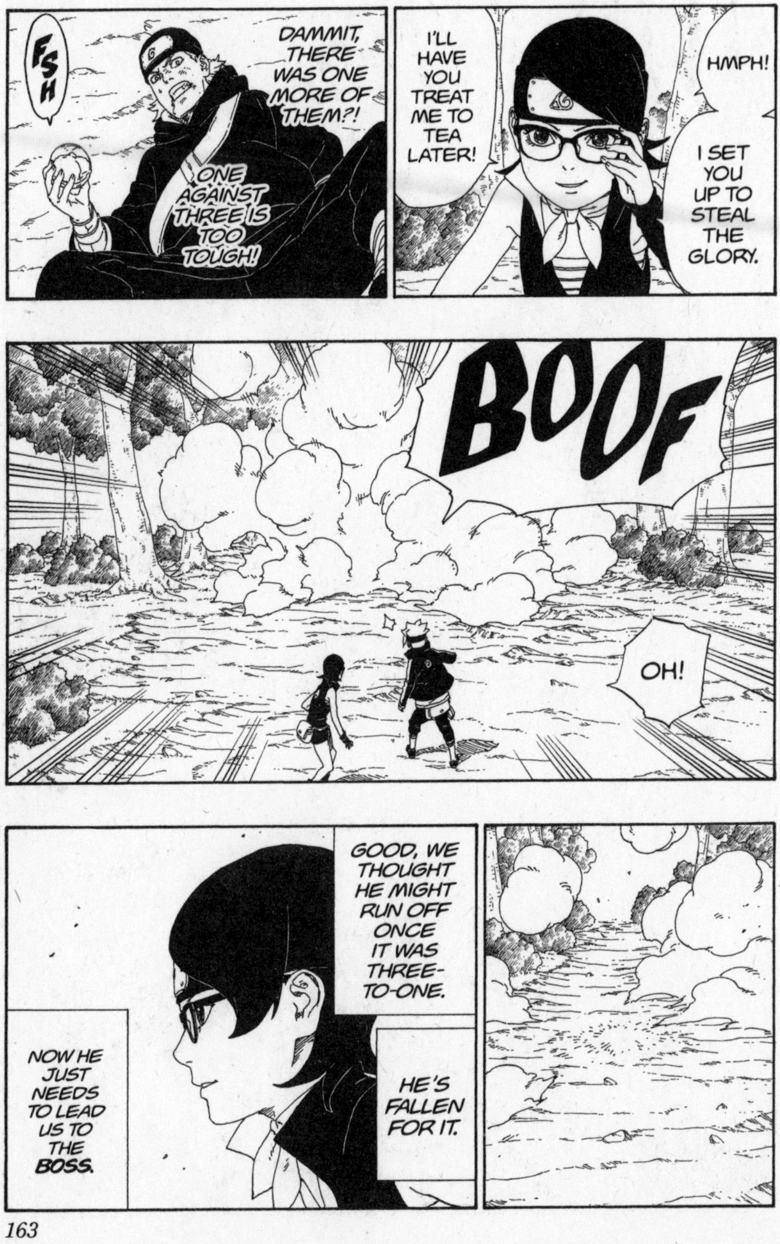
HMPH!
I SET YOU UP TO STEAL THE GLORY.
I'LL HAVE YOU TREAT ME TO TEA LATER!
DAMMIT, THERE WAS ONE MORE OF THEM?!
FSH
ONE AGAINST THREE IS TOO TOUGH!
BOOF
OH!
GOOD, WE THOUGHT HE MIGHT RUN OFF ONCE IT WAS THREE-TO-ONE.
HE'S FALLEN FOR IT.
NOW HE JUST NEEDS TO LEAD US TO THE BOSS.

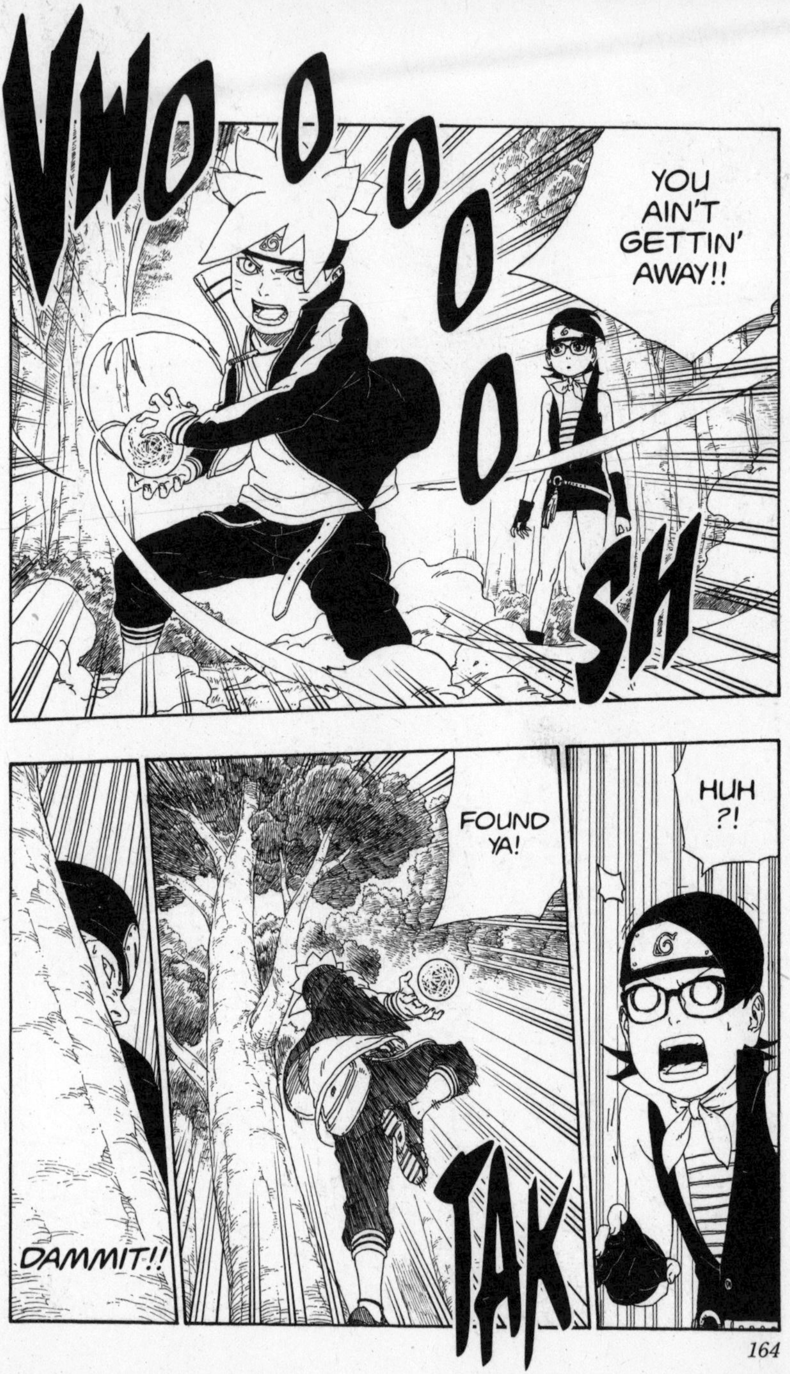
YOU AIN'T GETTIN' AWAY!!
VWOOOOOOSH
HUH?!
FOUND YA!
TAK
DAMMIT!!

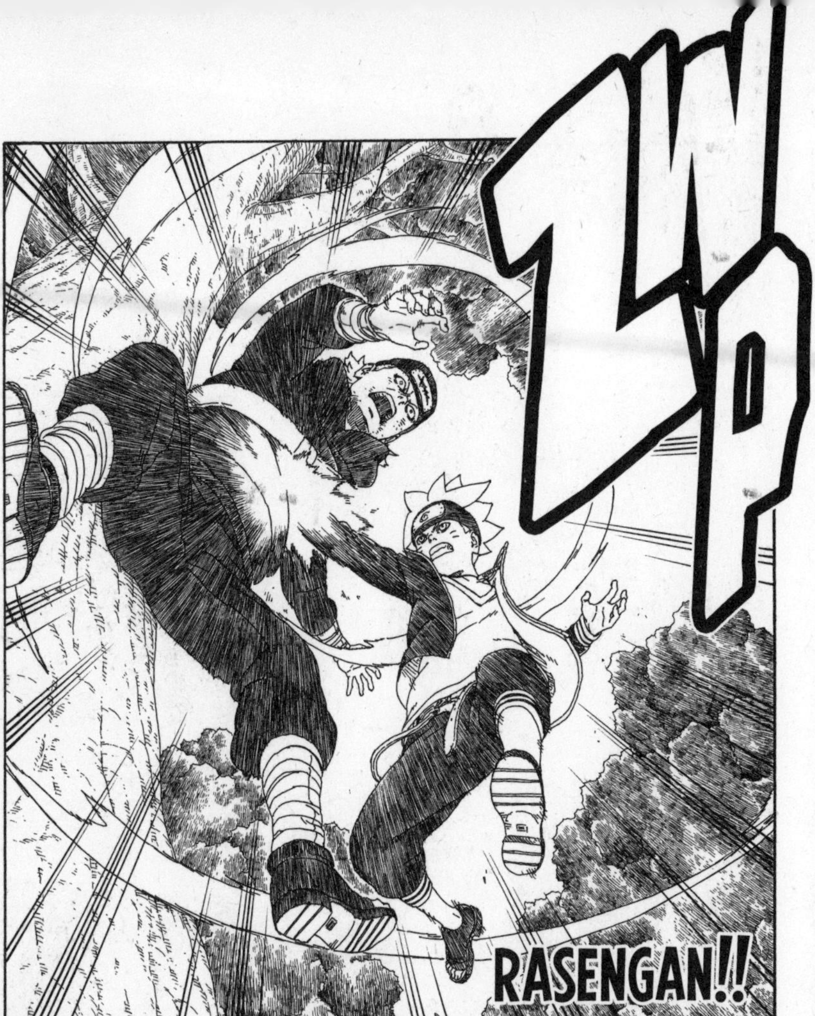
ZWIP
RASENGAN!!

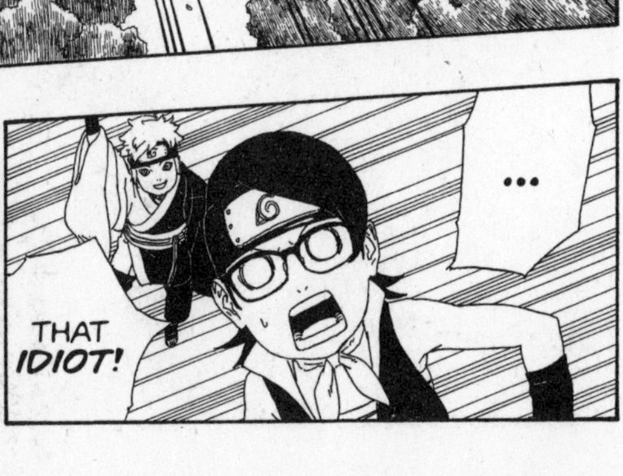
...
THAT IDIOT!

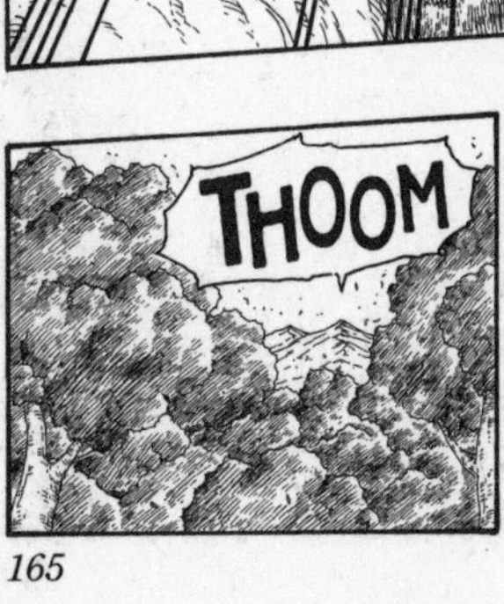
THOOM

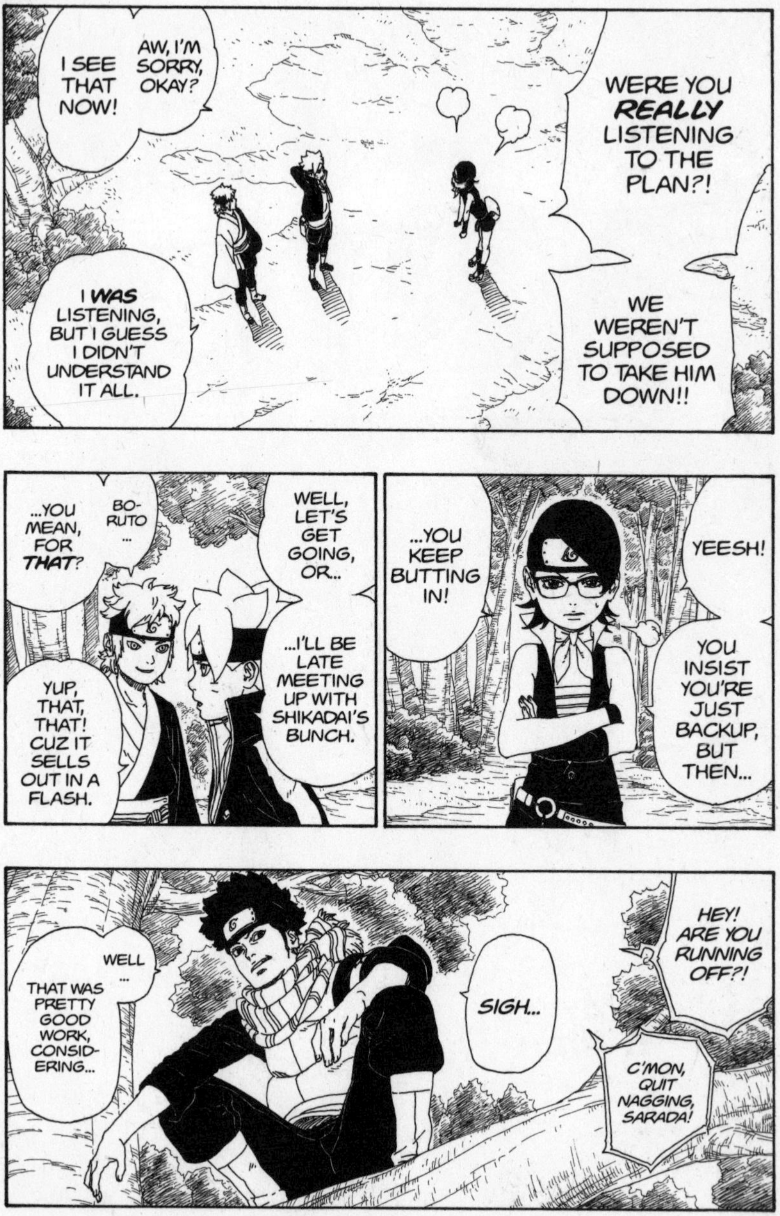
WERE YOU REALLY LISTENING TO THE PLAN?!
WE WEREN'T SUPPOSED TO TAKE HIM DOWN!!
AW, I'M SORRY, OKAY?
I SEE THAT NOW!
I WAS LISTENING, BUT I GUESS I DIDN'T UNDERSTAND IT ALL.
YEESH!
YOU INSIST YOU'RE JUST BACKUP, BUT THEN...
...YOU KEEP BUTTING IN!
WELL, LET'S GET GOING, OR..
...I'LL BE LATE MEETING UP WITH SHIKADAI'S BUNCH.
BO-RUTO...
...YOU MEAN, FOR THAT?
YUP, THAT, THAT! CUZ IT SELLS OUT IN A FLASH.
HEY! ARE YOU RUNNING OFF?!
C'MON, QUIT NAGGING, SARADA!
SIGH...
WELL...
THAT WAS PRETTY GOOD WORK, CONSIDERING...

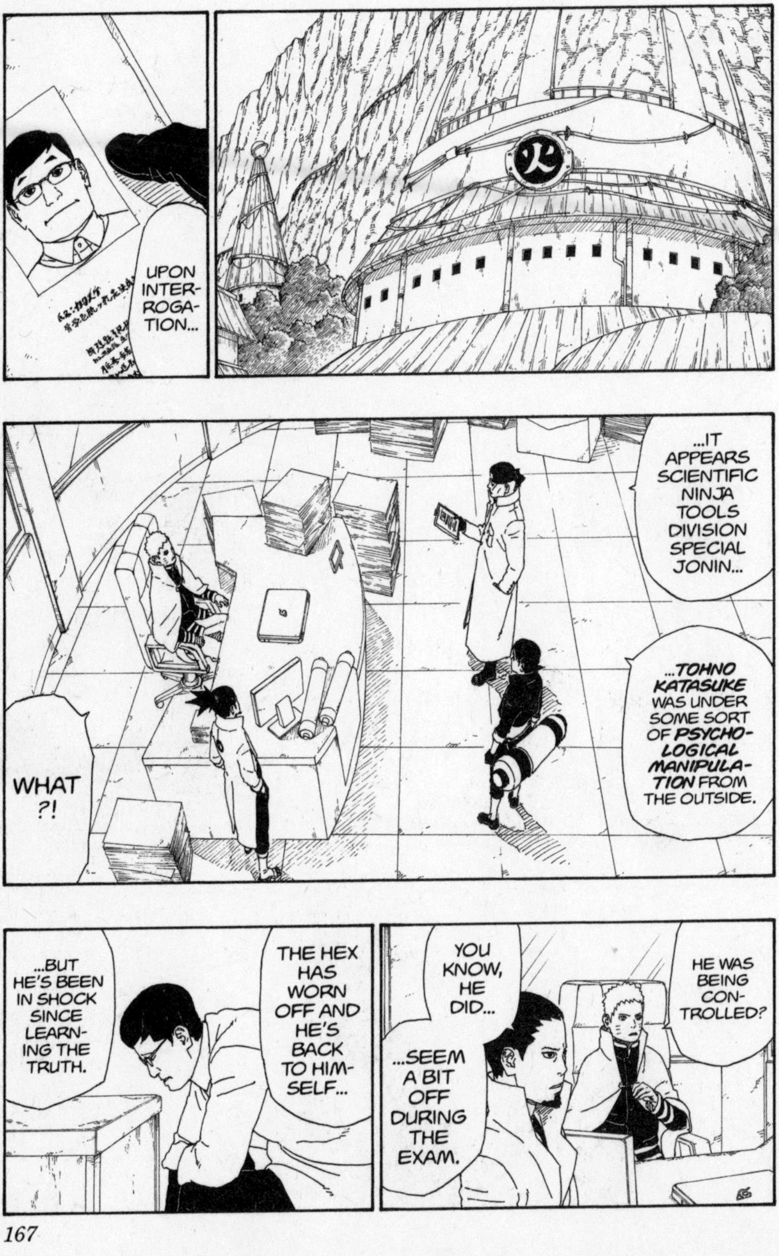
UPON INTERROGATION...
...IT APPEARS SCIENTIFIC NINJA TOOLS DIVISION SPECIAL JONIN...
...**TOHNO KATASUKE** WAS UNDER SOME SORT OF **PSYCHOLOGICAL MANIPULATION** FROM THE OUTSIDE.
WHAT?!
HE WAS BEING CONTROLLED?
YOU KNOW, HE DID...
...SEEM A BIT OFF DURING THE EXAM.
THE HEX HAS WORN OFF AND HE'S BACK TO HIMSELF...
...BUT HE'S BEEN IN SHOCK SINCE LEARNING THE TRUTH.

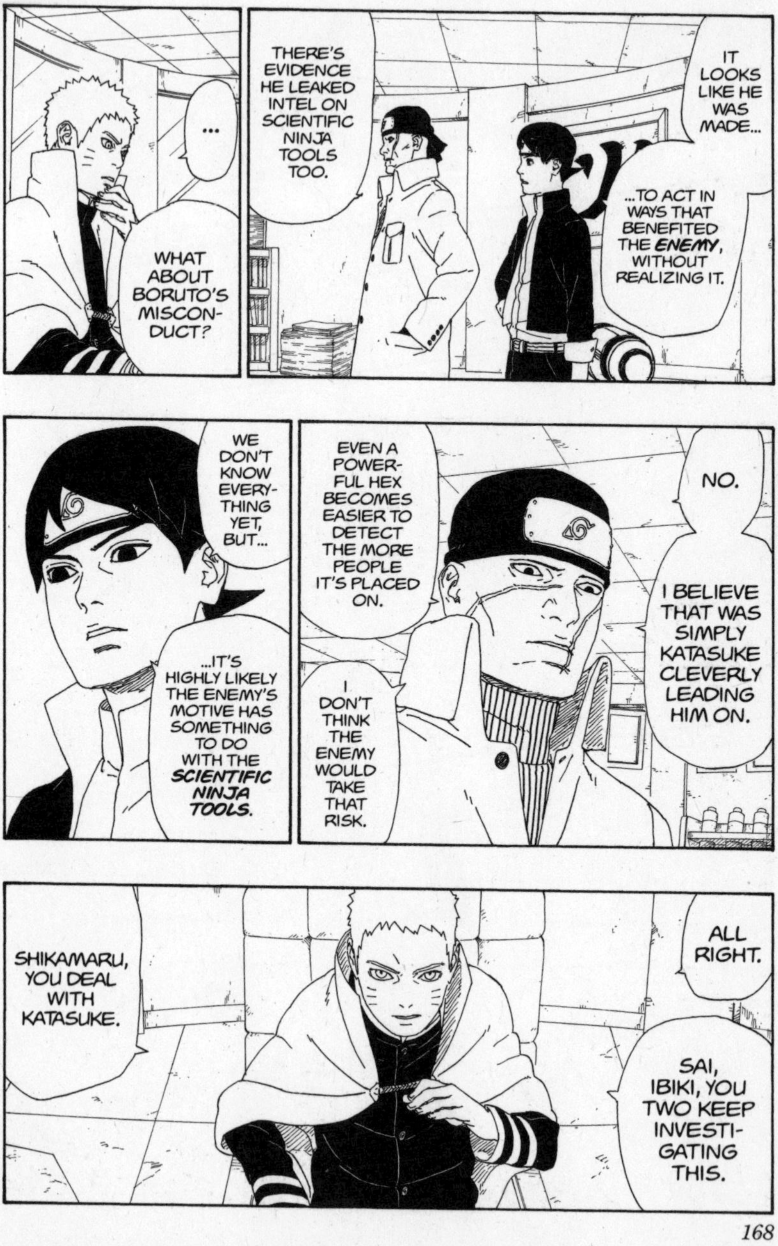
IT LOOKS LIKE HE WAS MADE...
...TO ACT IN WAYS THAT BENEFITED THE ENEMY, WITHOUT REALIZING IT.
THERE'S EVIDENCE HE LEAKED INTEL ON SCIENTIFIC NINJA TOOLS TOO.
...
WHAT ABOUT BORUTO'S MISCONDUCT?
NO.
I BELIEVE THAT WAS SIMPLY KATASUKE CLEVERLY LEADING HIM ON.
EVEN A POWERFUL HEX BECOMES EASIER TO DETECT THE MORE PEOPLE IT'S PLACED ON.
I DON'T THINK THE ENEMY WOULD TAKE THAT RISK.
WE DON'T KNOW EVERYTHING YET, BUT...
...IT'S HIGHLY LIKELY THE ENEMY'S MOTIVE HAS SOMETHING TO DO WITH THE ***SCIENTIFIC NINJA TOOLS***.
ALL RIGHT.
SHIKAMARU, YOU DEAL WITH KATASUKE.
SAI, IBIKI, YOU TWO KEEP INVESTIGATING THIS.

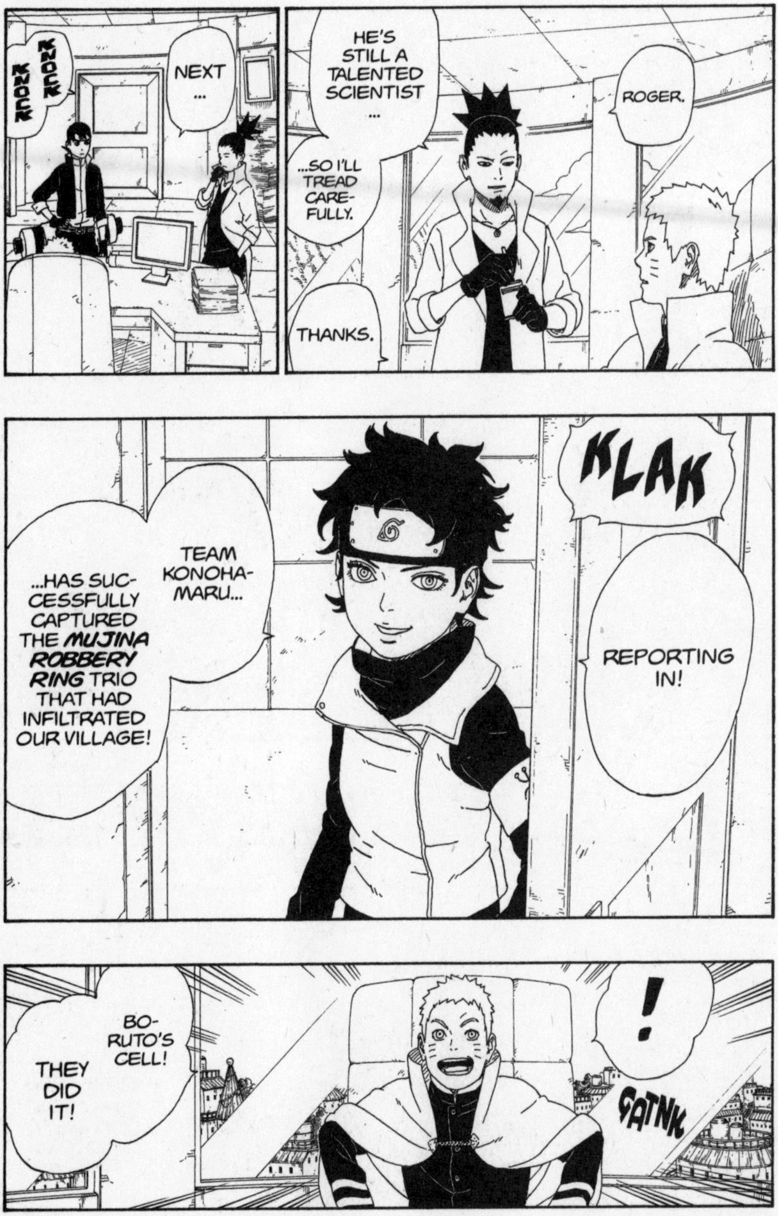
ROGER.
HE'S STILL A TALENTED SCIENTIST...
...SO I'LL TREAD CAREFULLY.
THANKS.
NEXT...
KNOCK KNOCK
KLAK
REPORTING IN!
TEAM KONOHAMARU...
...HAS SUCCESSFULLY CAPTURED THE *MUJINA ROBBERY RING* TRIO THAT HAD INFILTRATED OUR VILLAGE!
!
GATNK
BORUTO'S CELL!
THEY DID IT!

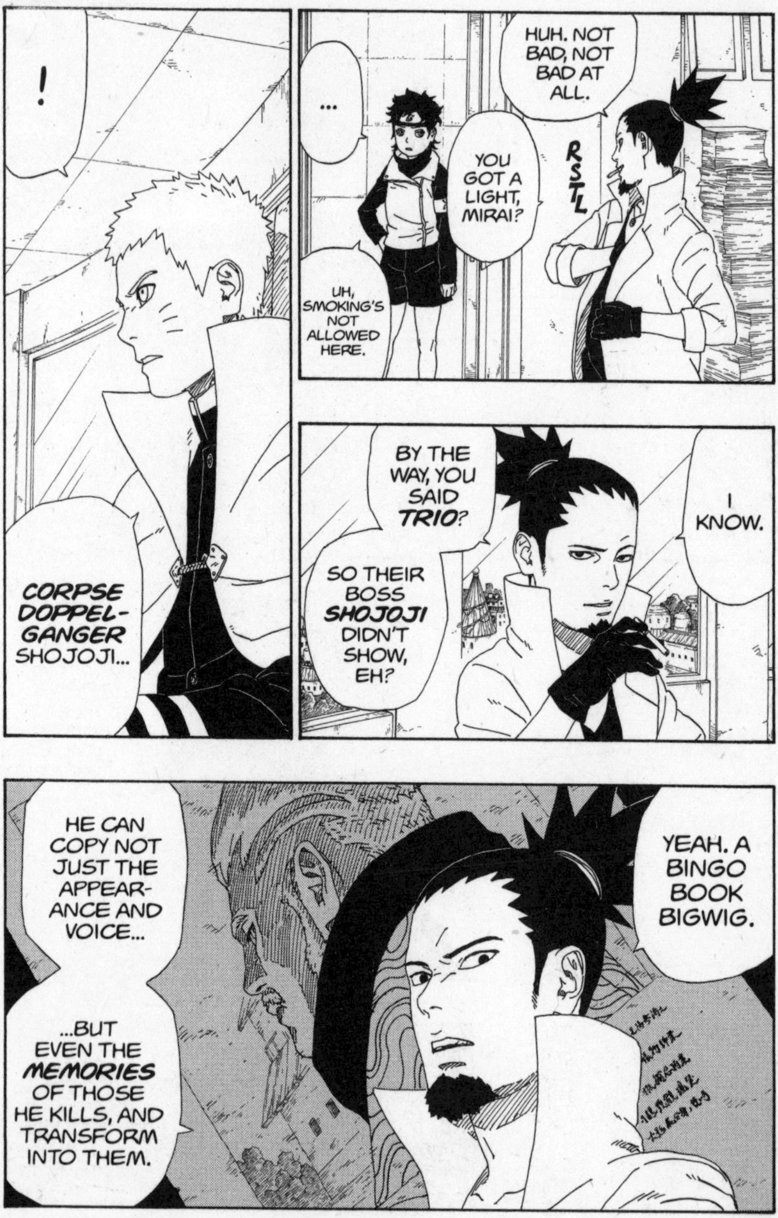
HUH. NOT BAD, NOT BAD AT ALL.
RSTL
YOU GOT A LIGHT, MIRAI?
...
UH, SMOKING'S NOT ALLOWED HERE.
BY THE WAY, YOU SAID TRIO?
I KNOW.
SO THEIR BOSS SHOJOJI DIDN'T SHOW, EH?
!
CORPSE DOPPEL-GANGER SHOJOJI...
YEAH. A BINGO BOOK BIGWIG.
HE CAN COPY NOT JUST THE APPEAR-ANCE AND VOICE...
...BUT EVEN THE MEMORIES OF THOSE HE KILLS, AND TRANSFORM INTO THEM.

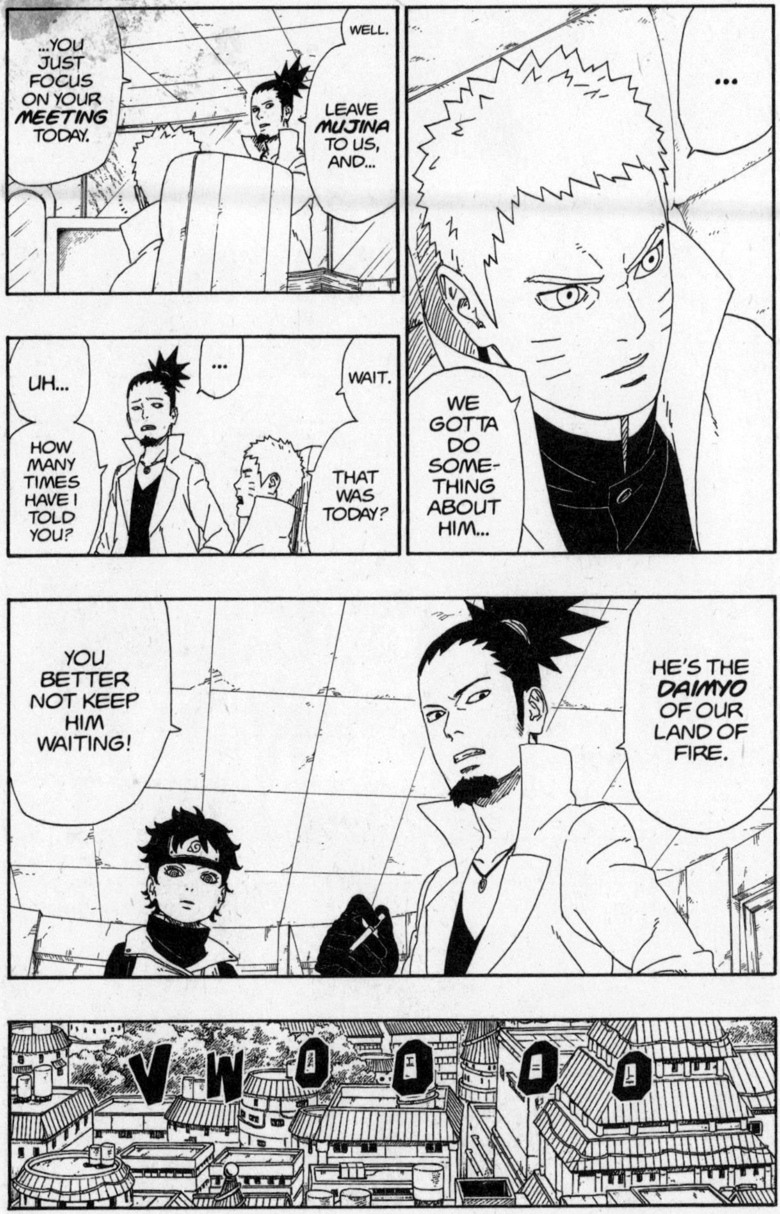
...
WE GOTTA DO SOMETHING ABOUT HIM...
WELL.
LEAVE MUJINA TO US, AND...
...YOU JUST FOCUS ON YOUR MEETING TODAY.
WAIT.
THAT WAS TODAY?
...
UH...
HOW MANY TIMES HAVE I TOLD YOU?
HE'S THE DAIMYO OF OUR LAND OF FIRE.
YOU BETTER NOT KEEP HIM WAITING!
VWOOOO

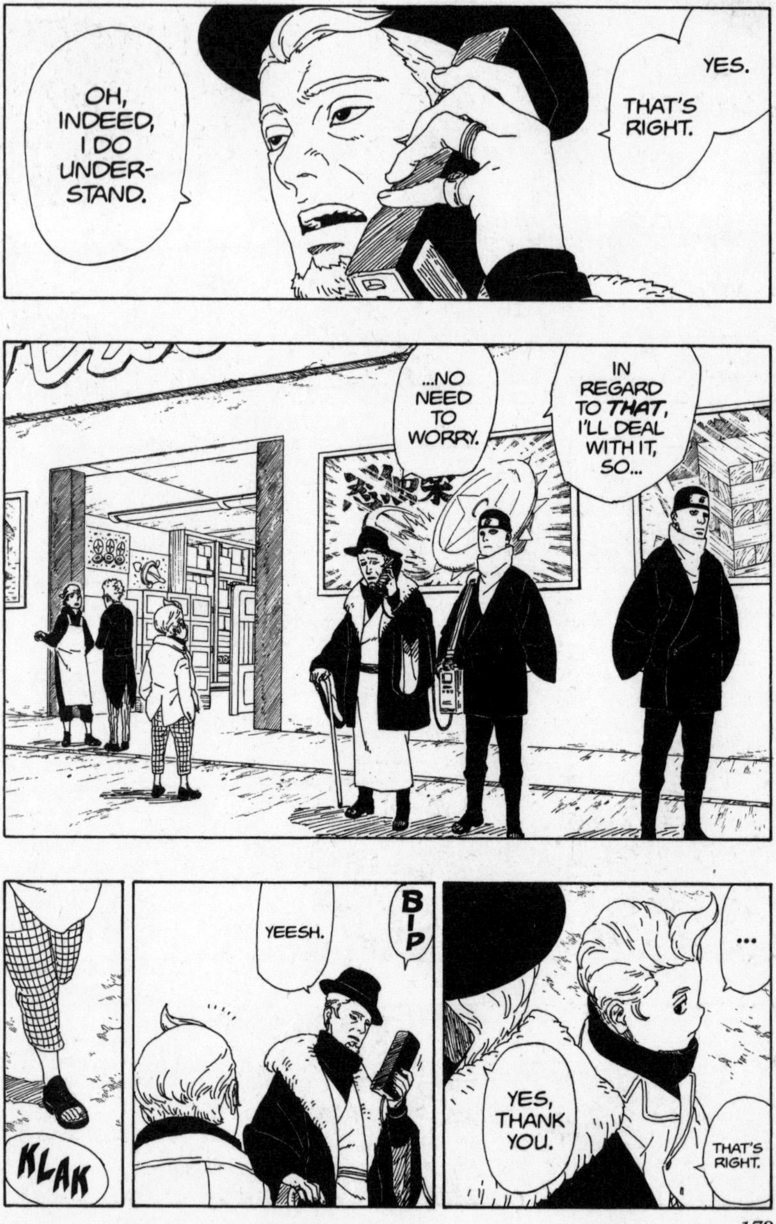
YES.
THAT'S RIGHT.
OH, INDEED, I DO UNDER-STAND.
IN REGARD TO *THAT*, I'LL DEAL WITH IT, SO...
...NO NEED TO WORRY.
...
THAT'S RIGHT.
YES, THANK YOU.
BIP
YEESH.
KLAK

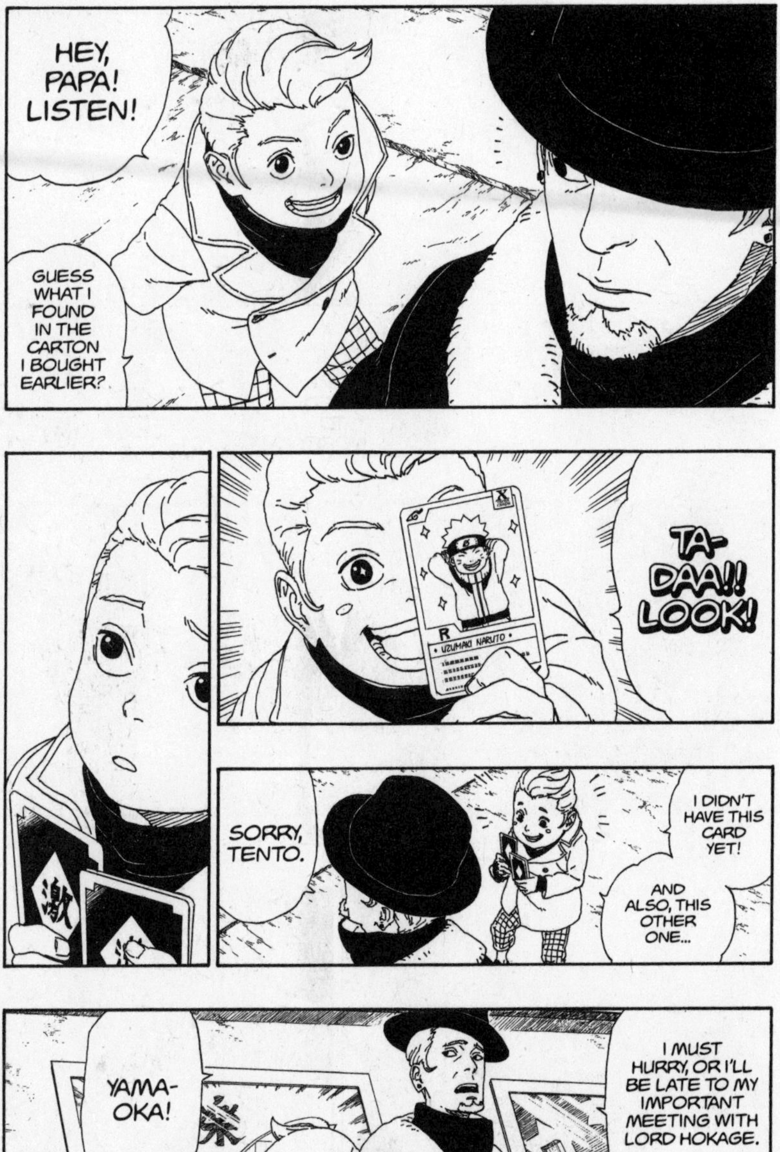
HEY, PAPA! LISTEN!
GUESS WHAT I FOUND IN THE CARTON I BOUGHT EARLIER?
TA-DAA!! LOOK!
I DIDN'T HAVE THIS CARD YET!
AND ALSO, THIS OTHER ONE...
SORRY, TENTO.
I MUST HURRY, OR I'LL BE LATE TO MY IMPORTANT MEETING WITH LORD HOKAGE.
YAMA-OKA!

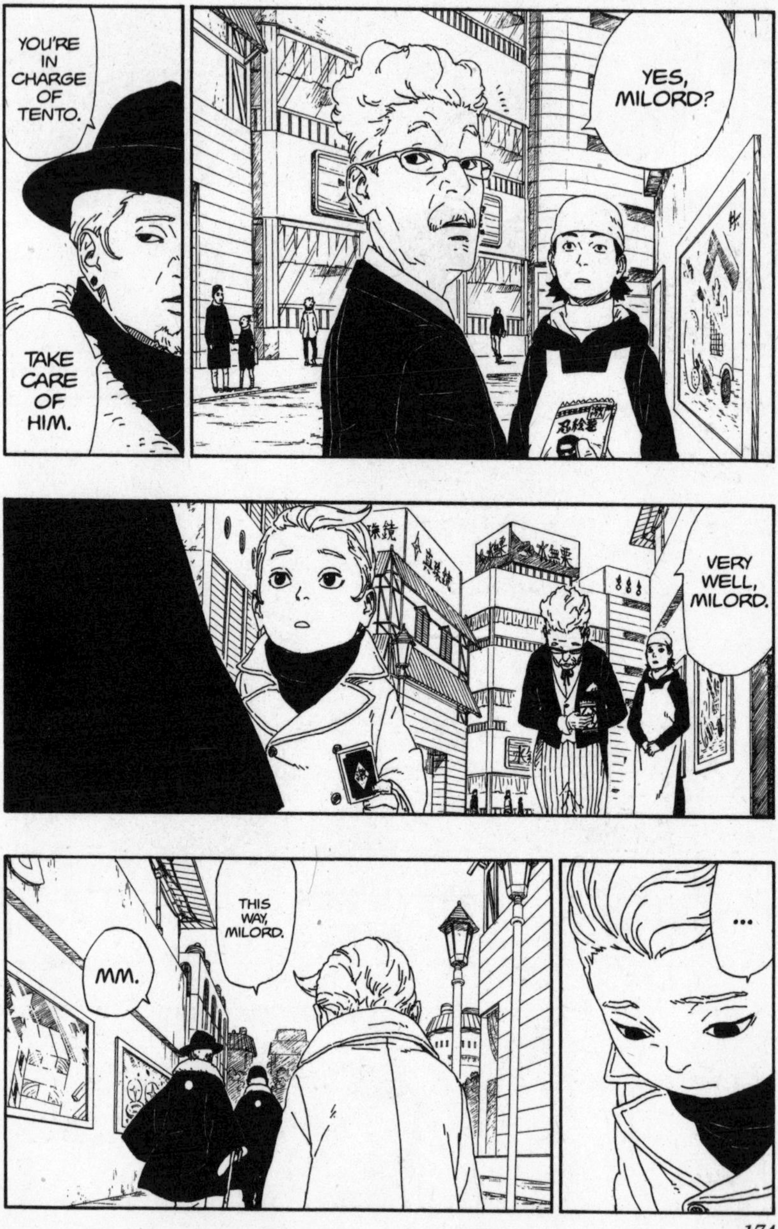
YES, MILORD?
YOU'RE IN CHARGE OF TENTO.
TAKE CARE OF HIM.
VERY WELL, MILORD.
...
THIS WAY, MILORD.
MM.

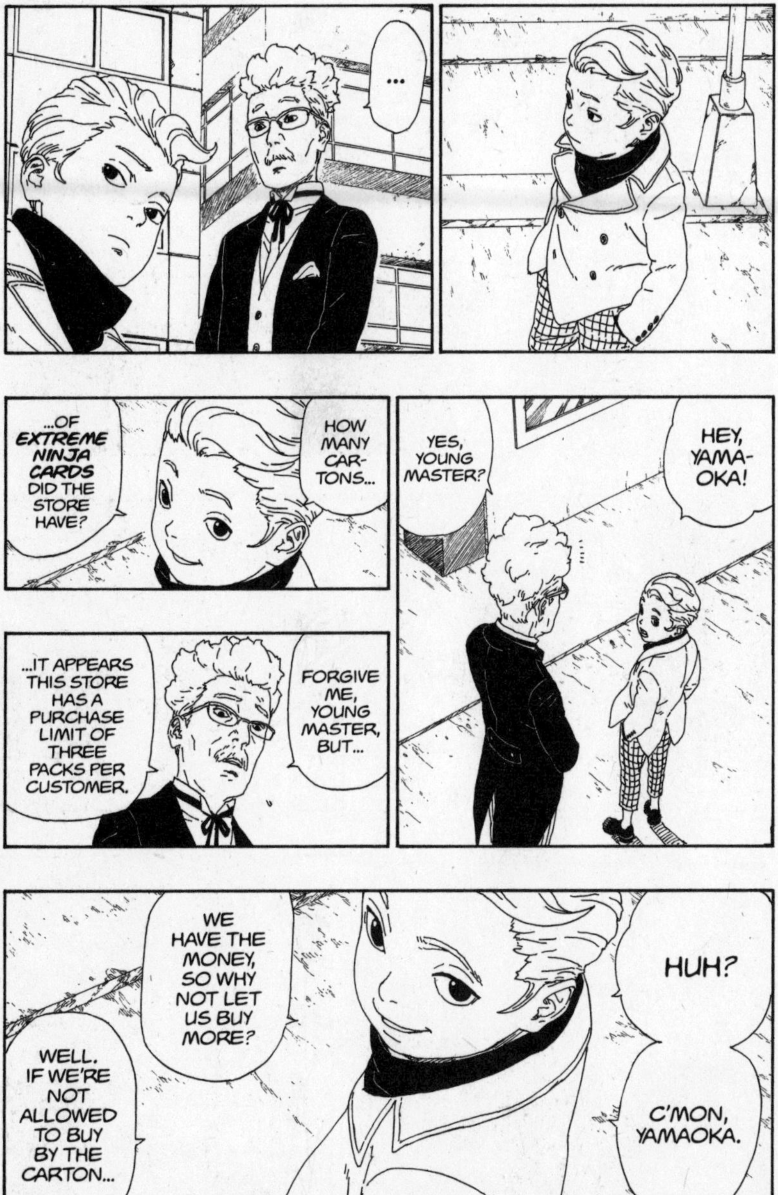
...
HEY, YAMAOKA!
YES, YOUNG MASTER?
HOW MANY CARTONS...
...OF ***EXTREME NINJA CARDS*** DID THE STORE HAVE?
FORGIVE ME, YOUNG MASTER, BUT...
...IT APPEARS THIS STORE HAS A PURCHASE LIMIT OF THREE PACKS PER CUSTOMER.
HUH?
C'MON, YAMAOKA.
WE HAVE THE MONEY, SO WHY NOT LET US BUY MORE?
WELL. IF WE'RE NOT ALLOWED TO BUY BY THE CARTON...

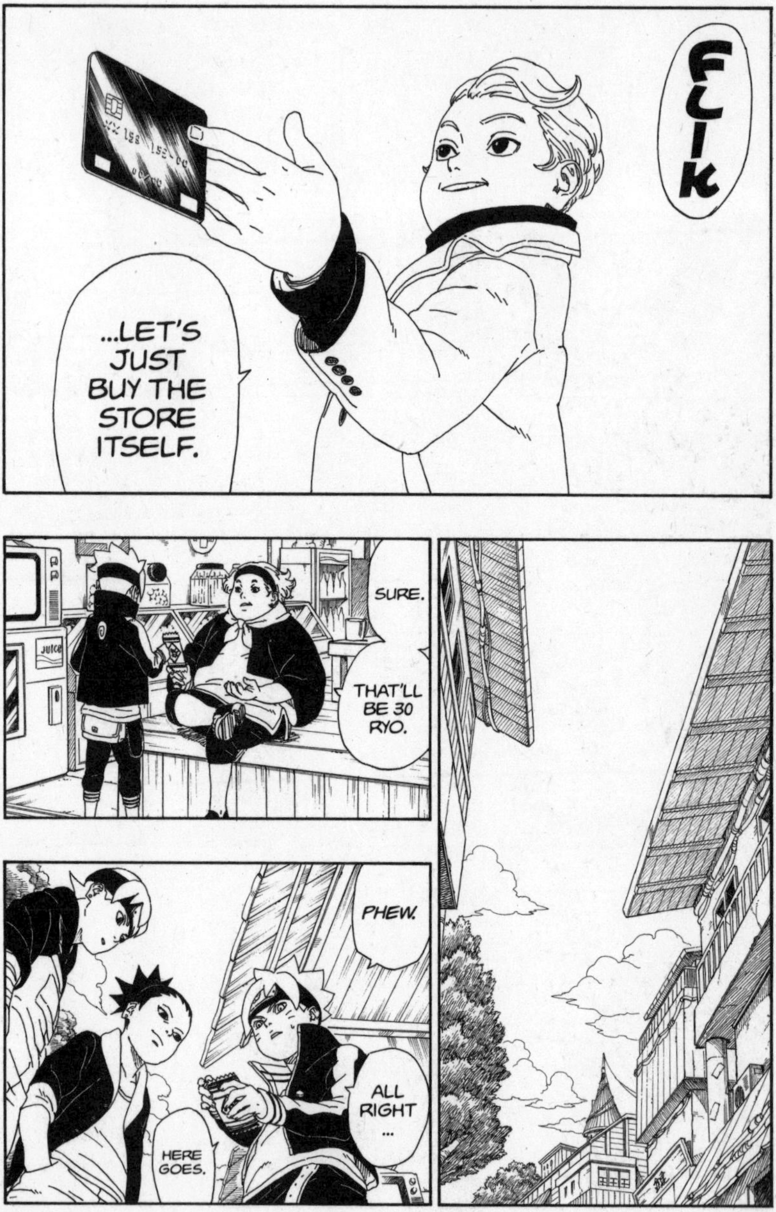
FLIK
...LET'S JUST BUY THE STORE ITSELF.
SURE.
THAT'LL BE 30 RYO.
PHEW.
ALL RIGHT ...
HERE GOES.

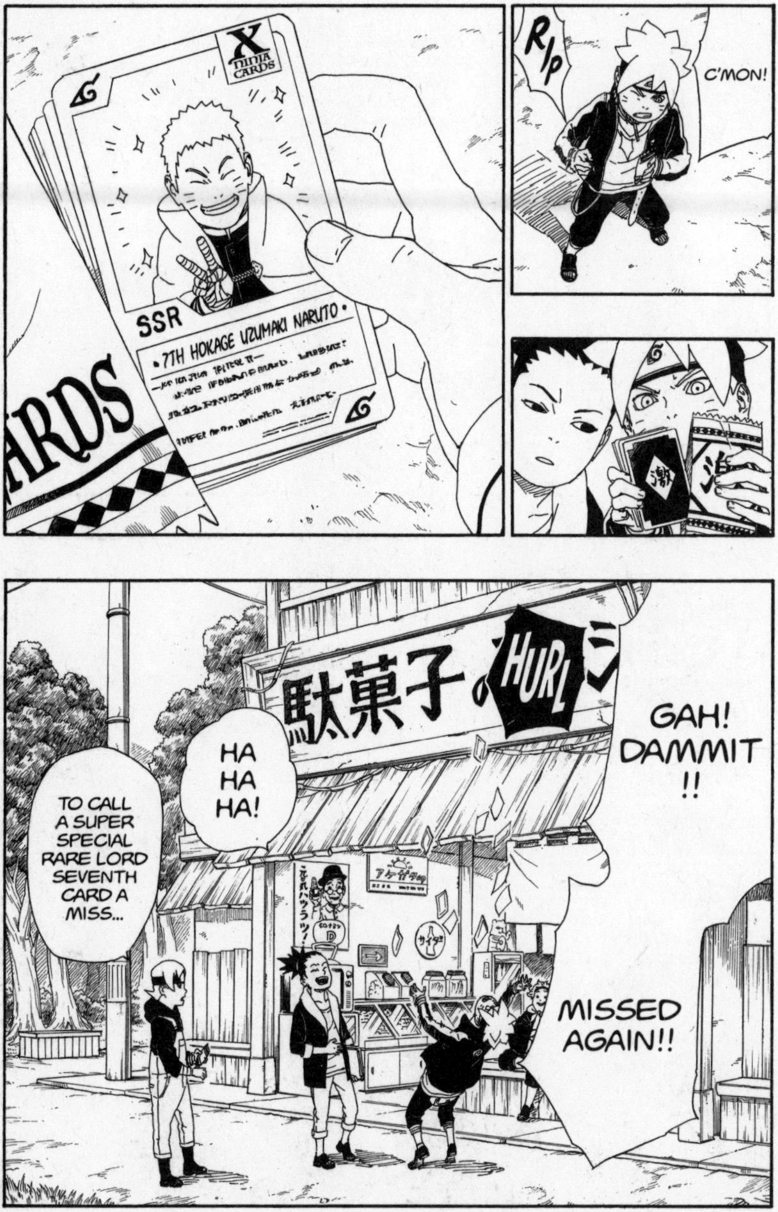
RIP
C'MON!
X NINJA CARDS
SSR
7TH HOKAGE UZUMAKI NARUTO
GAH! DAMMIT!!
HURL
駄菓子の
MISSED AGAIN!!
HA HA HA!
TO CALL A SUPER SPECIAL RARE LORD SEVENTH CARD A MISS...

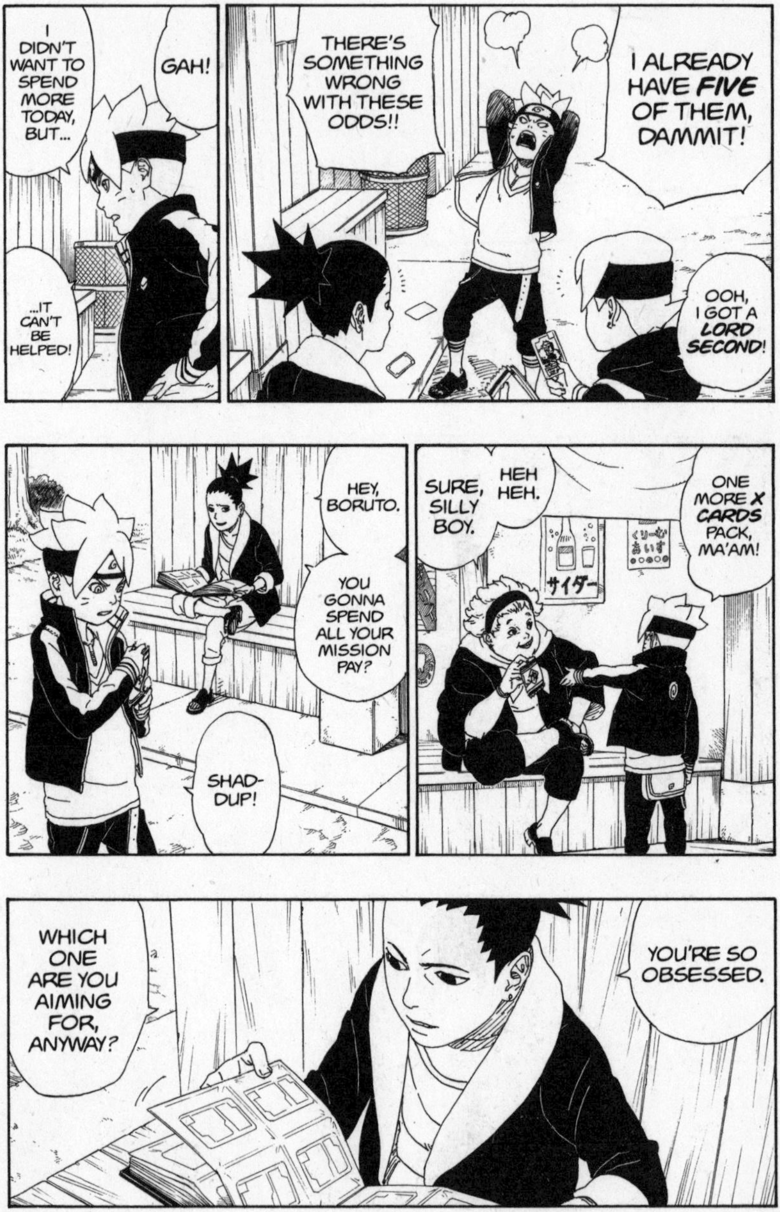
I ALREADY HAVE **FIVE** OF THEM, DAMMIT!
THERE'S SOMETHING WRONG WITH THESE ODDS!!
OOH, I GOT A **LORD SECOND**!
GAH!
I DIDN'T WANT TO SPEND MORE TODAY, BUT...
...IT CAN'T BE HELPED!
ONE MORE **X CARDS** PACK, MA'AM!
HEH HEH.
SURE, SILLY BOY.
くりーむあいす
サイダー
HEY, BORUTO.
YOU GONNA SPEND ALL YOUR MISSION PAY?
SHAD-DUP!
YOU'RE SO OBSESSED.
WHICH ONE ARE YOU AIMING FOR, ANYWAY?

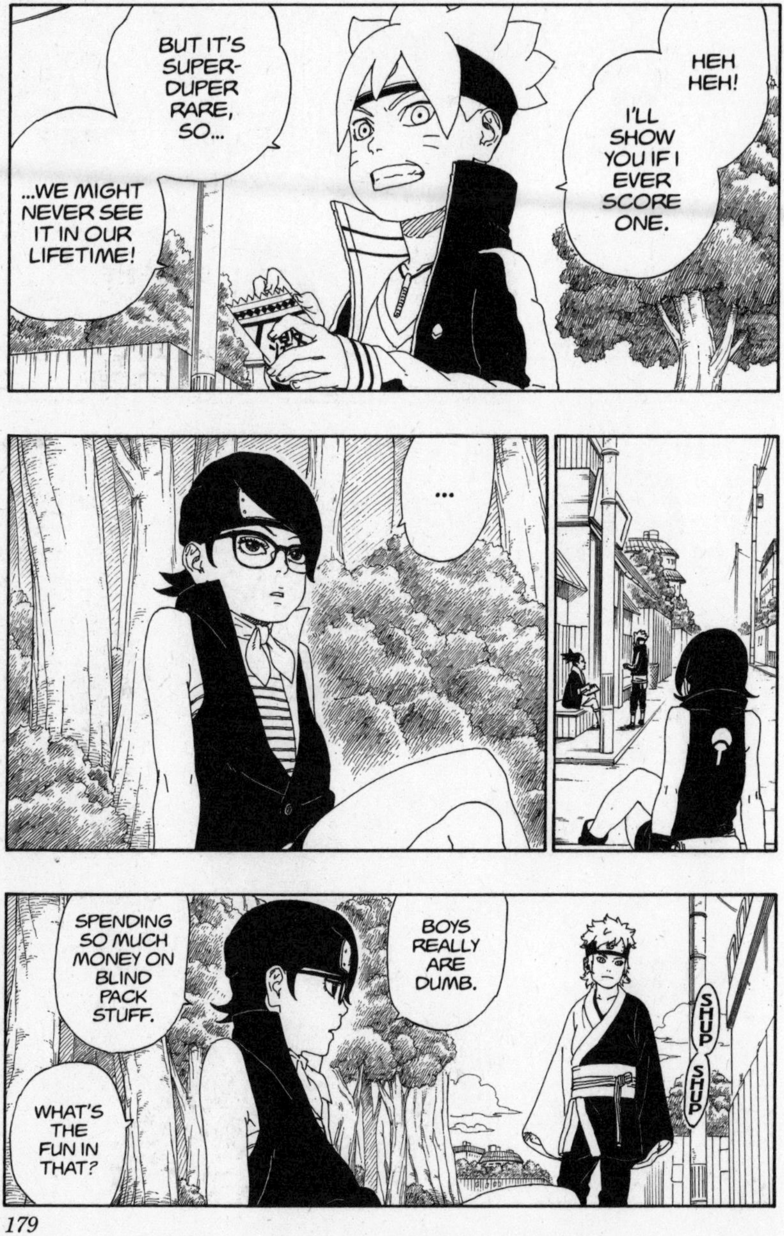
HEH HEH!
I'LL SHOW YOU IF I EVER SCORE ONE.
BUT IT'S SUPER-DUPER RARE, SO...
...WE MIGHT NEVER SEE IT IN OUR LIFETIME!
...
SHUP
SHUP
BOYS REALLY ARE DUMB.
SPENDING SO MUCH MONEY ON BLIND PACK STUFF.
WHAT'S THE FUN IN THAT?

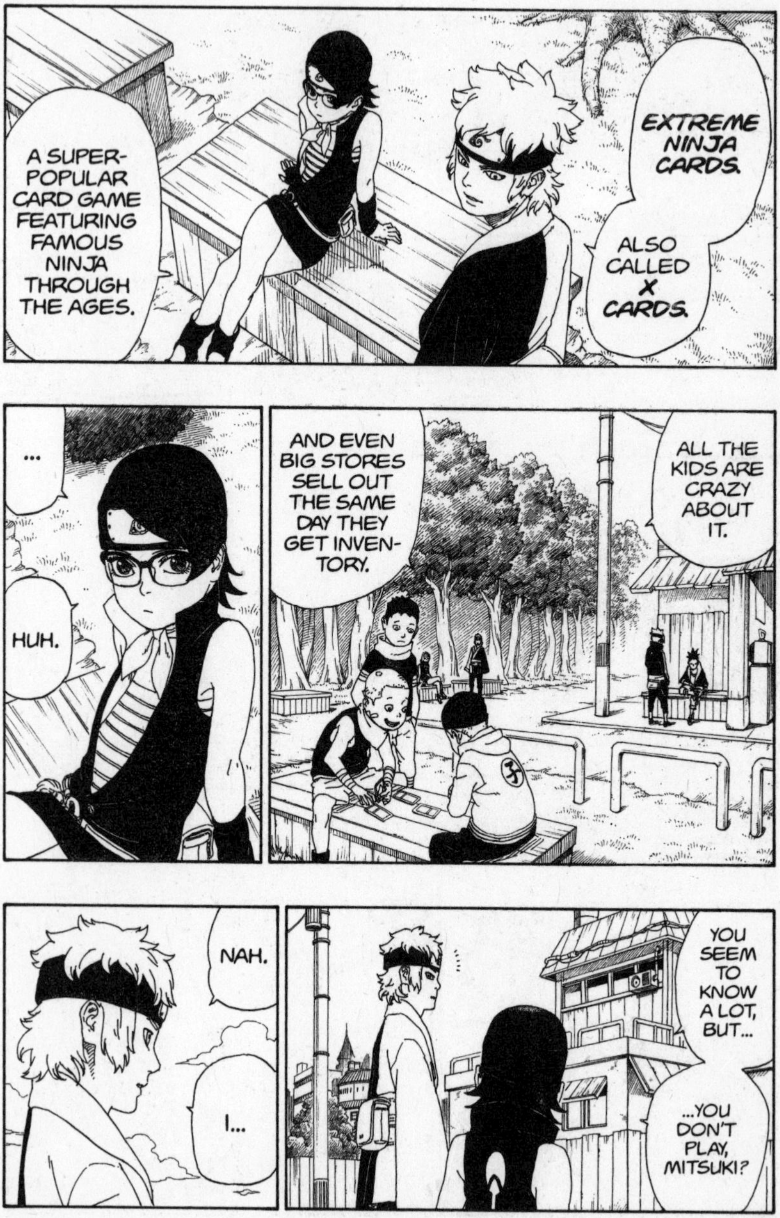
EXTREME NINJA CARDS.
ALSO CALLED X CARDS.
A SUPER-POPULAR CARD GAME FEATURING FAMOUS NINJA THROUGH THE AGES.
ALL THE KIDS ARE CRAZY ABOUT IT.
AND EVEN BIG STORES SELL OUT THE SAME DAY THEY GET INVENTORY.
...
HUH.
YOU SEEM TO KNOW A LOT, BUT...
...YOU DON'T PLAY, MITSUKI?
NAH.
I...

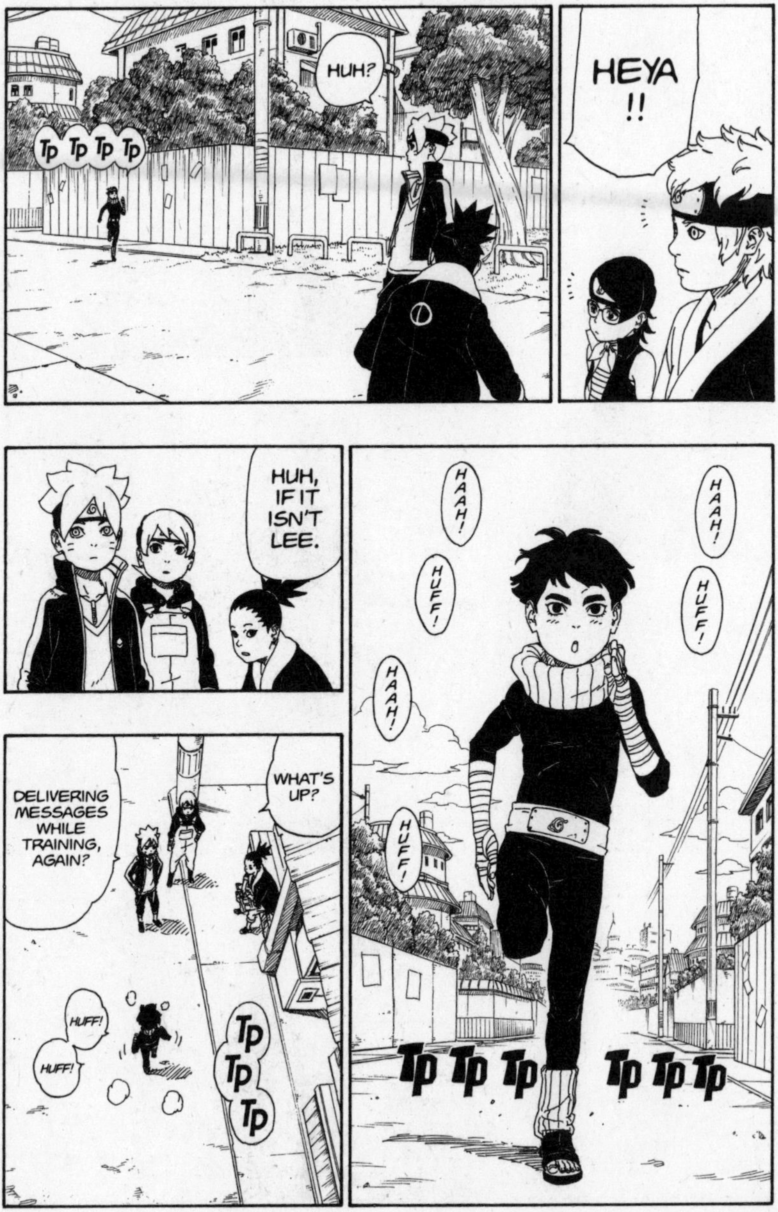
HEYA !!
HUH?
Tp Tp Tp Tp
HAAAH!
HUFF!
HAAAH!
HUFF!
HAAAH!
HUFF!
Tp Tp Tp Tp Tp Tp
HUH, IF IT ISN'T LEE.
WHAT'S UP?
DELIVERING MESSAGES WHILE TRAINING, AGAIN?
Tp Tp Tp
HUFF!
HUFF!

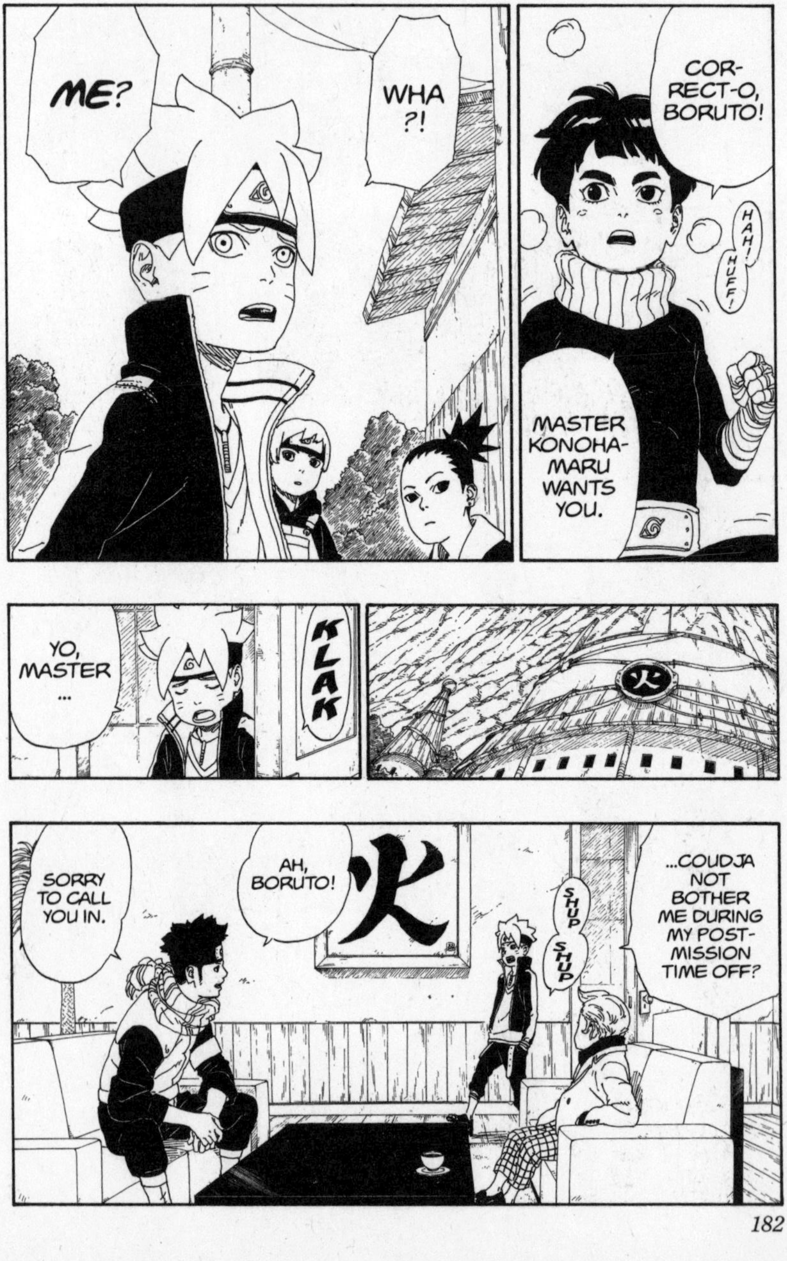
COR-RECT-O, BORUTO!
HAH! HUFF!
MASTER KONOHA-MARU WANTS YOU.
WHA ?!
ME?
KLAK
YO, MASTER ...
...COUDJA NOT BOTHER ME DURING MY POST-MISSION TIME OFF?
SHUP SHUP
AH, BORUTO!
SORRY TO CALL YOU IN.

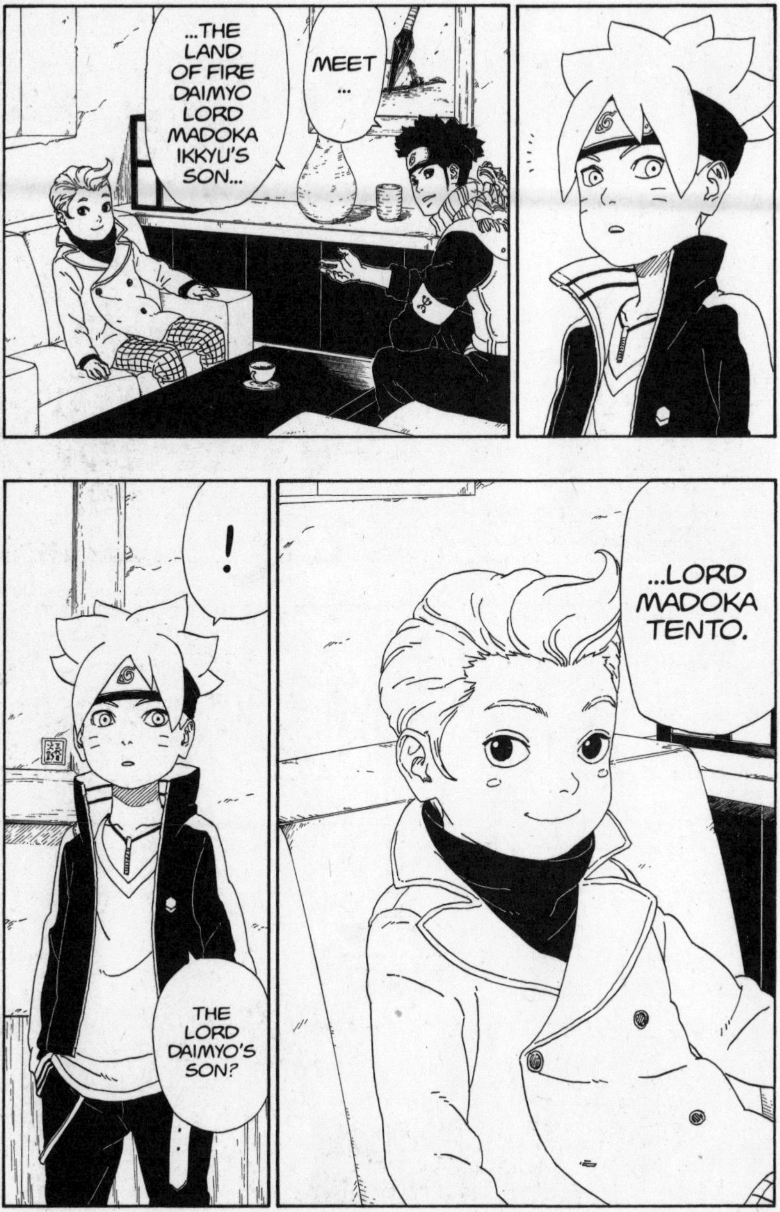
MEET ...
...THE LAND OF FIRE DAIMYO LORD MADOKA IKKYU'S SON...
...LORD MADOKA TENTO.
!
THE LORD DAIMYO'S SON?

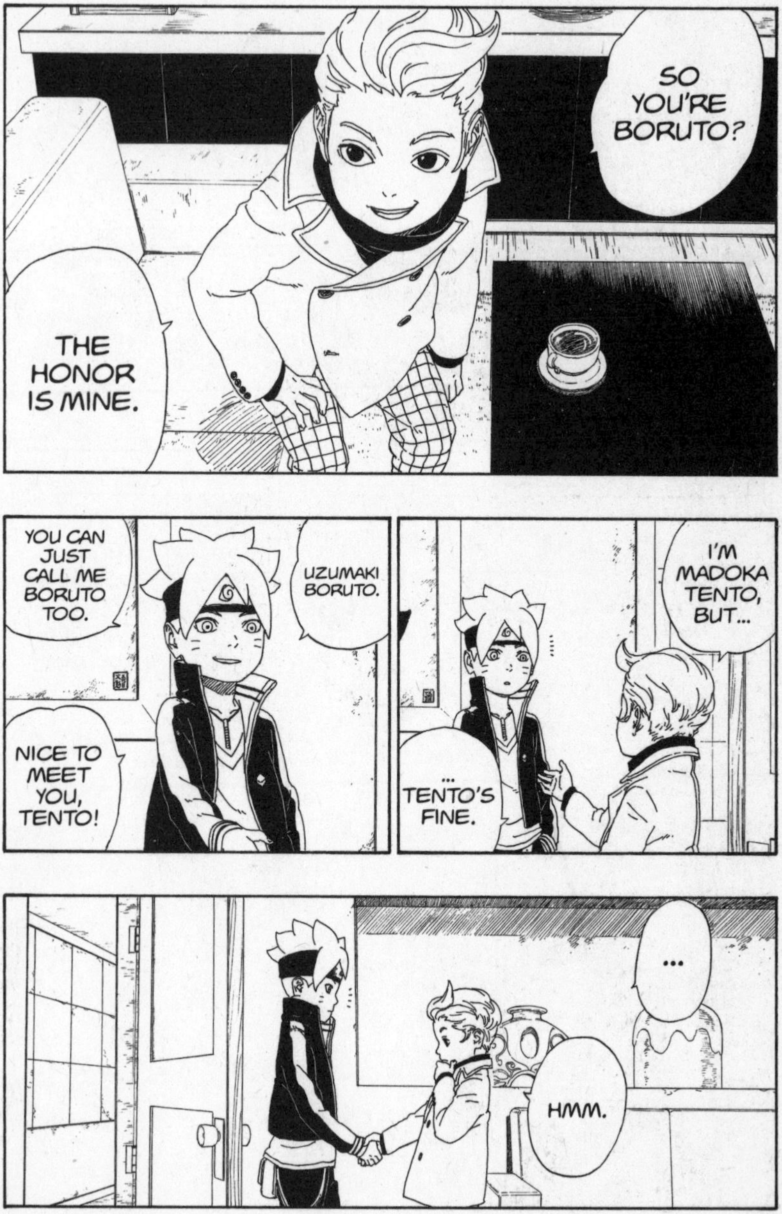
SO YOU'RE BORUTO?
THE HONOR IS MINE.
I'M MADOKA TENTO, BUT...
... TENTO'S FINE.
UZUMAKI BORUTO.
YOU CAN JUST CALL ME BORUTO TOO.
NICE TO MEET YOU, TENTO!
...
HMM.

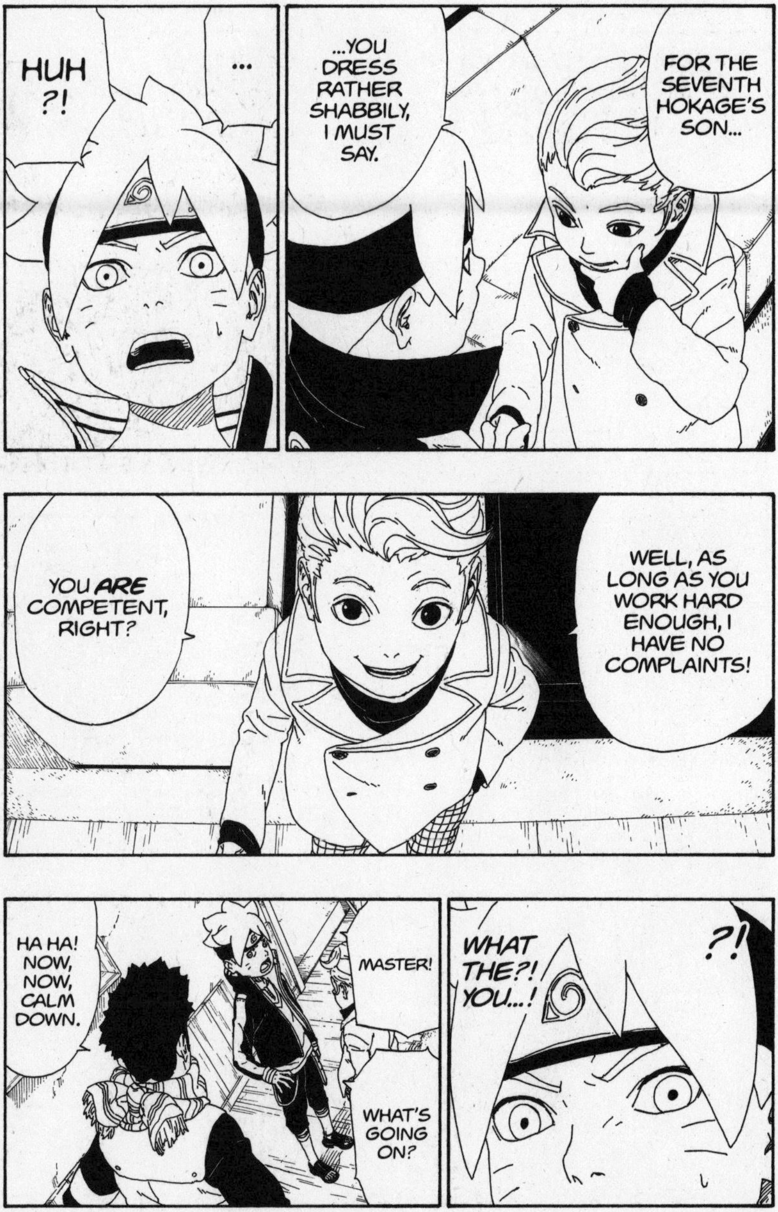
FOR THE SEVENTH HOKAGE'S SON...
...YOU DRESS RATHER SHABBILY, I MUST SAY.
...
HUH ?!
WELL, AS LONG AS YOU WORK HARD ENOUGH, I HAVE NO COMPLAINTS!
YOU **ARE** COMPETENT, RIGHT?
?!
WHAT THE?! YOU...!
MASTER!
WHAT'S GOING ON?
HA HA! NOW, NOW, CALM DOWN.

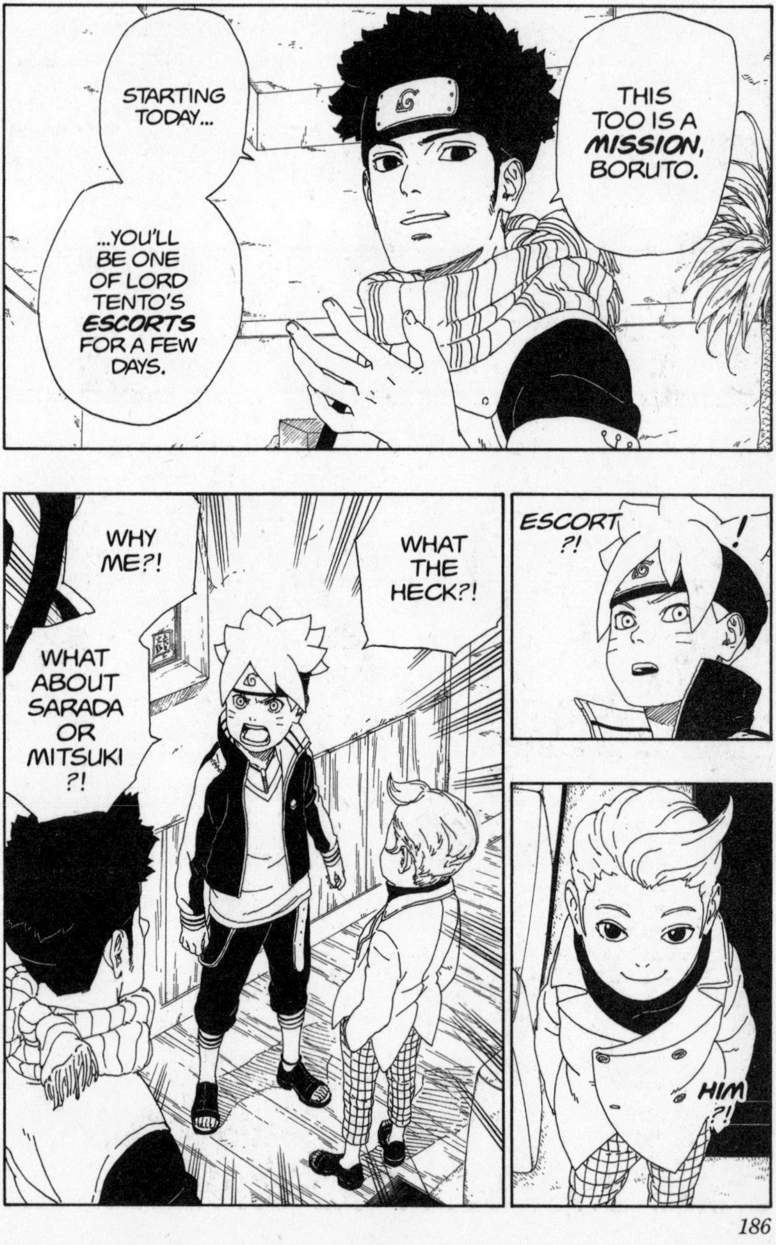
THIS TOO IS A MISSION, BORUTO.
STARTING TODAY...
...YOU'LL BE ONE OF LORD TENTO'S ESCORTS FOR A FEW DAYS.
ESCORT ?!
!
HIM ?!
WHAT THE HECK?!
WHY ME?!
WHAT ABOUT SARADA OR MITSUKI ?!

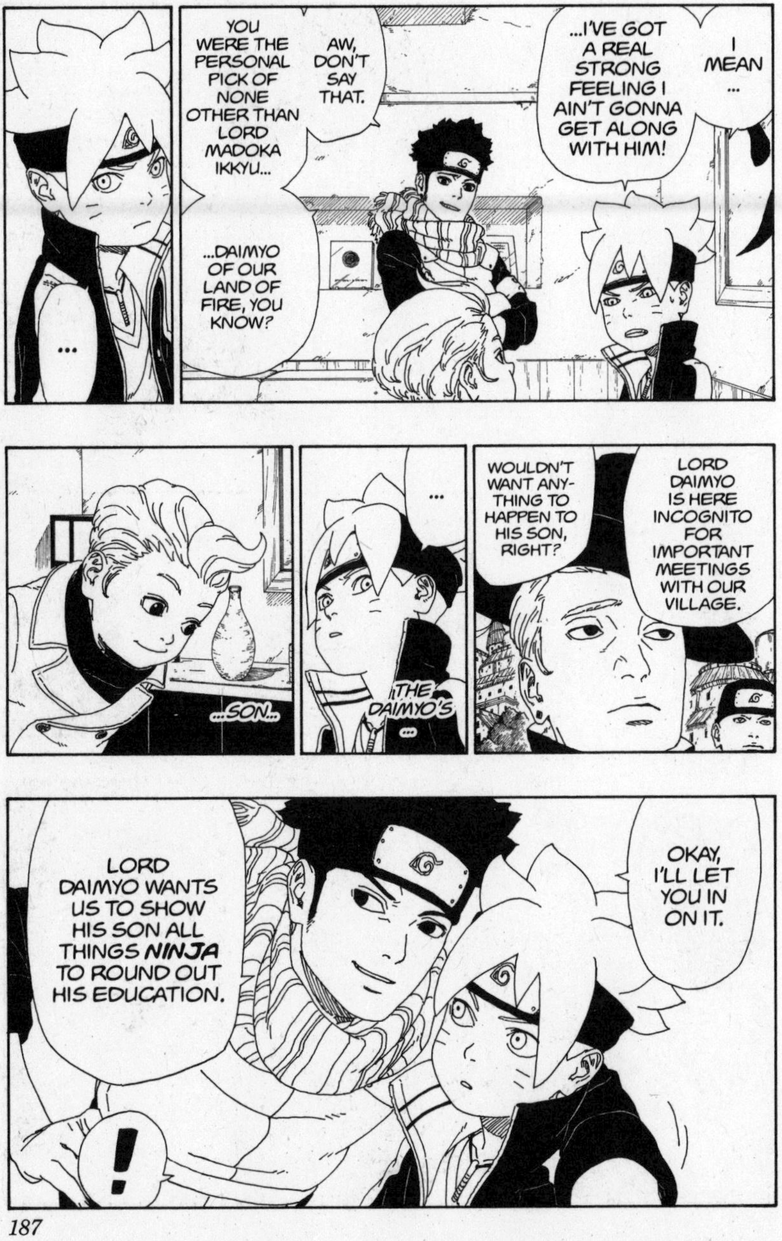
I MEAN ...
...I'VE GOT A REAL STRONG FEELING I AIN'T GONNA GET ALONG WITH HIM!
AW, DON'T SAY THAT.
YOU WERE THE PERSONAL PICK OF NONE OTHER THAN LORD MADOKA IKKYU...
...DAIMYO OF OUR LAND OF FIRE, YOU KNOW?
...
LORD DAIMYO IS HERE INCOGNITO FOR IMPORTANT MEETINGS WITH OUR VILLAGE.
WOULDN'T WANT ANYTHING TO HAPPEN TO HIS SON, RIGHT?
...
THE DAIMYO'S ...
...SON...
OKAY, I'LL LET YOU IN ON IT.
LORD DAIMYO WANTS US TO SHOW HIS SON ALL THINGS *NINJA* TO ROUND OUT HIS EDUCATION.
!

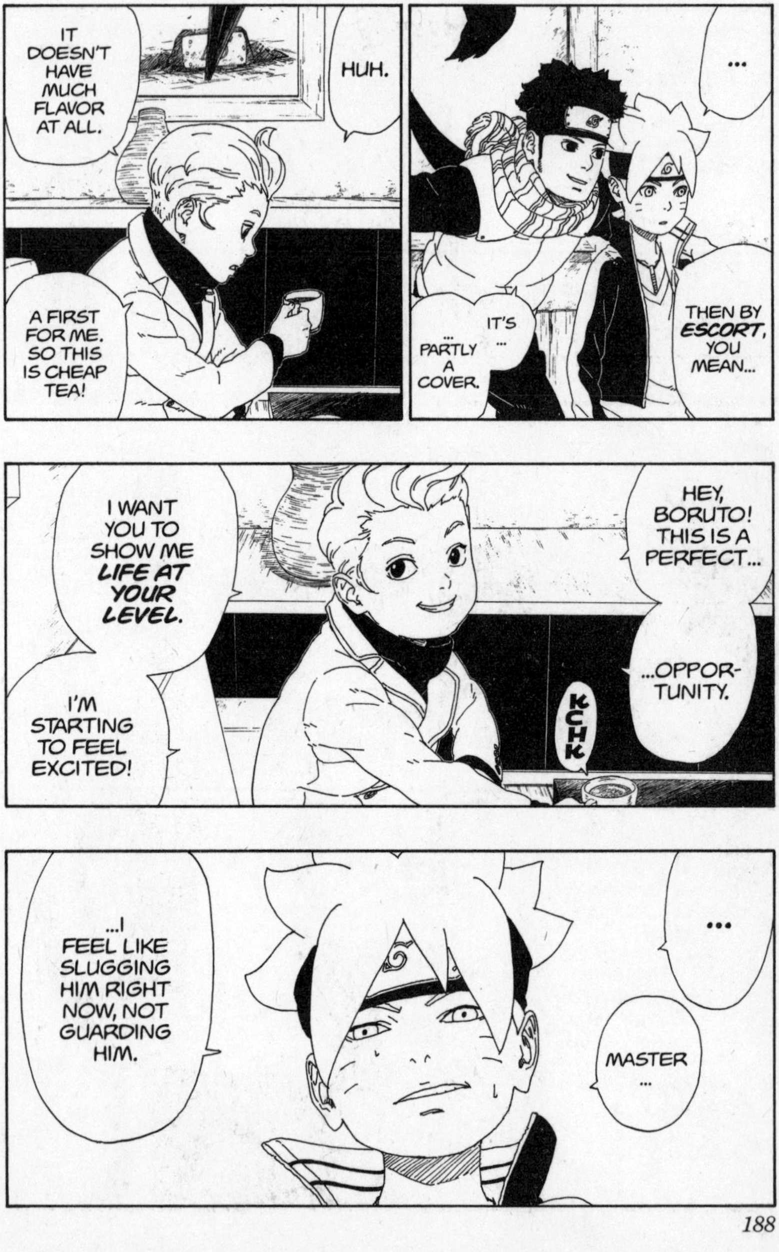
...
THEN BY ESCORT, YOU MEAN...
IT'S ... ... PARTLY A COVER.
HUH.
IT DOESN'T HAVE MUCH FLAVOR AT ALL.
A FIRST FOR ME. SO THIS IS CHEAP TEA!
HEY, BORUTO! THIS IS A PERFECT...
...OPPORTUNITY.
KCHK
I WANT YOU TO SHOW ME LIFE AT YOUR LEVEL.
I'M STARTING TO FEEL EXCITED!
...
MASTER ...
...I FEEL LIKE SLUGGING HIM RIGHT NOW, NOT GUARDING HIM.

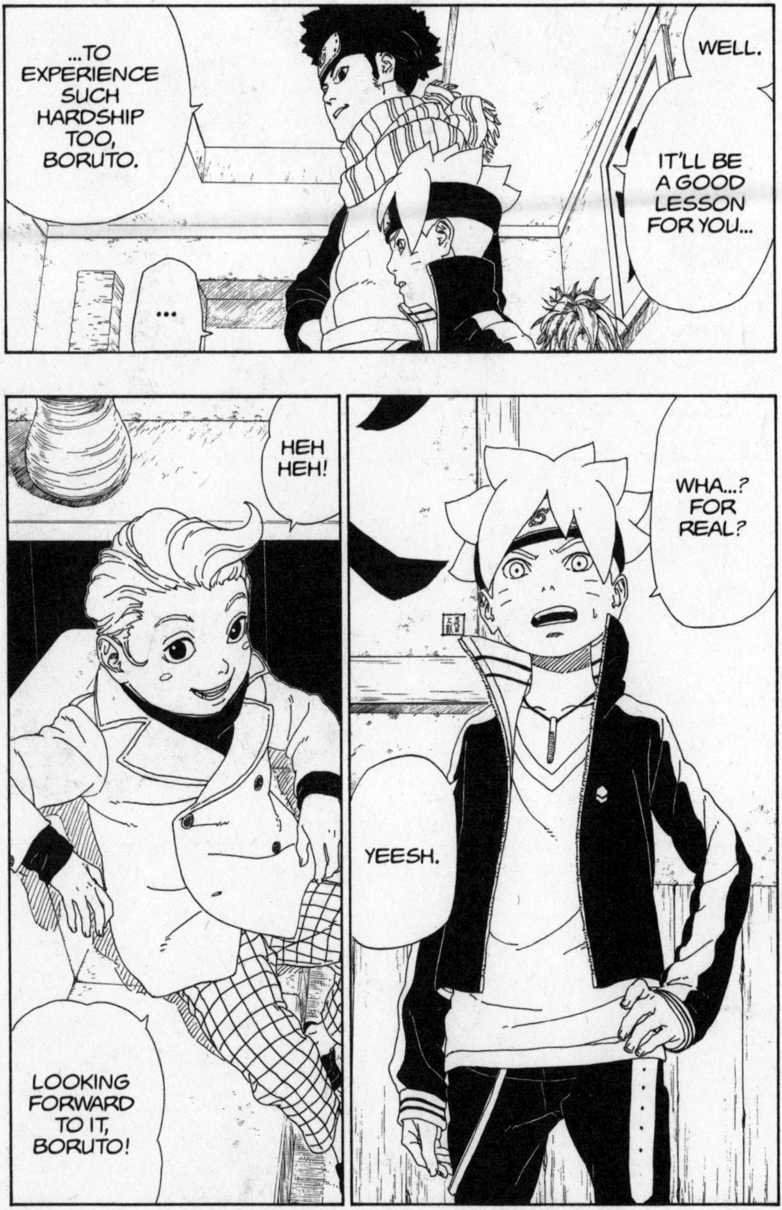
WELL.
IT'LL BE A GOOD LESSON FOR YOU...
...TO EXPERIENCE SUCH HARDSHIP TOO, BORUTO.
...
WHA...? FOR REAL?
YEESH.
HEH HEH!
LOOKING FORWARD TO IT, BORUTO!

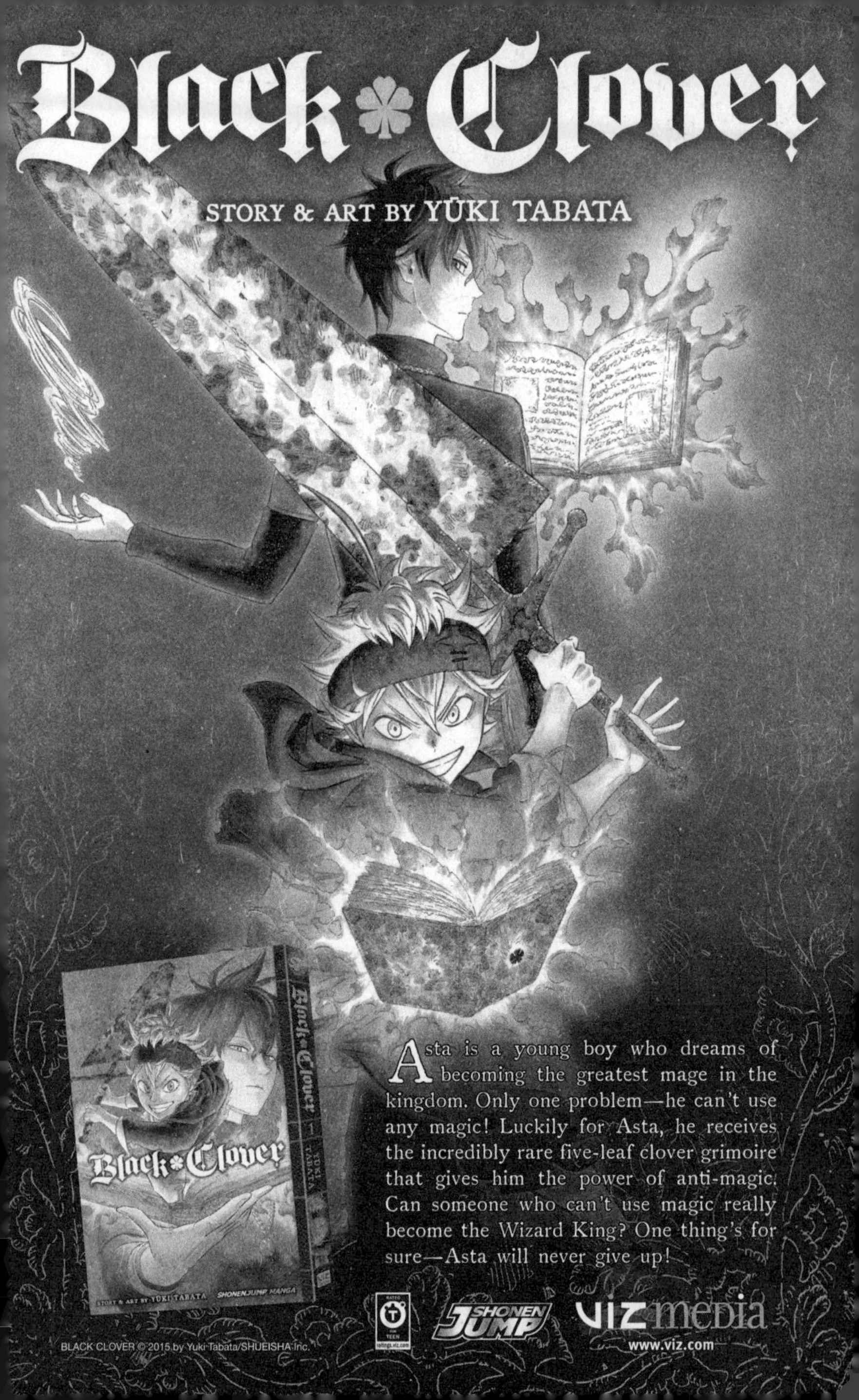
Black Clover
STORY & ART BY YŪKI TABATA
Black Clover
1
YUKI TABATA
STORY & ART BY YUKI TABATA
SHONENJUMP MANGA
Asta is a young boy who dreams of becoming the greatest mage in the kingdom. Only one problem—he can't use any magic! Luckily for Asta, he receives the incredibly rare five-leaf clover grimoire that gives him the power of anti-magic. Can someone who can't use magic really become the Wizard King? One thing's for sure—Asta will never give up!
SHONEN JUMP
VIZ media
BLACK CLOVER © 2015 by Yuki Tabata/SHUEISHA Inc.
www.viz.com

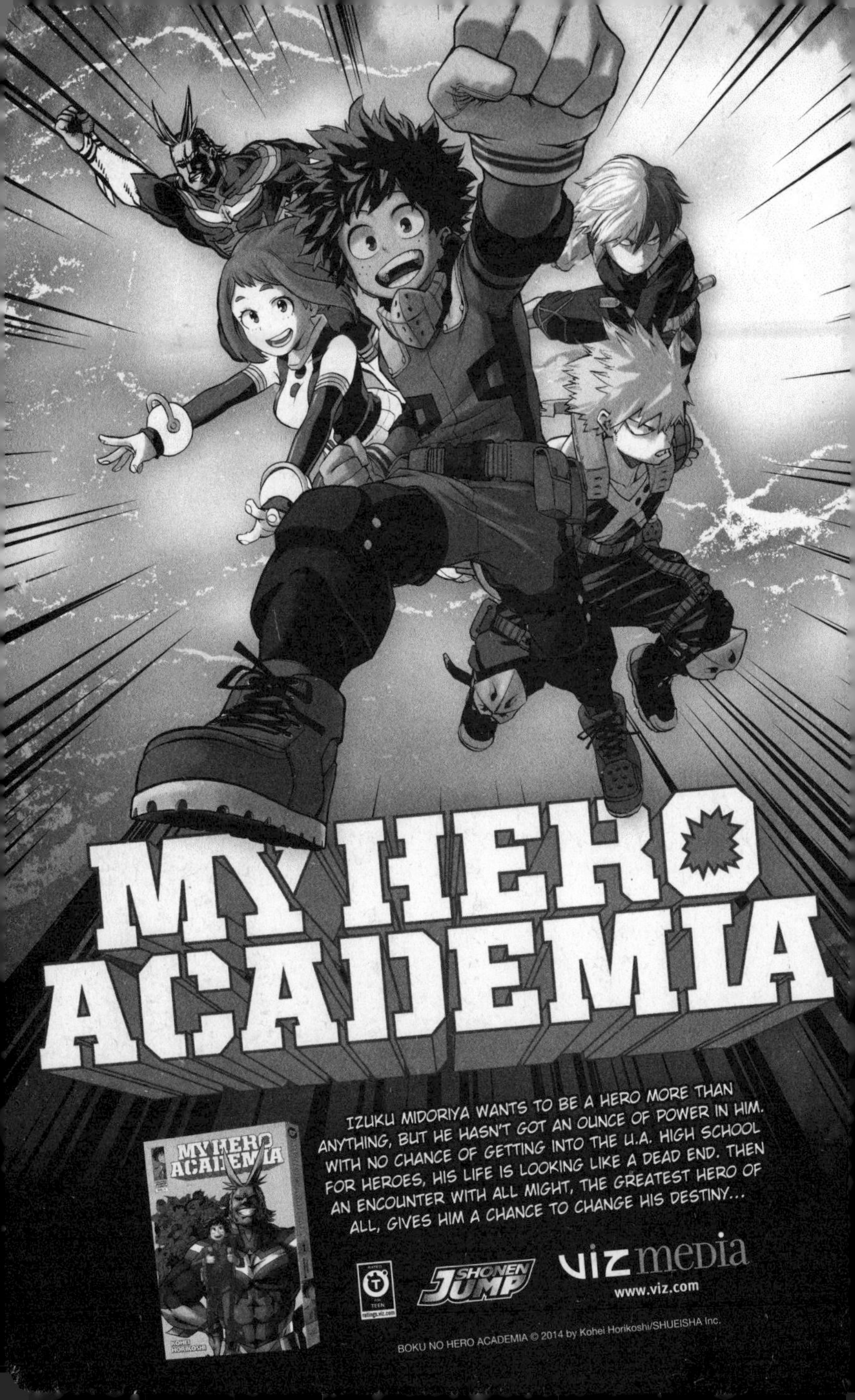
MY HERO ACADEMIA
IZUKU MIDORIYA WANTS TO BE A HERO MORE THAN ANYTHING, BUT HE HASN'T GOT AN OUNCE OF POWER IN HIM. WITH NO CHANCE OF GETTING INTO THE U.A. HIGH SCHOOL FOR HEROES, HIS LIFE IS LOOKING LIKE A DEAD END. THEN AN ENCOUNTER WITH ALL MIGHT, THE GREATEST HERO OF ALL, GIVES HIM A CHANCE TO CHANGE HIS DESTINY...
MY HERO ACADEMIA
KOHEI HORIKOSHI
TEEN
ratings.viz.com
SHONEN JUMP
viz media
www.viz.com
BOKU NO HERO ACADEMIA © 2014 by Kohei Horikoshi/SHUEISHA Inc.

YOU'RE READING
IN THE
WRONG DIRECTION!!

WHOOPS! Guess what? You're starting at the wrong end of the comic!

...It's true! In keeping with the original Japanese format, **Boruto** is meant to be read from right to left, starting in the upper-right corner.

Unlike English, which is read from left to right, Japanese is read from right to left, meaning that action, sound effects and word-balloon order are completely reversed... something which can make readers unfamiliar with Japanese feel pretty backwards themselves. For this reason, manga or Japanese comics published in the U.S. in English have sometimes been published "flopped"—that is, printed in exact reverse order, as though seen from the other side of a mirror.

By flopping pages, U.S. publishers can avoid confusing readers, but the compromise is not without its downside. For one thing, a character in a flopped manga series who once wore in the original Japanese version a T-shirt emblazoned with "M A Y" (as in "the merry month of") now wears one which reads "Y A M"! Additionally, many manga creators in Japan are themselves unhappy with the process, as some feel the mirror-imaging of their art alters their original intentions.

We are proud to bring you **Boruto** in the original unflopped format. Turn to the other side of the book and let the ninjutsu begin...!

—Editor

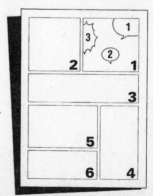